Zionism Unsettled
A CONGREGATIONAL STUDY GUIDE

ABOUT THIS PUBLICATION

In 2011, the Israel/Palestine Mission Network of the Presbyterian Church (U.S.A.) (theIPMN.org) established a working group to explore the history, doctrine, and various forms of Zionism. Around the same time, Friends of Sabeel North America (FOSNA.org) invited IPMN to collaborate in developing for publication a collection of essays on Jewish and Christian Zionism. The resulting book, *Zionism and the Quest for Justice in the Holy Land*, is scheduled for publication by Wipf and Stock in 2014.

   Zionism Unsettled is a congregational study guide that may be used alone or in conjunction with the longer book, *Zionism and the Quest for Justice in the Holy Land*. This congregational study guide consists of two parts: this booklet and its accompanying free DVD. These companion resources follow the general chapter outline of *Zionism and the Quest for Justice in the Holy Land* while introducing additional material that highlight issues of particular interest. Each section in this study guide is followed by a set of questions to help stimulate productive group discussion. A Leader's Guide with more information about using this resource appears on page 64.

Copyright IPMN, January 2014   •   ISBN No. 978-1-4675-9321-2   •   PDS No. 26466-14-001

Contents

1 · Toward a New Framework

The Zionist solution to the Jewish question has created a whole new set of problems, which it has so far proved incapable of solving.[4]

ADAM SHATZ

The Israel/Palestine conflict is now in its seventh decade. The so-called peace process has devolved into a cover under which irreversible territorial and demographic facts on the ground are being implemented with impunity by Israel. "We are engaged," writes Ian Lustick, "in negotiations to nowhere."[1]

Diplomatic posturing in support of a two-state solution notwithstanding, Israel's expansion into territory classified under international law as occupied has brought about a *de facto* one-state entity under Israeli jurisdiction. Rashid Khalidi of Columbia University is one of many analysts to note that the current situation is unstable. He writes, "a 'one-state solution' based on enduring discrimination and oppression is ultimately unsustainable."[2]

Anne Paq

"Only Israeli Jews are full citizens of that land," Khalidi explains, "while 5 million Palestinians live in a state of subjugation or exile and 1.2 million Palestinian Arabs live in Israel as second-class citizens."

Mainstream media coverage of the Palestine/Israel conflict is abundant, perhaps even disproportionate, given the number of conflicts that afflict the world. And yet, for all the ink that has been spilled in dissecting the conflict, much of the analysis to date fails to reckon with the genesis of this seemingly intractable impasse. What has been almost entirely absent from the mainstream conversation about Israel/Palestine is open, frank discussion about the ways in which ideology—that is, political and religious doctrine—has been a driving force of the conflict.

Outside mainstream circles, however, fearless and constructive discussion on the role of ideology in the creation of the contemporary Palestine/Israel political situation is alive and well—in fact, it predates by half a century the 1948 establishment of the modern state of Israel.

For Israel, the situation on the ground has trended inexorably toward territorial expansion and subjugation of the Palestinian people by military occupation. At the same time, from the Palestinian perspective, the trend has been growing dispossession and deprivation of basic human rights. Alongside these negative developments, a positive trend is being seen: contemporary voices are breaking the taboos that have stigmatized and punished critical examination of Zionism and its consequences. Palestinians, who have as a people experienced Zionism as a *Nakba*, or "Catastrophe," [see box, page 6] have struggled since 1948 to be recognized as victims of Zionism, the ideological movement established to remedy Jewish victimization.

Nur Masalha, a Palestinian historian (and Israeli citizen), echoes a widely-felt Palestinian complaint about reflexive Western acceptance of the Zionist framework when he writes, "Upholding the Zionist narrative of denial is still seen in the West as neutral, while anything more critical is seen as biased." Masalha continues, "Zionism was (and remains) not just about the colonization of Palestinian land, but also about colonizing minds—Jewish, Arab, European, American."[3]

Perhaps it is not surprising that Masalha, like many Palestinians, identifies Zionism as a root cause of the ongoing struggle for self-determination between Palestinians and Israelis. What is unexpected is the number and diversity of Jews who have chosen to speak out about the consequences of Zionism—despite enormous communal pressure not to do so. It is a promising development that in our own time these diverse Jewish voices, with increasing

What is the *Nakba*?

Nakba is the Arabic word for "Catastrophe" and refers to the massive ethnic cleansing of over 750,000 Palestinians, the confiscation of Palestinian land, and the destruction of over 500 Palestinian villages by Israeli forces in 1947-48 when the British vacated Palestine and Israel became a state. The Hebrew term for the Nazi Holocaust, Shoah, also translates as "Catastrophe." The interconnection and causality between the Jewish and Palestinian catastrophes has led some to observe that the Palestinians are, in some ways, secondary victims of the Nazi Holocaust.

confidence and assertiveness, are examining the role of Zionism in shaping the history of the contested tract of land known by its inhabitants as both Palestine and Israel.

QUESTIONING ZIONISM

In the foreword to his indispensable anthology, *Prophets Outcast: A Century of Dissident Jewish Writing about Zionism and Israel*, Adam Shatz identifies the central dilemma of the Israel-Palestine conflict: "The Zionist solution to the Jewish question has created a whole new set of problems, which it has so far proved incapable of solving."[4] Shatz writes,

> Jewish critics of Israel have predicted with uncanny precision the steady deterioration of Arab-Jewish relations under Zionism, the seemingly inexorable drift toward territorial expansionism and theocratic fanaticism in Israel, and the consequent erosion of Jewish ethics.[5]

Shatz's anthology contains essays by Ahad Ha'am (1891), Yitzhak Epstein (1907), Sigmund Freud (1930), Leon Trotsky (1934 and 1937), Abraham Leon (1940), Albert Einstein (1930, 1938, and 1948), and Martin Buber (1948), all predicting and lamenting the inevitable collision of Jewish and Palestinian interests in the evolution of Zionism from a far-fetched theoretical framework to a politically-empowered Jewish resettlement project.

In a 2009 *Los Angeles Times* article, "Zionism is the Problem," journalist Ben Ehrenreich echoed the opinion of his numerous Jewish and non-Jewish

antecedents—but, importantly, in a major US daily newspaper. For several decades now, Ehrenreich wrote,

> To question not just Israel's actions, but the Zionist tenets on which the state is founded, has …been regarded an almost unspeakable blasphemy. Yet it is no longer possible to believe with an honest conscience that the deplorable conditions in which Palestinians live and die in Gaza and the West Bank come as the result of specific policies, leaders or parties on either side of the impasse. The problem is fundamental: Founding a modern state on a single ethnic or religious identity in a territory that is ethnically and religiously diverse leads either to politics of exclusion…or to wholesale ethnic cleansing. Put simply, the problem is Zionism.[6]

Within the past few years, influential Jewish public intellectuals and academics including Tony Judt, Peter Beinart, Henry Siegman, and David Remnick have mounted important challenges to mainstream perceptions of Israel. Their contributions have appeared primarily in elite, long-form periodicals (*New York Review of Books*, *London Review of Books*, *Nation*, *New Yorker*), partly because thoughtful analysis cannot reduce the conflict to the sound byte-size articles favored by mainstream media. These articles are among the numerous factors helping to bring about a gradual change in the public discourse.

One applauds the distance traveled by these authors, whose personal ideological frameworks have been formed by the early exposure to Zionism typical of many Jewish youth of their generation—one might even say, arguably, indoctrination. In questioning Israeli policies, these thinkers have, to their credit, knowingly walked into the "buzz-saw"[7] of delegitimization with which organized Israel-advocacy groups attack critics of the Jewish state. Praiseworthy and courageous as they are, one laments these writers' tardy acceptance of views long considered obvious by Palestinians and others familiar with their history. For all the critical insight that Jewish writers bring to the process of moving the public consciousness, it is important not to privilege their voices at the expense of others' lest Jewish analysts inadvertently dictate the pace at which once-unthinkable notions become normalized and accepted as self-evident.

These thinkers represent a range of attitudes: some draw the line at rejecting Zionism itself, clinging instead to a version of Zionism (*i.e.*, Labor or liberal) that has been swept aside and rendered politically irrelevant by the triumph within Israel of maximalist Jewish nationalism. Given the political reality on the ground in Palestine/Israel, the growing split between self-identified Zionists and non-Zionists among Israel's most vocal critics may be a distinction without a difference.

In December 2012, online journalist Philip Weiss (a self-identified non-Zionist) called out the mainstream media for practicing censorship by its silence about Zionism. The media give plenty of coverage to other religious issues from evangelism to stem-cell research to radical Islam, he wrote, so why not do the same with Zionism?[8] In January 2013, Israeli historian Ilan Pappe compared the public failure to deal with Zionism to a doctor who, instead of diagnosing and treating his sick patient, merely gives him pills to dull the pain.[9]

In a February 2013 lecture at the Carnegie Endowment, Ian Lustick compared Israel's national ideology to a map with directions to a desired destination. He said,

> Zionist ideology was, in its day, a valuable problem identifier and guide to the solutions for those problems for desperate Jews. But except for the foundational principle that Jews are normal and deserve the rights of any other people, the traditional discourse of Zionism as theory and guide is an obstacle to Jewish welfare and security.... Israel can live in a post-Zionist age by adapting to the world as it is, or it can die in one. As it is said among Jews: 'Choose life.'[10]

Caren Aviv and David Shneer, like Lustick, find the map analogy useful. In their book, *New Jews: The End of the Jewish Diaspora*, they note with concern that

> in some quarters, questioning the Jewish map is downright heresy. So much of Jewish life, thought, and scholarship revolves around the idea that Israel is, has been, and always will be at the center of the Jewish universe.[11]

While these critical observations about Zionism may seem new to most readers, in fact, they are not. Forty-seven years ago, in a prescient *New York Review* essay titled "Holy War," the eminent American Jewish journalist I.F. Stone wrote,

> Israel is creating a kind of moral schizophrenia in world Jewry. In the outside world the welfare of Jewry depends on the maintenance of secular, non-racial, pluralistic societies. In Israel, Jewry finds itself defending a society...in which the ideal is racial and exclusionist.[12]

THROUGH TRUTH TO RECONCILIATION

In the 1969 essay cited above, I.F. Stone lifts up a challenge to his fellow Jews and, by extension, all humankind:

> For me the Arab problem is also the No. 1 Jewish problem. How we act toward the Arabs will determine what kind of people we become: either oppressors and racists in our turn like those from whom we have suffered, or a nobler race able to transcend the tribal xenophobias that afflict mankind.[13]

It is important for American communities of Christians, Jews, and Muslims to not only listen to what Palestinians (such as Khalidi, Masalha, and Edward Said[14]) and Jews (such as Lustick, Ehrenreich, and Stone) say about Zionism and the struggle in Palestine/Israel, but also, for several reasons, to enter into the discussion.

First, Christian anti-Semitism was a major factor in the rise of Jewish Zionism. Second, American Christian Zionists are now major political supporters of Israeli government policies that harm Palestinians and impede a just peace. Third, the United States has not been an impartial broker of peace in the Middle East. The US ensures that Israel has a "military edge" in the region and continues to fund aspects of Israel's military occupation of Palestine, including the expansion of illegal Jewish settlements on Palestinian land. And finally, the time is overdue to break the taboo that has constrained members of synagogues, churches, and mosques to remain silent on the subject of Zionism for fear of fraying interfaith relationships. It is time to speak the truth in love to one another.

The theme that unites and underlies this congregational study is the toxic relationship between theology and politics in all three Abrahamic faiths. Judaism, Christianity, and Islam all suffer from a common condition: theological and ethical exceptionalism [see box, page 8]. Although this resource focuses primarily on Zionism, exceptionalism is not unique to Zionism; rather it is present wherever exceptionalist religious ideology is fused with political power. Christian exceptionalist beliefs and actions contributed to the Nazi Holocaust, the genocide of Native Americans, and countless other instances of tragic brutality. Exceptionalist doctrines and behaviors within Islam have contributed to grievous human rights abuses such as the massacres during

Exceptionalism is not unique to Zionism. It is present wherever exceptionalist religious ideology is fused with political power.

What is Exceptionalism?

All three Abrahamic religions claim to be exceptional in some ways. Exceptionalism is the belief that "my people" are unusual, unique, or special. On the positive side, all three Abrahamic religions have a special calling to be a blessing for all the nations. Rabbinic Judaism coined the term *tikkun olam*, (repairing or healing the world) to express this call. On the negative side, exceptionalism exempts the chosen from the need to conform to normal rules, laws, or general principles that we use to hold other peoples accountable.

Exceptionalist beliefs have a sacred quality and lead to exceptionalist attitudes and actions involving double standards in behavior and often in law. When holding political power, each Abrahamic faith has been susceptible to the merger of theological and ethical exceptionalism that puts believer-insiders above the law they expect nonbeliever-outsiders to obey. Christian exceptionalism has often taken the form of anti-Semitism, the theological support of slavery followed by Jim Crow segregation, as well as ethnic cleansing and genocide against American Indians. The dark side of Zionist exceptionalism today is the ethnic cleansing and land confiscation of Palestinians justified by an appeal to God's will derived from biblical texts.

The Israeli settlement Shim'a and its nearby outpost Mitzpe Eshtamoa are built on more than 160 dunams (40 acres) of land confiscated by the Israeli government from a Palestinian extended family that makes its livelihood from grazing and agriculture in the South Hebron Hills region of the West Bank. Settlers have harrassed and physically assaulted the Palestinian landowners, destroyed olive trees, and restricted them from accessing their own land. In this photo taken on May 20, 2013, a Star of David formed by settlers out of local stones brands the Palestinians' land as Jewish.

springtimeinpalestineandisrael.wordpress.com

the closing days of the Ottoman Empire which crescendoed with the Armenian genocide in 1915.[15]

History has demonstrated with tragic repetition the straight line from sacred claims of special status to separation, prejudice, discrimination, and violence toward other peoples.

Jews know from historical first-hand experience about the perils of theocratic fanaticism harnessed by state power—after all, Jews have repeatedly suffered at the hands of Christians (and, to a much lesser extent Muslims) when these religions gained political dominance in lands with Jewish minorities. With their own people's history in mind, Jewish critics of Israel have warned of the disastrous potential of Jewish state power.

We believe that justice, peace, and reconciliation will become possible for the Jewish, Muslim, and Christian inhabitants of the Holy Land when Israel and its supporters around the world comprehend the impossibility of resolving the crisis through the exercise of power, and radicalized Muslims relinquish the dream of an Islamic theocracy. The transformation will emerge, too, as Jews and non-Jews build new interpretations of the *Shoah,* since the horror of that genocide underlies much of what is known and accepted about the course of postwar Jewish history.

FROM DENIAL TO RECOGNITION

Palestinian-American scholar Edward Said laments the psychological scarring inflicted by trauma, and

> *I believe with all my heart that when Israel frees itself from its obsession with the Shoah and its exclusivity, the world also will be much freer.*[18]
>
> AVRAHAM BURG

how that trauma can manifest itself as an ongoing cycle of victimization. "I can admit the notion that the distortions of the Holocaust created distortions in its victims, which are replicated today in the victims of Zionism itself, that is, the Palestinians,"[16] Said writes, pointing to the urgent need to unpack the psychological burden of the Nazi Holocaust as a means of healing Palestinian-Israeli relationships.

Israeli writer Akiva Eldar identifies the pathology inherent in Zionism that drives the conflict when he writes,

> ...the fact that Israel sees itself as a victim justifies its aggression and injustice. With the help of guilt-neutralizing mechanisms, Israelis disengage the circumstantial link between an action and its consequences, and absolve themselves of responsibility.[17]

Edward Said offers a hopeful alternative:

> Understanding what happened to the Jews in Europe under the Nazis means understanding what is universal about a human experience under calamitous conditions. It means compassion, human sympathy, and utter recoil from the notion of killing people for ethnic, religious, or nationalist reasons.[18]

Like Eldar and Said, Avraham Burg, former chairman of the Jewish Agency for Israel and speaker of

The fundamental assumption of this study is that no exceptionalist claims can be justified in our interconnected pluralistic world.

the Knesset, calls for an expanded, inclusive understanding of the Nazi genocide in contemporary life.

> I believe with all my heart that when Israel frees itself from its obsession with the *Shoah* and its exclusivity, the world also will be much freer. Israel's role will be to watch and sound the alarm and to stand beside the persecuted where they are, without regard to friend or foe.[19]

The Israeli government, however, maintains a policy of making distinctions between "our" suffering and "theirs." Within Israel, *Nakba* commemoration among the Palestinian residents of Israel is a punishable offense. Selective archaeological exploration of the land is a politicized act that contributes to what Nadia Abu El-Haj describes as the "formation and enactment of [Israel's] colonial-national historical imagination and…the substantiation of its territorial claims." State-sponsored archaeologists seek out and preserve the traces of ancient Jewish inhabitation; meanwhile, the remains of Arab and Byzantine inhabitation are overlooked, neglected, concealed, and even destroyed.[20]

"The Zionist narrative of denial," a term coined by Palestinian scholar Nur Masalha, is alive and well. The Israeli government further promotes denial and double-standards among its Jewish citizenry by failing to teach Israelis about the mass uprooting and dispossession of Palestine's indigenous people that occurred just a few years after the liberation of the Nazi death camps.

Others have added their voices to those of Eldar and Said, calling for an expanded, inclusive understanding of the Nazi genocide in contemporary life, so that "Never again!" applies not only to Jews but to all peoples, including Palestinians, and a renunciation of the morally hazardous claims of a hierarchy of victimhood.

How can one compare the suffering of the African slave trade, the decimation of native peoples throughout the Americas, or the suffering inflicted upon Jews during the Nazi Holocaust? Disagreement over the criteria for such a moral calculus as well as the appropriate weight to assign each criterion leads to an ethical quagmire, producing even more animosity and recrimination between peoples who have suffered outrageous bondage and loss of life.

This study explores the theological and ethical exceptionalism of Jewish and Christian Zionism, which have been sheltered from open debate despite the intolerable human rights abuses rooted in their core beliefs. The challenge of interfaith relations is to find a way to respect theological differences and the historical experiences that gave rise to them while preventing them from becoming excuses for injustice toward those who find themselves on the outside. The fundamental assumption of this study is that no exceptionalist claims can be justified in our interconnected, pluralistic world.

Jerusalem is a holy place for Jews, Muslims, and Christians.

Anne Paq

Palestine, Israel, and the United Nations

In principle the United Nations was established to provide a diplomatic alternative to violence in the resolution of conflicts. In practice, the United Nations has yielded little diplomatic benefit for the Palestinian people.

Israel has abided by UN prescriptions only when useful to achieving its military, territorial, and demographic goals. More frequently, however, Israel has violated UN authority.

Apart from a lengthy list of resolutions condemning Israeli military transgressions and violations of human rights, Israel has suffered no punitive sanctions for its rogue behavior.[1,2]

Ironically, the Universal Declaration of Human Rights was adopted by the newly created UN in 1948 as a response to the Nazi Holocaust. Now, Israel and the US are the main obstacles to implementing its mandate for Palestinians.

PARTITION

Palestinians rejected the right of the United Nations to impose a partition plan in Palestine. On February 6, 1948, the Arab Higher Committee communicated to the UN Secretary General its position that the UN "has no jurisdiction to order or recommend the partition of Palestine. There is nothing in the Charter to warrant such authority, consequently the recommendation of partition...[is] null and void."[3] The demand that the UN refer the matter of jurisdiction to the International Court of Justice in

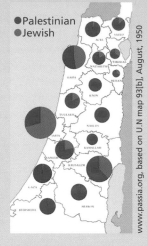

Mandate Palestine population distribution by subdistrict, 1946

● Palestinian
● Jewish

www.passia.org, based on U.N map 93[b], August, 1950

adherence to the Charter was unheeded.

DISPROPORTIONALITY

The United Nations Special Committee on Palestine (UNSCOP) 1947 partition plan granted a disproportionate share of territory to the Zionists relative to either their population or their land ownership at the time. The future Jewish state was granted 55% of the total land area and the future Arab state, 45%. At the time of partition, Palestinian Arabs owned approximately 93% of the land in Palestine; Jews, 7%. The Negev region of southern Palestine, where less than 1% of the land was held in Jewish ownership, was allotted to the future Jewish state because it coincided with the Zionists' desire to control a port on the Red Sea.

SEPARATION BARRIER

The 2004 International Court of Justice (ICJ) ruling against the separation

barrier Israel has constructed on expropriated Palestinian land within the West Bank calls on Israel to "cease the construction of the wall in the Occupied Palestinian Territories, including East Jerusalem; dismantle the structure therein situated; rescind all legislative and regulatory acts relating to the wall; and make reparations for all damage caused by the construction of the wall."[4] Barrier construction, land seizure, and concomitant infringements by Israel on Palestinian freedom of movement continue unabated.

THE US VETO

As Israel's powerful ally, the US has wielded its veto in the UN Security Council to overturn numerous resolutions condemning Israeli actions toward Palestinians and neighboring countries that otherwise would have passed[5,6]. The power of the US veto to neutralize the will of the majority has sidelined the United Nations in its role as keeper of peace in the region.

RESOLUTIONS VIOLATED

While Israel claims legitimacy as a state based on the UN-sanctioned partition plan, Israel has since 1948 consistently disregarded the international body's demands[1,2]. The United Nations Security Council resolutions violated by Israel in the wake of the 1967 war are:

237 · June 14, 1967 – Calls on Israel "to ensure the safety, welfare and security of the inhabitants where military operations have taken place" during the war launched by Israel on June 5, 1967, "and to facilitate the return of those inhabitants who have fled the areas since the outbreak of hostilities."

242 · November 22, 1967 – Emphasizes "the inadmissibility of the acquisition of territory by war," emphasizes that member states have a commitment to abide by the UN Charter, and calls for the "[w]ithdrawal of Israeli armed forces from territories occupied" during the June 1967 war.

252 · May 21, 1968 – "Deplores the failure of Israel to comply with" General Assembly resolutions 2253 and 2254, considers Israel's annexation of Jerusalem "invalid," and calls upon Israel "to rescind all such measures already taken and to desist forthwith from taking any further action which tends to change the status of Jerusalem."

259 · September 27, 1968 – Expresses concern for "the safety, welfare and security" of the Palestinians "under military occupation by Israel," deplores "the delay in the implementation of resolution 237," and requests Israel to receive the Special Representative and facilitate his work.

267 · July 3, 1969 – Recalls resolution 252 and General Assembly resolutions 2253 and 2254, notes that "since the adoption of the above-mentioned resolutions Israel has taken further measures tending to change the status of the City of Jerusalem," reaffirms "the established principle that acquisition of territory by military conquest is inadmissible," "[d]eplores the failure of Israel to show any regard for the resolutions," "[c]ensures in the strongest terms all measures taken to change the status of the City of Jerusalem," "[c]onfirms that all legislative and administrative measures and actions taken by Israel which purport to alter the status of Jerusalem, including expropriation of land and properties thereon, are invalid and cannot change that status," and urgently calls on Israel to rescind the measures taken to annex Jerusalem.

The Palestinian Liberation Organization was granted UN "permanent observer" status in 1974 as a non-state "entity." On September 23, 2012, Palestinian President Mahmoud Abbas presented Palestine's application for full membership as a member state to UN Secretary-General Ban Ki-moon. The Security Council was deadlocked, given the certainty of a US veto, and the Palestinian application was not brought to a vote. Blocked from receiving full UN membership, Palestine was granted "observer state" status in November 2012. The status change is granted by the General Assembly, in which no country wields veto power. Palestinians used their new status to join the United Nations Educational, Scientific and Cultural Organization (UNESCO), after which Israel and the United States withdrew funding.[7]

2 · Political Zionism

Political Zionism means different things to different people:

- The nationalist movement to create in Palestine "a Jewish and democratic state."[2]
- "The establishment in Palestine of a national home for the Jewish people."[3]
- "…[T]he first manifestation of the approach of our redemption."[4]
- "An ideology of Jewish nationalism. Refers primarily to the establishment and building up of a politically independent Jewish state in the historic land of Israel."[5]
- "The national movement for the return of the Jewish people to their homeland and the resumption of Jewish sovereignty in the Land of Israel."[6]

Ben-Gurion always refrained from issuing clear or written expulsion orders; he preferred that his generals "understand" what he wanted.[1]

- "…[T]he preoccupation with Jewish vulnerability and suffering [*i.e.*,'our eternal victimhood'], and the sense of entitlement to the land [of Israel]."[7]
- Privilege allotted to one group and denied to other groups based on ethnicity and/or religion, *i.e.*, state-sponsored ethnic discrimination and ethnic cleansing.[8]

Each of these definitions has a different emphasis and implies a different historical and ideological understanding of Zionism. To sort out these conflicting understandings of political Zionism, Sections 2 and 3 will examine the ideas and practices of five major leaders[9] who shaped the Zionist project from its beginning in the 1890s through the present: Theodor Herzl, Vladimir Jabotinsky, David Ben-Gurion, Menachem Begin, and Binyamin Netanyahu.

THEODOR HERZL: FOUNDER OF ZIONISM

On January 5, 1895, Theodor Herzl (1860-1904), a Viennese journalist, watched the show trial at *L'École Militaire* in Paris as Captain Alfred Dreyfus, a Jew on the general staff of the French army who had been falsely accused of treason, was stripped of his military rank and banished to Devil's Island as a mob cried "Death to the Jews." Shocked to the core by the intractable anti-Semitism of Europe, Herzl

The Balfour Declaration

Political Zionism pulled off its first major diplomatic victory during World War I when, in 1917, Zionist leaders Chaim Weitzmann and Nahum Sokolow persuaded the British government to issue a declaration favoring "the establishment in Palestine of a national home for the Jewish people." Britain's motives were mixed. Both Prime Minister Lloyd George and Foreign Secretary Arthur Balfour, the declaration's writer, had been influenced by Christian Zionism, which advocated the return of Jews to Palestine. At the same time, the emigration of Jews from Britain would please British anti-Semites who wished to be rid of what they called "the Jewish Problem."

While Balfour's letter to Lord Rothschild prescribed that "nothing shall be done which may prejudice the civil and religious rights of existing non-Jewish communities in Palestine," it did not contain any pledge of *political* rights for either Jewish or non-Jewish communities. Palestinian Arab leaders denounced the Balfour Declaration, stating "...we always sympathized profoundly with the persecuted Jews and their misfortunes in other countries..., but there is wide difference between such sympathy and the acceptance of such a nation...ruling over us and disposing of our affairs."[10]

> Foreign Office,
> November 2nd, 1917.
>
> Dear Lord Rothschild,
>
> I have much pleasure in conveying to you, on behalf of His Majesty's Government, the following declaration of sympathy with Jewish Zionist aspirations which has been submitted to, and approved by, the Cabinet
>
> "His Majesty's Government view with favour the establishment in Palestine of a national home for the Jewish people, and will use their best endeavours to facilitate the achievement of this object, it being clearly understood that nothing shall be done which may prejudice the civil and religious rights of existing non-Jewish communities in Palestine, or the rights and political status enjoyed by Jews in any other country'
>
> I should be grateful if you would bring this declaration to the knowledge of the Zionist Federation.
>
> Arthur James Balfour

ABOUT THIS SECTION

This section is a condensed and edited version of an essay by the Rev. Dr. Walt Davis and Dr. Pauline Coffman entitled "Political Zionism from Herzl (1890s) to Ben-Gurion (1960s)," in Wagner and Davis, eds., *Zionism and the Quest for Justice in the Holy Land.*

Dr. Davis is Professor of the Sociology of Religion (emeritus) at San Francisco Theological Seminary. Dr. Coffman is Professor and Director (retired) of the School of Adult Learning, North Park University in Chicago. Both were author/editors of *Steadfast Hope: The Palestinian Quest for Just Peace* (2009, 2011).

set off on a personal quest that would lead to the creation of the state of Israel half a century later.

In 1896 Herzl wrote *The Jewish State,* calling for the creation of a national homeland for all Jews. The following year he convened the first international Zionist Congress, which began the implementation of this goal by establishing the World Zionist Organization. The central tenets of Herzl's Zionism were:

- Anti-Semitism is a permanent, endemic, and ineradicable element of European cultures;
- Jewish life and culture in the *Galut* (exile) is distorted, producing passive, servile, and self-deprecating masses;
- Only a Jewish state can provide safety and well-being for Jews and reverse the negation of the *Galut* by creating a "New Jew";
- Therefore, once a Jewish state is created, Jews should eventually immigrate to it, thus bringing an end to anti-Semitism.

OPPOSITION TO POLITICAL ZIONISM

From the earliest days of political Zionism prominent Jewish writers have opposed it. In his own day, Herzl's greatest opponent, Ahad Ha'am (a cultural Zionist), predicted that the pursuit of an independent state would erode "the true spirit of Judaism" (the ethical teaching of the Hebrew prophets) and "beget in us a tendency to find the path of glory in the attainment of material power and political domination."[11] Later on, other cultural Zionists, including Rabbi Judah Magnes (one of the founders of Hebrew University in Jerusalem) and social philosopher Martin Buber, would join Ha'am in warning that moral degeneration might be the end result of Jewish nationalism and the desire to become "like all the nations."[12]

Zionism was a small minority movement within world Jewry in the early 1900s. Although 35,000 Jews, mostly from Russia, moved to Palestine between 1882 and 1903—this was later named the First *Aliyah*[13]—almost half of these new arrivals later left the country because of illness, Arab resistance, and other hardships. The Second *Aliyah,* 1904-1914, brought 40,000 Jews from the Russian empire and a generation of socialist leaders who would form the backbone of the Labor Zionist movement, which envisioned agricultural labor by Jews as the means for "redeeming" Israel and the creation of an "egalitar-

This 1931 propaganda poster was distributed by the *Irgun* in central Europe. The map includes both Mandatory Palestine and the Emirate of Transjordan, areas which the *Irgun* claimed in their entirety for a future Jewish state.

ian Jewish society from which Arabs were excluded."[14] This generation of immigrants to Palestine would lead the fight for independence and govern Israel from statehood in 1948 until 1977.

ZE'EV JABOTINSKY: FOUNDER OF REVISIONIST ZIONISM

The Russian-born Ze'ev (Vladimir) Jabotinsky (1880-1940) rejected the idealism of socialist Labor Zionism. In 1925 he founded an opposition party, the Revisionists, forerunner of today's Likud Party, which would eventually be elected to power in Israel in 1977 under the leadership of Menachem Begin. (The current Prime Minister, Binyamin Netanyahu, also belongs to the Likud Party and strongly identifies with the Revisionist tradition.)

Jabotinsky's most influential essay, *The Iron Wall,* was written in 1923, long before the Nazi genocide would provide Zionists with the fundamental rationale for establishing a nation state in Palestine as a haven for the Jewish people, with little regard for the impact on the existing Palestinian population and culture. No colonization can succeed by ignoring the 'iron law' of armed force, Jabotinsky believed. "That is morality for you," he asserted.

> Zionism is a colonizing adventure, and therefore it stands or falls by the question of armed force. It is important to build, it is important to speak

ARCHITECTS OF ZIONISM

Theodor Herzl

Vladimir Jabotinsky

David Ben-Gurion

Hebrew, but unfortunately, it is even more important to be able to shoot....[15]

Israeli scholar Benjamin Beit-Hallahmi summarizes Jabotinsky's position:

The Labor Zionist attitude towards the natives and their predicament was one of denial. The right-wing approach, developed by Jabotinsky, stated bluntly that the conflict was real, that dispossession was real and inevitable, but it was justified to fulfill Zionist plans....[Its] attitude was one of defiance and confidence. The natives would have to accept their fate—namely an historical defeat. Right-wing Zionism has been quite open, even proud, about the colonialist role of Zionism and about its inherent violence vis-à-vis the natives of Palestine....Jabotinsky...did not play games nor mince his words. He called a spade a spade and Zionism armed colonialism. Jabotinsky never denied the conflict between Zionism and the Palestinians. On the contrary, he made it into one of the basic assumptions of his political program.[16]

Although Ben-Gurion and other Labor Zionists managed to modulate and even neutralize Jabotinsky's influence in the 1920s and 1930s, his fundamental doctrine of military force is firmly embedded today not only in the Israeli Defense Forces, the Likud Party, and other parties on the right, but also in other more centrist parties as well.

DAVID BEN-GURION: LABOR ZIONISM

David Ben-Gurion (1886-1973) is regarded as the founding father of the state of Israel. He immigrated to Palestine from Poland in 1906 to join the growing number of Zionist communal farm workers. In the 1920s and '30s he rose to leadership in key Zionist organizations including the powerful socialist labor federation (the *Histadrut*) and the Hebrew Defense Organization (the *Haganah*). From 1935-1948 Ben-Gurion headed the Jewish Agency which became a virtual Jewish government-in-formation. This put him in line to become the first Prime Minister and Minister of Defense in 1948, positions he held for much of the time until his retirement in 1963.

From the time of his early years in Palestine until the end of World War II, Ben-Gurion repeatedly gave voice to the dominant ideology of Labor Zionism: the revolutionary task of creating a new Jew in a new Jewish state where pioneer Zionists would honor

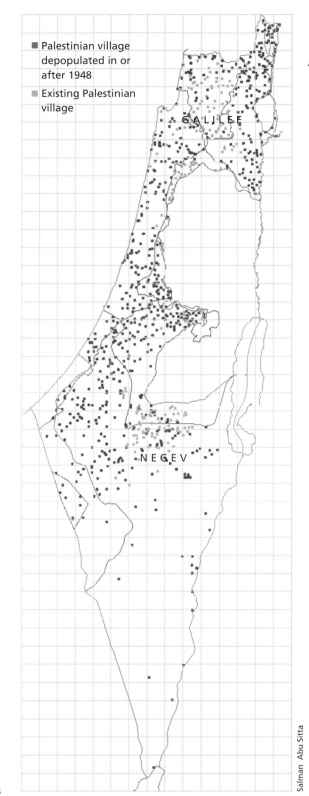

■ Palestinian village depopulated in or after 1948

■ Existing Palestinian village

GALILEE

NEGEV

Salman Abu Sitta

"Judaizing" the Land

More than 500 Palestinian villages were depopulated by Jewish soldiers and paramilitaries in 1948 (the Israeli *Nakba*-awareness organization *Zochrot* numbers the destroyed localities at 678). The villages were destroyed not only to make it impossible for the Palestinians who had fled their homes to return, but also to erase the evidence of recent Palestinian inhabitation from the landscape of the young Jewish state.

Now, 65 years later, the Zionist quest for demographic control of the land is still underway—not only in the occupied territories, but within Israel itself. State planners pursue the goal of ensuring a "contiguous Jewish presence" in every area within Israel. In the Galilee and Negev, regions with high concentrations of Arabs, "Judaization" policies benefit Jewish Israelis while restricting the growth and development of the Palestinian population. Much of this discriminatory development occurs on agricultural land expropriated from Palestinian villages by the state—expropriations which have stripped their Arab residents of their former livelihoods. [Read more on page 60.]

labor, conquer the land, restore Jewish dignity, be free from fear generated in gentile nations, and have opportunity for individual creativity. It would be a socialist, collectivist, egalitarian, Hebrew-speaking society.

Like Herzl before him, Ben-Gurion was sensitive to world opinion and carefully avoided public statements about "the Arab problem," namely, how a Jewish homeland would compromise the rights of native Palestinians.[17] However, during the Arab

Revolt of 1936-39, caused by Palestinian fears of dispossession and Jewish dominance, Ben-Gurion asked Elimelech Avnir, the *Haganah* military commander in Tel Aviv, to draw up guidelines for the complete takeover of Palestine should the British relinquish their governing role. At a meeting of the Jewish Agency Executive in June 1938, Ben-Gurion declared, "I am for compulsory transfer; I do not see anything immoral in it."[18]

The growing Nazi threat to European Jewry contributed to Ben-Gurion's willingness to sacrifice Arab rights in Palestine. A decade later, Ben-Gurion would adopt a draconian plan to rid the new state of as many Palestinians as possible.

In November 1947 the United Nations adopted a plan to partition Palestine into areas designated for a Jewish state and an Arab state. Each state would consist of both Jewish and Arab citizens, but tragically no provision was made for an interim United Nations military force to protect the rights of the minorities during the transition. As expected, war broke out between Jewish and Arab forces when Israel declared independence in May 1948.

Two months prior to independence, Ben-Gurion and his advisors had already adopted the *Haganah's Plan Dalet*, which called for the systematic and total expulsion of Palestinians from their homeland.[19] From December 1947 until the armistice between Israel and its Arab neighbors in 1949, this strategy of ethnic cleansing would force all the inhabitants from more than 500 Palestinian villages, totally and deliberately destroy the structures in 400 Palestinian villages, create 750,000 Palestinian refugees, kill most who resisted the dispossession of lands and homes, and prevent the return of Palestinian refugees to their homes after the cessation of hostilities.

ABSORBING NEW IMMIGRANTS

In the first decade of the life of the new state, the Jewish population almost doubled. Holocaust survivors poured in from Europe. Hundreds of thousands of Sephardic and Mizrahi[20] Jews from Morocco, Algeria, Tunisia, Egypt, Syria, Iraq, and other Middle Eastern countries flooded Israel to escape the actual violent blowback or fear of blowback as the region became inflamed at the perceived injustice of the enforced partition of Palestine, the creation of a Jewish state, the ethnic cleansing of Palestinians in 1947-48, and the Sinai War of 1956.

By 1961 45% of the Israeli population comprised Jews from North Africa and Arab countries and formed what has been called "Second Israel," a lower class of clerks, small retailers, car mechanics, taxi drivers, vegetable peddlers, and agricultural workers employed by the *kibbutzim* (collectivized communal farms). The culture clash with the majority of Ashkenazi (European) Jews was intense. The Jews of "Second Israel" were religious rather than secular,

Unsung Hero of the Warsaw Ghetto Uprising

At the time of his death in Poland in 2009, Marek Edelman (b. ca. 1920) was the last surviving leader of the 1942 Warsaw Ghetto Uprising. A pre-war member of the Jewish Socialist Bund and lifelong anti-Zionist, Edelman was, like others that declined to embrace the postwar Zionist framework, a victim of "the [Israeli] nationalization of the narrative of the uprisings as well as the expunging of its incompatible, non-Zionist components."[23] In his later life, Edelman further alienated the Zionist orthodoxy by speaking out in solidarity with the Palestinian people and cautioning that Jewish self-defense in Israel was in danger of crossing the line into oppression.

Nahum Goldmann Museum of the Jewish Diaspora, Tel Aviv

1919. A class at the Alliance Israëlite Universelle School for Girls, Tangier, Morocco. At its peak in the 1950s, the Moroccan Jewish population numbered 300,000 within a general population of some 8 million. Unlike elsewhere in the Arab world, the creation of Israel did not spark widespread animosity or attacks on Jews. Recruiters for the young Jewish state were active in Morocco as elsewhere in the Middle East—many Jews left after being told by Zionist agents they were in danger. Emigrating Moroccan Jews chose the US, France, and Israel as their destinations; many are reported to look back fondly on the cordial relations they enjoyed with their Moroccan Muslim neighbors. Today, Morocco is home to approximately 2,500 Jews.[21, 22]

modest in dress, opposed to gender equality, unaccustomed to the collectivist approach to communal life and child-rearing, and market oriented rather than socialist.

Some of the *Mizrahi* (Arab Jews) were well-known Arabic-language poets and writers who joined with Palestinian poets to form a union of Arabic writers. Early attempts at cultural cooperation between Palestinians and Arab Jews did not endure, as many Mizrahi realized that "self de-Arabization was the key factor that would ensure their full integration into the more veteran Israeli Jewish society…."[24]

CLOAKING SECULAR NATIONALISM WITH SACRED MESSIANISM

As early as 1951 Ben-Gurion realized that to provide housing and jobs for all anticipated immigrant refugees and cover Israel's trade deficits, he would need foreign investment and aid grants. At the risk of subverting the planned economy of the *Histadrut* (federation of labor unions), he launched the Israel Bonds Campaign and encouraged Jews in the Diaspora to start up private companies in Israel. He also recognized the need for a unifying institution other than the socialist Histadrut to initiate a process of cultural assimilation so that the diverse cultures of world Jewry could begin to form a new national identity. The unifying institution he chose was the military—infused as it was with a spirit of national pride, discipline, obedience, courage, and sacrifice. He called the new pragmatism "statism" and began creating a state cult or civil religion of patriotic nationalism to unify and mobilize a population so diverse that few other unifying ideals existed. The intention was to make room for the rich diversity of economic, political, religious, and cultural differences without undermining national unity. Many Labor Zionists were furious at the gradual marginalization of socialist institutions and influence and their replacement with capitalist institutions.

BEN-GURION AND THE BIBLE

Although he was a thoroughgoing secularist, Ben-Gurion also contributed to the sacred character of Israeli civil religion by interlacing nationalism with Biblical literalism. He

> regarded the creation of a Jewish state in Palestine as a reflection of the biblical stories of exodus from exile in Egypt and the conquest of the land

of Canaan…."[The Bible is] the single most important book in my life," he declared.[25]

From the early 1950s until his retirement from public life in 1963, he conducted Bible studies every two weeks in the Prime Minister's residence or his *kibbutz* in the Negev, lecturing to a wide range of political leaders and scholars. In his memoirs Ben-Gurion noted the role of religious motivation in the recruitment of Jewish immigrants to Israel:

> Without a messianic, emotional, ideological impulse, without the vision of restoration and redemption, there is no earthly reason why even oppressed and underprivileged Jews…should wander off to Israel of all places….The immigrants were seized with an immortal vision of redemption, which became the principal motivation of their lives.[26]

Tellingly, Ben-Gurion's favorite book of the Bible was Joshua, which recounts the Israelite conquest of the land, the annihilation of the Canaanites, the settlement of the land by the twelve tribes of Israel, and a ceremony in which all the people promise to be faithful to their covenant with God. In this manner, the secular Ben-Gurion appropriated the biblical stories for a nationalistic civil religion that would later buttress the expansionism of both religious and secular settlers after the Six-Day War in June 1967.[27]

1950. This Romanian Jew, a survivor of the Nazi concentration camps, immigrated to Israel, where he settled with his congregation, *Agudah Israel*, in a village recently "cleansed" of Palestinians.

Gamma-Keystone

REFLECTION

1. What questions arise for you from reading and reflecting on this section?

2. Discuss the role of European nationalism and anti-Semitism in the creation of Zionism.

3. How, why, and when did Zionism, a secular nationalist movement, become a religious movement?

4. Discuss the role of the British in the establishment of Zionism in Palestine. What have been the consequences of the exertion of control by external powers over the region?

5. What were the consequences for Palestinians and Jews of the 1947 vote of the United Nations to authorize the partition of Palestine?

6. What were the objections that cultural Zionists raised against political Zionism?

Constantinian Religion

> *The ultimate sin is silence in the face of injustice.*
>
> ELIE WIESEL

Some historians identify the conversion of Emperor Constantine to Christianity in 312 C.E. as the decisive date after which anti-Jewish contempt became systemic and pathological. James Carroll's influential study *Constantine's Sword: The Church and the Jews* explores what happened when European Christian ethnic-religious prejudice became institutionalized and invested with state power. Carroll's study of "Constantinian Christianity" is also a scathing critique of and apology for centuries of Christian mistreatment of the Jewish people.

Christianity is only one of several world religions to have harnessed religious ideology to political power. And in the same way that Carroll, a Roman Catholic, has examined Christian history, Jews continue to examine the moral and religious consequences for Judaism inherent in the rise of political Zionism.

CRITICS OF CONSTANTINIAN JUDAISM

Martin Buber (1878–1965), a Jewish religious philosopher who profoundly influenced Protestant theologians Reinhold Niebuhr and Paul Tillich, opposed the imposition by force of political Zionism on Palestine's diverse, multi-ethnic society. In the aftermath of Israel's military victory in 1948, Buber lamented, "The cry of victory does not have the power of preventing the clear-eyed from seeing that the soul of the Zionist enterprise has evaporated…." He continued prophetically, "Yes, a goal has been reached, but it is not called Zion….[The] day will yet come when the victorious march of which our people is so proud today will seem to us like a cruel detour."[1]

Judah Magnes (1877–1948), a prominent US-born Reform rabbi who emigrated to Israel, was a committed cultural Zionist who helped found both the American Jewish Committee and Hebrew University in Jerusalem. His vocal opposition to the fusing of Judaism and nationalism inherent in the establishment of a specifically Jewish state made him the target of heckling and attacks in the press.

Several branches of ultra-orthodox Judaism have rejected Israel's legitimacy since its founding. "Of all the crimes of political Zionism," writes one ultra-orthodox critic of Israel,

> the worst and most basic…is that from its beginning Zionism has sought to separate the Jewish people from their G-d, to render the divine covenant null and void, and to substitute a 'modern' statehood and fraudulent sovereignty for the lofty ideals of the Jewish people.[2]

Rabbi Brant Rosen, a Reconstructionist, is currently "working…toward a theology of Jewish liberation that reclaims the universal vision of the Prophets and provides a progressive spiritual alternative to the fusing of religion and state power."[3]

That these voices are not widely embraced as an integral part of the spectrum of Jewish thought is a reflection of the near-total success of mainstream Zionist institutions in suppressing dissenting perspectives. Increasingly, however, Jews are challenging the right of the old guard to determine the limits of acceptable speech and action.[4]

Theologian Marc Ellis, himself the target of delegitimization and intimidation campaigns by hawkish monitoring groups, finds that the Jewish ethical tradition is "now facing its own moral crisis as Jewish identity becomes increasingly uncritically identified with the governmental politics of America and Israel." "Holocaust theology," says Ellis, describes a worldview that, in our time, "continues as normative in the Jewish community." Jews who dissent from the mainstream assumptions, Ellis writes, risk "excommunication" because of their failure to adhere to the "theological prerequisite to community membership."[5]

The modern Christian Church has learned many lessons from its own history of anti-Jewish contempt. And yet, these lessons are incomplete; the process of reckoning with the Church's complicity in the destruction of European Jewry has rendered many Christians mute in the face of Israel's mistreatment of the Palestinians.

THE INTERFAITH ECUMENICAL DEAL

Marc Ellis calls this syndrome "the interfaith ecumenical deal" or "the interfaith ecumenical dialogue, the post-Holocaust place where Jews and Christians have mended their relationship." Ellis writes,

> Israel was huge in this dialogue. Christians supported Israel as repentance for anti-Semitism and the Holocaust. Then as Israel became more controversial with [Israeli] abuse of Palestinians, Christians remained silent. Non-support and, worse, criticism of Israeli policies, was seen by the Jewish dialoguers as backtracking to anti-Semitism. That's where the dialogue became a deal: Silence on the Christian side brings no criticism of anti-Semitism from the Jewish side.[6]

Carroll's work in *Constantine's Sword* rightly identifies the transgressions of Christians and the Church toward the Jews over centuries. Carroll's exposé is incomplete because it errs, like many well-intentioned partners in the "ecumenical deal," in failing to recognize that Israeli policies are also an expression of "Constantinian religion." When Carroll complains that Church leaders seem "interested only in partial memory and a limited reckoning with the past,"[7] one might fault him and other Christian participants in the "ecumenical deal" for exempting Israel from scrutiny.

Carroll's book explores what happened when "the power of the empire became joined to the ideology of the Church." For Church and empire both, Carroll concludes, it "led to consequences better and worse—although not for Jews, for whom, nothing good would come."[8] Few in our time would dispute the obvious corollary: the fusion of state power with Judaism has led to consequences better and worse—although decidedly worse for Palestinians.

Marc Ellis lifts up a vision of what might occur when Church leaders "have finally learned the central lesson of Christian complicity in the Holocaust." The lesson, Ellis writes, is not only that Christians have erred toward the Jewish people, but that more universally, "The ultimate sin is silence in the face of injustice."[9]

3 · The Concept and Practice of a Jewish State

JUNE 1967: THE THIRD ARAB-ISRAELI WAR

From 1949 to 1967 there were three Arab-Israeli wars. The first war ended when the Armistice of 1949 left Egypt in control of the Sinai and the Gaza Strip and Jordan in control of the West Bank and East Jerusalem. The war of 1956 ended with UN troops policing the separation of Egyptian and Israeli forces along the Suez Canal, with an ongoing pattern of belligerence continuing in the following years.

Tensions between Egypt and Israel reached the boiling point in early June 1967. Many in Israel and around the world feared that Egypt, which had been rearmed by the Soviet Union, might inflict a lethal blow on the small state of Israel. The General Staff of the Israeli military, knowing that Egypt wasn't prepared for war, confronted the Israeli cabinet with the demand for an immediate preemptive strike against Egypt.

The Israeli strike began on June 5, 1967. In six days the war was over, with Israel achieving an overwhelming victory. Israeli forces destroyed the military capabilities of Egypt, Jordan, and Syria; took Gaza and the Sinai from Egypt; pushed Jordan out of East Jerusalem and the West Bank; and occupied the Syrian Golan Heights.

On June 8, 1967, an editorial in the liberal Israeli newspaper *Haaretz* declared: "The glory of past ages no longer is to be seen at a distance but is, from now on, part of the new state." The following day, General Moshe Dayan, a self-declared secularist who led the capture of East Jerusalem, could not repress the messianic sentiments which he shared with secular and religious Israelis: "We have returned to our holiest places, we have returned in order not to part from them ever again."[1]

THE REVISIONIST LOGIC TAKES HOLD

After the Six-Day War Israel annexed Palestinian East Jerusalem (6.4 square kilometers) and 28 Palestinian villages (an additional 64 square kilometers) on land adjacent to East Jerusalem. The annexation was immediately condemned by United Nations

Security Council resolutions 237 and 242 as well as General Assembly resolutions 2253 and 2254. Israeli non-compliance with the UN demand for withdrawal from territories occupied during the war elicited UNSC resolutions 252 (1968) and 267 (1969) restating the same demands and condemnations. In 1980 the Israeli Knesset passed the Jerusalem Basic Law, declaring Jerusalem to be Israel's "eternal and indivisible" capital. This action provoked the UN Security Council Resolution 478, which declared Israel's annexation "null and void." Nevertheless, every Israeli prime minister since 1967 has declared that Greater Jerusalem will always remain a part of the state of Israel.

THE REASSERTION OF NATIONAL MESSIANISM

Soon after the Six Day War the idea of "Greater Israel" gained wide support. In 1967 the Labor government gave a boost to the religious Zionist movement by resurrecting biblical nomenclature, replacing the name "West Bank" with "Judea and Samaria." The Education Ministry issued to schools new maps of *Eretz Yisrael* that included "Judea and Samaria" without clear boundaries to the state and without the "Green Line" demarcation of the 1949 armistice.

According to [Gush Emunim's] spiritual leaders, a greater authority existed above that of the state.... the law could be broken if this served "higher" aims.[2]

Rabbi Moshe Levinger (left) and Hanan Porat, two of the founding leaders of *Gush Emunim*, advocated the view that "God had promised the West Bank to the Jewish people and that it was their duty to settle it." Since Levinger and Porat established an Israeli settler base in Hebron in 1968, Religious Zionist extremism has moved from the margins to the mainstream and shaped the Israeli state settlement project in the occupied territories. On Porat's death in 2011, Prime Minister Binyamin Netanyahu praised him for having "dedicated his life to building up the land of Israel, and to educating generations of students about Religious Zionism and loving the land of Israel and the Jewish people."[3]

ABOUT THIS SECTION

This section is a condensed and edited version of an essay by the Rev. Dr. Walt Davis and Dr. Pauline Coffman entitled "The Triumph of Revisionist Zionism" in Wagner and Davis, eds., *Zionism and the Quest for Justice in the Holy Land.*

Dr. Davis is Professor of the Sociology of Religion (emeritus) at San Francisco Theological Seminary. Dr. Coffman is Professor and Director (retired) of the School of Adult Learning, North Park University in Chicago.

These changes had the effect of erasing Palestine not only from maps but also from the minds of Israelis. At the same time, by providing biblical justification for the military conquest of Palestine, it demonstrated the intentional merger of political and religious Zionism.

The nationalist religious settler movement took a leap forward in 1974 with the formation of *Gush Emunim* (Bloc of the Faithful), a messianic religious group committed to the establishment of Jewish religious settlements in the West Bank, Gaza, and the Golan Heights. The new Zionism of Greater Israel gained official sponsorship when the Likud Party was elected to power in 1977 under Prime Minister Menachem Begin, marking a shift to the right in Israeli politics that continues to the present. The government began to provide financial incentives for the establishment of settlements in the West Bank, now identified as "Judea and Samaria." The purpose was to solidify Jewish control of what was claimed to have been Israelite territory in biblical times and to prevent the establishment of a Palestinian state.

In their recent book, *Chosen Peoples*, Todd Gitlin and Liel Liebovitz conclude that Israeli national messianism, whether in its overt religious form or in the form of a civil religion, reflects a conscious or unconscious recognition of divine election to be God's chosen people. Gitlin and Liebovitz write, "Zionism's inability to shake the messianic ideal became manifest in the hold that the West Bank settlers exercised on the conscience of the whole nation."[4] In spite of its thoroughly secular origin, Zionism flourished, especially after 1967, because of the inextricable blending of its political and religious agenda. This is one example of the similarities between Zionism, South African apartheid, and Jim Crow segregation in the Southern US: All three ideologies are a political-religious blend, providing religious justification for the politics of racial or ethnic discrimination.

THE CONSOLIDATION OF AMERICAN ZIONISM

During the 1940s the American Jewish Committee (AJC), the most influential Jewish civic organization of the time, comprising largely members of the Reform movement, remained anti-Zionist. In January 1948 the AJC committee on Palestine expressed grave concern that "the Zionists will now make an attempt to organize the community along Zionist lines and will try to capture the communal organiza-

There are similarities between Zionism, South African apartheid, and Jim Crow segregation in the Southern US.

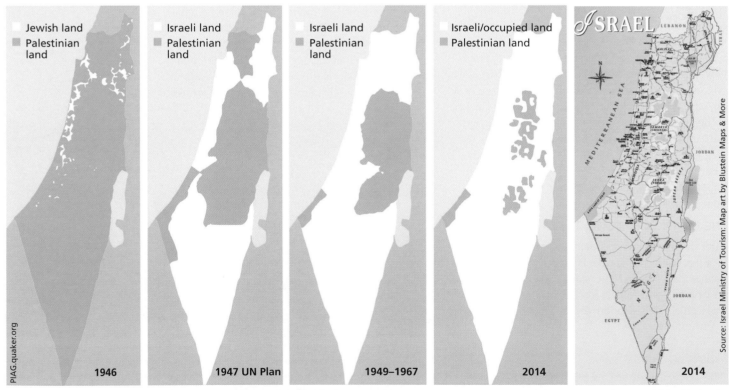

PIAG.quaker.org

Jewish land / Palestinian land — **1946**

Israeli land / Palestinian land — **1947 UN Plan**

Israeli land / Palestinian land — **1949–1967**

Israeli/occupied land / Palestinian land — **2014**

ISRAEL — **2014**

Source: Israel Ministry of Tourism: Map art by Blustein Maps & More

The inexorable expansion of Israeli control over former Mandate Palestine is, by now, virtually complete. Fully half the population within this land area is not Jewish.[5] For Israelis committed to the principle of a Jewish state, the population issue poses a demographic threat to the ethno-religious character of the state. Palestinians are faced with the prospect of, at best, second-class status in a state that classifies them as outsiders and, at worst, deprivation in isolated enclaves without autonomy or self-determination. As Palestinian population centers in the occupied West Bank have become isolated "bantustans" administered under a discriminatory, two-tier legal system that privileges Jewish Israelis, an inevitable—if contested—comparison has been made to apartheid-era South Africa.

tions."[6] This concern was prophetic. The Anti-Defamation League (ADL), which until then had been generally aligned with the AJC, quickly switched sides in the months leading up to Israeli statehood. Since Israeli statehood, the ADL has equated anti-Zionism with anti-Semitism.[7]

Right-wing Revisionist Zionism and Israeli political-religious nationalism found a ready audience in the US following the Six-Day War. Jewish theologian Marc Ellis writes, "Israel was not central to [American] Jewish identity. It only emerged as the central Jewish concern after the 1967 war."[8] Now most if not all of the 51 member groups affiliated with the Conference of Presidents of Major Jewish Organizations[9] are Zionist, committed to the suppression of any criticism of Israel in the mainstream American media, in American civil society, and even within their own organizations. In fact, they now designate any criticism of Israel as a delegitimization of the state of Israel.

MENACHEM BEGIN: FIRST LIKUD PRIME MINISTER

In October 1973, during the Muslim holy month of Ramadan and on *Yom Kippur,* the holiest day in the Jewish calendar, Egypt and Syria launched a surprise attack on Israel that lasted almost three weeks. Israel was caught off guard and suffered over 10,000 casualties. This fourth Arab-Israeli war marked the political twilight of Labor Zionism. With the next election in 1977 Menachem Begin (1913-1992) became prime minister as the *Likud* party soundly defeated Labor and its allies. Now the Israeli settlements in the occupied territories, declared illegal repeatedly by the international community, had an ardent champion as head of government. The number of settlements and settlers grew exponentially with government sponsorship and financing, becoming the lynchpin of Israel's military occupation of the West Bank, East Jerusalem, and the Golan Heights. By 1981 when Begin was elected for a second term, the consolidation of "Greater Israel" had become the number-one priority of the Begin government. Since the Six-Day War in 1967 this policy has fed the zeal of nationalist religious settlers who have had a disproportionately large influence in political Zionism's move to the right.

Before World War I Begin had commanded the European Revisionist movement's paramilitary group, *Betar,* in Czechoslovakia and Poland. A devoted disciple of Jabotinsky, Begin came to Palestine in 1942 and quickly rose to commander of the Revisionist paramilitary *Irgun.* He led the *Irgun* from 1943 until 1948 in an armed revolt against the British, and, in 1947-48, planned attacks on Palestinian towns and villages. Bernard Avishai of Hebrew University notes that in Begin's chronicle of *Irgun,* which Ben-Gurion and others labeled a terrorist group,

Menachem Begin

Life without access to livelihood: such is the legacy Begin bequeathed to Palestinians.

Menachem Begin addresses an *Irgun* rally in Israel, 1948 (note *Irgun* emblem, lower left). *Irgun* terrorism targeted both British officials of the Mandate and Palestinians. During the period 1937-1948 *Irgun* operatives carried out bombings, shootings, kidnappings, assassinations, and massacres of unarmed civilians. In demostrating that terrorism can be an effective strategy for forcing political change, the *Irgun* inspired political terror movements elsewhere around the world.

Begin glorified armed revolt: 'Out of the blood and tears and ashes a new specimen of Jew was born, a specimen completely unknown to the world for over eighteen hundred years: the FIGHTING JEW.'..."[10]

Begin's most significant achievement as prime minister was the peace agreement with Egypt, brokered by President Jimmy Carter between Begin and Anwar Sadat in September 1978 at Camp David. Sadat had taken the initiative by his historic trip to Jerusalem in November 1977. Begin resisted responding to Sadat's peace initiative until public pressure forced his hand. The Camp David Accords called for peace between Egypt and Israel, the return of the Sinai to Egypt (which Israel had controlled since 1967), and full Palestinian autonomy. Shortly after signing the peace accords in April 1979, Begin approved new Jewish settlements near the West Bank cities of Ramallah and Nablus. Even more insulting to Sadat and the peace agreement,[11] the Prime Minister's office prepared plans that would give Palestinians "autonomy over their persons but not over their resources."[12] Israel would maintain exclusive control over the West Bank aquifers, public land, roads and communications, immigration, and public order. Life without access to livelihood: such is the legacy Begin bequeathed to Palestinians.

Begin's fall from power came quickly, tarnished as he was by poor stewardship of the Israeli economy and the 1982 invasion-gone-awry of Lebanon to root out the Palestinian Liberation Organization, including the tragic massacre of thousands of Palestinians and Lebanese. The death of his wife in late 1982 caused Begin great grief, and a year later he resigned from office and withdrew from public life.

BINYAMIN NETANYAHU: TOWARD A SINGLE, JEWISH, APARTHEID STATE

The themes that run consistently through the leadership of the current Prime Minister of Israel, Binyamin "Bibi" Netanyahu (1949–) reflect a steady hardening to the right for political Zionism. Israeli politics are driven by actual and manipulated fear of annihilation (another Holocaust), radical separation from Arab Palestinians, and a clear policy of the expansion of settlements in the occupied territories to encircle Jerusalem and claim as much Palestinian land as possible. It is hard to find any evidence that recent Israeli governments have any intention of negotiating a just peace with Palestinians.

Prime Minister Netanyahu became the standard-bearer for right-wing political Zionism after joining the Likud party in 1993 and winning election as the leader. In 1996 he was Likud's candidate for Prime Minister, the first Israeli election in which Israelis directly elected their Prime Minister. A wave of suicide bombings in 1996 helped spread his campaign message: "Netanyahu—making a safe peace."[13]

Binyamin Netanyahu

It is hard to find any evidence that recent Israeli governments have any intention of negotiating a just peace with Palestinians.

Netanyahu was elected Prime Minister, but had to form a coalition with the ultra-orthodox parties in order to govern because his party, Likud, did not win a majority in the Knesset.

In September 1993 the Oslo Accords were signed by Yasser Arafat for the Palestinian Liberation Organization (PLO) and Yitzhak Rabin for Israel, giving to the newly created "Palestinian Authority" (PA) limited autonomy in Jericho and Gaza. Netanyahu made it clear from the start of his term as Prime Minister that he disagreed with the Oslo Accords and emphasized a policy of "three no's": no withdrawal from the Golan Heights, no division of Jerusalem which Israeli had annexed in 1967,[16] and no preconditions whatsoever for negotiations.[17] Under pressure from the US to make concessions on West Bank settlements in order to keep momentum for peace, Netanyahu signed two agreements with Palestinians—the Hebron Protocol and the Wye River Memorandum. His supporters felt betrayed and accused him of trading "land for peace." As a result of these concessions and a number of scandals in his personal life he lost the next election.

NETANYAHU'S BACKGROUND

A look at Netanyahu's background is helpful. He is the son of Benzion Netanyahu (1910–2012), who was a professor of Jewish history at Cornell University, editor of *Encyclopaedia Hebraica*, and a senior aide to Ze'ev Jabotinsky, who has been called the ideological father of the Likud Party. Netanyahu's father and grandfather were leaders in the Zionist movement and served in the Israeli military. "Leaving no room for compromise, Benzion argued that Jews inevitably faced discrimination that was racial, not religious, and that compromising with Arabs was futile."[18]

A specialist in the history of Jews in Spain, Benzion thought "Jewish history was a history of holocausts" and believed Arabs would choose to respond only to force and to exterminate Jews if they had the chance.[19]

In the *Jewish Journal*, David Myers, chair of the history department at UCLA, writes,

We might call this the Amalekite view of Jewish history, referring to the hated biblical foes of the Israelites whose existence—and even memory—should be blotted out (Exodus 17:14). The historian's [Benzion's] belief that the Jews have been subjected to constant genocidal threats did not lead him to a passive fatalism, as if there were nothing that the Jews could do in the face of

March 2013. Netanyahu (left) poses with settler leaders celebrating the official recognition of outpost settlements in Rechilim and Nofei Nehemia. "We are facing an attack on the settlement enterprise and against our existence in the State of Israel," Netanyahu said.[14] Peace Now reports that "during the first eight months of the new Netanyahu government, there has been a non-stop settlement construction and approval boom."[15]

Jerusalem Post: Meir Berachia/Samaria Regional Council

Amalek. Rather, it inspired his own militant Zionism, which demanded a persistent willingness to wage war against one's enemies.[20]

Myers believes Netanyahu's statements about the threat of Iran are an indication that he shares his father Benzion's Amalekite worldview. Iran is not just a grave threat; Netanyahu compares it to Amalek, the most terrifying of Jewish persecutions.[21]

NETANYAHU'S SECOND AND THIRD TERMS AS PRIME MINISTER: 2009 – 2013

Netanyahu's second term began in February 2009 when Likud was able to control a majority of the seats in the Knesset by forming an alliance with Avigdor Lieberman's *Yisrael Beiteinu* ("Israel is our Home"). This political party, popular with Russian immigrants like Lieberman, is further to the right than Likud and is associated with xenophobia.

During the 2009-2013 period the Knesset passed over a dozen discriminatory laws. The Association for Civil Rights in Israel notes that because of this tide of anti-democratic legislation,

> the basic principles of the Israeli democratic system are being undermined. There is an ongoing infringement on issues such as freedom of expression, human dignity, and equality; on the possibility of upholding the pluralism of views and thoughts; on freedom of assembly and protest....[22]

These laws illustrate the steady hardening of right wing politics in Israel.[23]

NETANYAHU AND THE "JEWISH STATE"

In the last decade, Netanyahu has been demanding, as the outcome of any negotiations with Palestinians, their recognition of Israel as a "Jewish state." Glenn Kessler's October 2010 *Washington Post* article traces the history of this diplomatic demand. "Nine years ago," Kessler explains,

> then-Secretary of State Colin L. Powell delivered a speech on the Middle East in which he briefly called on Palestinians to recognize Israel as a "Jewish state." Powell doesn't recall how the phrase ended up in his speech, but David Ivry, then the Israeli ambassador to the United States, says he persuaded an aide to Powell to slip it in.[24]

President George W. Bush picked up the "Jewish state" concept in his speeches and used it in a controversial exchange of letters with Israeli Prime Minister Ariel Sharon in 2004. Obama has also adopted the phrase, most recently in a speech on September 23, 2010, before the UN General Assembly.[25]

For the Israeli government of Prime Minister Binyamin Netanyahu, Palestinian recognition of Israel as a "Jewish state" would mean acceptance that the Jews have existed in the Middle East for

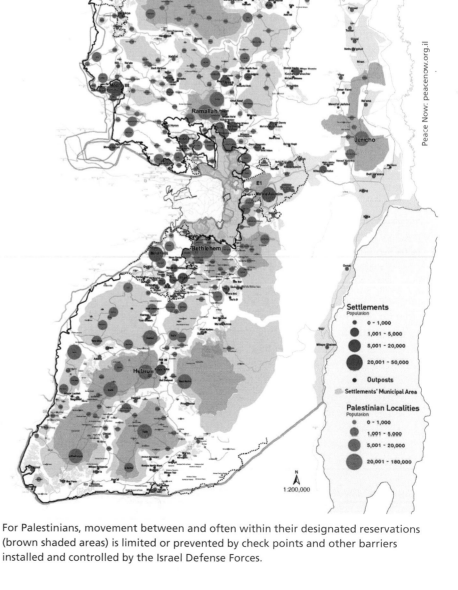

Israeli Settlements in the Occupied West Bank and East Jerusalem
as of November 2011

Peace Now: peacenow.org.il

Settlements
Population
- 0 – 1,000
- 1,001 – 5,000
- 5,001 – 20,000
- 20,001 – 50,000
- Outposts

Settlements' Municipal Area

Palestinian Localities
Population
- 0 – 1,000
- 1,001 – 5,000
- 5,001 – 20,000
- 20,001 – 180,000

N
1:200,000

For Palestinians, movement between and often within their designated reservations (brown shaded areas) is limited or prevented by check points and other barriers installed and controlled by the Israel Defense Forces.

thousands of years—and that Palestinian refugees have no claim to return to property they fled or were forced to flee when Israel was founded six and a half decades ago.

In addition, Palestinian and Arab officials contend that labeling Israel a "Jewish state" calls into question the rights of Palestinians with Israeli citizenship, who comprise 20 percent of Israel's population.[26]

Since the Powell speech, this insistence on explicit Palestinian recognition of a "Jewish state" has become almost routine, but it is relatively *new* language for negotiations and for the international community. The phrase has become part of the American lexicon and appears to be settled American policy, if judged by US presidential campaigns and UN speeches. This demand presents a major obstacle for peace because, just as Jews want a "right of return" to the land, so too do the millions of Palestinian refugees who have languished in refugee camps for three generations. Non-Zionists point out that a "Jewish state" is an *ethnocracy*, not a democracy.

THE JANUARY 2013 ELECTION: "TO THE RIGHT, MARCH!"

Continuing the trend, parties on the right still make up about half of the new Knesset. On March 30, 2013, the new Finance Minister, Yair Lapid, announced a major settlement plan to build an additional 16,000 housing units in the illegal settlements,[27] and on March 27 the new Minister of Economics and Trade, Naftali Bennett, called the two-state solution "beautiful statements" but "sadly detached from reality" and vowed to "never surrender to popular opinion."[28]

Netanyahu's worldview is shaped by both the "Iron Wall" doctrine of Revisionist Zionism and a nationalist appropriation of the Bible as history. While he does not claim to be religious, Netanyahu has pragmatically co-opted the Zionist belief that emerged as the second generation of Zionists moved away from the secular/socialist ideology of Israel's founding generation and adopted a religious one— namely that Jews were "promised" the land of Israel by God as it is described in the Torah/Bible. Here is where political and religious Zionism merge. Divine redemption is now seen as national redemption through adversarial human struggle. In May 2012 *Prophecy News Watch* reported that Netanyahu had 'resurrected' the Bible Study Circle of Ben-Gurion.

"The Bible is a parable for humanity," Netanyahu said at the outset [of the Bible Study], and

If the Jews are able to cross the river of time, and in their vast odyssey cross the chasm of annihilation and come back to their ancestral home, that means there is hope for humanity....The Bible is the foundation of our existence. It unites the Jewish people, as it has throughout the generations. It also serves not only as a foundation but also as a map and compass.[29]

Mitri Raheb refers to this practice by secular Zionists as an effort to intentionally "brand" the State of Israel as a "biblical entity." This branding, Raheb notes, confuses many Christians who are not able to distinguish between biblical Israel and the newly created state of Israel.[30]

Nourit Peled-Elhanan, Hebrew University professor of language and education and author of *Palestine in Israeli Schools*, notes that this literalist view of the Bible as history is taught in Israeli schools and is responsible for "a clear socialization process" guided by a "racist education system."[31]

EQUALITY OR APARTHEID?

The five conditions for peace that would be acceptable to Palestinians in the occupied territories and the wider Arab world are: 1) an end to Jewish settle-

> *Religious Zionism is dead....It's as if they are saying that settlers express love of Israel. That's the great idiocy.*[32]
> RABBI DAVID HARTMAN

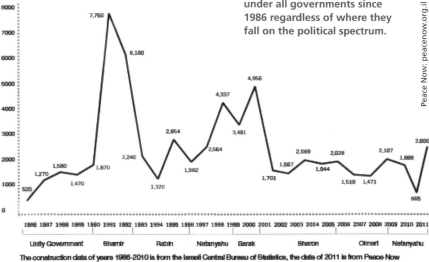

Settlers in Secular Settlements **15%**

Settlers in Ultra-Orthodox Settlements **29%**

Settlers in National-Religious Settlements **25%**

Settlers in Mixed, Religious-Secular Settlements **31%**

Palestinians note that the "peace process" has been a sham. Between the 1993 signing of the Oslo Accords and 2011, 43,304 new housing units were built in Israeli settlements on occupied land.

While the stereotypical Israeli settler is national-religious, settlers span a spectrum of religious and political affiliations (left).

Statistics compiled by Peace Now (below) also show that the settlement enterprise has prospered under all governments since 1986 regardless of where they fall on the political spectrum.

Peace Now: peacenow.org.il

The construction data of years 1986-2010 is from the Israeli Central Bureau of Statistics, the data of 2011 is from Peace Now

ments, 2) a return to 1967 borders with appropriate land swaps, 3) a shared Jerusalem, 4) resolution of the refugee issue, and 5) full rights for Palestinians with Israeli citizenship.[33] When we contrast these five conditions with the worldview of Netanyahu and the right-wing consensus dominant in Israel today, it is not surprising that the gulf appears to be expanding rather than narrowing.

Despite the resumption of peace talks that US Secretary of State John Kerry initiated in July 2013, there is a growing consensus—except, notably, in the US and Israel—that the existing *de facto* one-state situation/solution is irreversible and that the Israeli form of apartheid (segregation and separate development) is becoming increasingly entrenched. Brant Rosen, a congregational rabbi in Evanston, Illinois, and co-chair of the Jewish Voice for Peace Rabbinical Council, was recently interviewed by Mark Karlin about his new book, *Wrestling in the Daylight: A Rabbi's Path to Palestinian Solidarity*. Asked if he thought that "Israel is in the process of becoming an apartheid state," he replied,

> It's not just a potential risk; I think we're witnessing the cost of this apartheid process every day. Even so, most Zionists are unable or unwilling to admit that this is what inevitably comes from fusing Judaism and political nationalism [Zionism]. But if you really consider it, how could it be otherwise? At the end of the day, how can you have a Jewish state that does not somehow treat non-Jews as "other"?...That does not, on some level, create a system of institutional racism that privileges Jews over non-Jews?[34]

THE DREAM VS. THE REALITY

"If you will it, it is no dream," Theodor Herzl, architect of modern Zionism, declared at the end of his 1902 novel, *Old-New Land*. But in 1896 when he first proposed a Jewish state, most people thought he was nothing more than a dreamer.

The Zionist movement that Herzl launched gained much of its support as a response to the history of humiliation and shame engendered by European persecution and Christian anti-Semitism and from the fear that no Jew anywhere would ever be secure without a Jewish state. The *Shoah* reinforced this fear, turning it into a central Zionist doctrine. The new state of Israel acted on this fear-based doctrine in 1950 by passing the Law of Return, granting the right of citizenship to any Jew who immigrates to Israel. Successive Israeli governments have manipulated this fear for political advantage both in domestic and foreign policy issues.

The Zionist movement, like other colonial movements, required collective denial of what was being done to Palestinians, a denial that may even be characterized as self-inflicted blindness. The major American Jewish organizations[35] bear considerable responsibility for spreading this fear and blindness by their uncritical support for Israel over the years, especially since 1967.[36] What I.F. Stone wrote in 1975 about Zionism's psychological act of denial seems to apply to these organizations as well:

> Jewish life [in Palestine] went on *as if the Arabs weren't there*. In a profound sense, the *yishuv*, the Jewish community, had to pretend that the Arabs weren't there, or confront ethical problems too painful to be faced....[37]

Anglican Archbishop Desmond Tutu chaired the South African Truth and Reconciliation Commission that helped his nation begin a process of healing after half a century of brutal apartheid. He described this process of healing in his book *No Future Without Forgiveness*. In Israel/Palestine, as a step that must be undertaken before forgiveness can begin: No Future Without Moral Truth.[38] Speaking moral truth will require both courage and compassion. The time has come for us all to name the Christian theological and ethical failures that gave rise to Zionism, as well as the Jewish theological and ethical failures that Zionism has produced.

At the end of the day, how can you have a Jewish state that does not...on some level, create a system of institutional racism that privileges Jews over non-Jews? [39]

RABBI BRANT ROSEN

REFLECTION

1. What questions arise for you from reading and reflecting on this section?

2. In what ways do Jewish Israelis have more rights under Israeli law than Palestinian citizens of Israel? Given the different treatment granted its citizens based on ethnicity, is it accurate to call Israel a democracy?

3. Israel's secular Zionist founders stressed the continuity between the ancient biblical kingdom of Israel and the modern state of Israel. They also revived the use of ancient Biblical place names such as "Judea and Samaria." What are the consequences of using religious history to justify political and territorial claims?

4. Tony Judt, the late noted scholar and historian, wrote: "The problem with Israel, in short, is not—as sometimes suggested—that it is a European 'enclave' in the Arab world; but rather that it arrived too late. It has imported a characteristically late-nineteenth-century separatist project into a world that has moved on, a world of individual rights, open frontiers, and international law. The very idea of a 'Jewish state'—a state in which Jews and the Jewish religion have exclusive privileges from which non-Jewish citizens are forever excluded—is rooted in another time and place. Israel, in short, is an anachronism." Do you agree with Judt's assessment? Why or why not?

5. Zionism's dream was to establish a secure homeland for all Jews. In light of current realities in Israel Palestine, discuss how Zionism has succeeded and/or failed in achieving its goal.

6. If Israel chooses to pursue a two-state solution, which of the Palestinian demands below are an obstacle?

   • an end to Jewish settlements in Palestine
   • a return to the 1967 borders with appropriate land swaps
   • a shared Jerusalem
   • resolution of the refugee issue
   • full rights for Palestinians who are Israeli citizens

A Tale of Two Villages

On July 15, 1948, the Palestinian village of Ayn Hawd, 24 miles southeast of Haifa, was depopulated of its Palestinian residents in a sweeping Israeli military offensive of the region. Most of Ayn Hawd's residents fled, ending up in Jenin (now in the occupied West Bank) and Irbid (Jordan), where many of their descendants still live.

Some of Ayn Hawd's Palestinian residents fled a short distance and remained there in makeshift shelters on the cultivated land they owned. While most depopulated Palestinian Arab villages in the area were demolished by the Israeli military during and after the 1948 war, Ayn Hawd's buildings remained intact. Its Palestinian former residents, although living only a few kilometers away, were prevented at any point from reclaiming their homes.

In 1954 the village was given a Hebrew name, Ein Hod, and established as a (Jewish) artists' colony. Today, Ein Hod is a popular tourist destination; the village's former mosque is the site of a restaurant-bar.

Over time, the temporary structures built by Ayn Hawd's uprooted natives were replaced by more durable shelters, and, through natural population increase, the village of Ayn Hawd Aljadidah (Arabic for "New Ayn Hawd") grew. Until 1992, when Ayn Hawd was granted partial recognition, the village was "unrecognized" under Israeli law—a classification applied to many Palestinian villages established by the scattered remnants of displaced Palestinians who remained after the 1948 war within the borders of the Jewish state. As an unrecognized village, Ayn Hawd Aljadidah did not receive Israeli municipal services, including water, electricity, sewers, or an access road. The village was granted full recognition only in 2004.[1]

A shop in the Ein Hod artists' colony.

Noga Kadman

Badil Resource Center for Palestinian Residency and Refugee Rights

Jewish Israelis now live in the beautiful stone structures stolen from Ayn Hawd's Palestinian residents in 1948.

Unlike the three-quarters of a million Palestinians who fled beyond Israel's borders in 1948 and were prevented from returning to their homes, the residents of Ayn Hawd who remained in the vicinity suffered a different fate. Historian Nur Masalha describes the peculiar limbo in which such Palestinians found—and still find—themselves:

> In the post-1948 period the minority of Palestinians—those who remained behind, many of them internally displaced—became second-class citizens, subject to a system of military administration by a government that confiscated the bulk of their lands. Today almost a quarter of the 1.3 million Palestinian citizens of Israel… are "internal refugees."[2]

Many Palestinians living in Israel are considered "absentees," a legal classification that has served Israeli state interests by stripping Palestinians of their rights under law.

> The category of "absentees" was originally a juridical term for those refugees who were "absent" from their homes but "present" within the boundaries of the state as defined by the Armistice Agreements of 1949. The vast majority of the Palestinians so classified were not allowed to return to their homes, to reclaim their property, or to seek compensation. Instead the state promulgated the Law of Absentees' Properties in 1950, which legalized the plundering of their possessions. The looting of Arab property was given the guise of a huge land transaction that the state had conducted with itself.[3]

Today, the Jewish Israelis of Ein Hod inhabit the beautiful old stone structures abandoned in 1948 by their former Palestinian owners. In the same way that traces of Palestinian history have been consciously erased elsewhere from the Israeli landscape, the official Ein Hod town website says that the town was "founded in 1953 by a Romanian-born Dada artist Marcel Janco."[4]

The looting of Arab property was given the guise of a huge land transaction that the state had conducted with itself.[3]

4 · Christian Views of Jews and Judaism

Zionism emerged as a European movement because it was there that Christianity evolved over the course of 2,000 years from the belief system of a marginal, persecuted minority to an institution invested with state power, dominating a continent. This combination of religious belief and political power took the toxic form of hostility and violence toward Christian sects considered heretical by those in power as well as nonbelievers—primarily Jews, but also Muslims until their expulsion from Spain after the *Reconquista* of 1492. European Jews experienced the religious intolerance of the dominant Christian culture in a variety of ways: forced conversion, exclusion, execution, humiliation, caricature, ghettoization, pogroms, and genocide. Little wonder, then, that 19th-century European Zionists linked anti-Semitism to the necessity of a state in which Jews could, finally, determine their own fate.

EARLY CHRISTIAN ANTI-JEWISH RHETORIC

In the post-Holocaust world of today, Christians are almost universally aware of the lethal consequences of anti-Semitism. In spite of this, the seeds of anti-Semitism, both in society and in the interpretation of scripture, are still being sown among Christians. In an Easter homily, Mileto, the second century Bishop of Sardis in Asia Minor, proclaimed that the Law (Judaism), "which was once precious is now worthless" because it has been replaced by the Gospel. This message is still used in some contemporary Christian circles as part of the lectionary for Lent.[1] During World War II, the Nazis used homilies of St. John Chrysostom of the late fourth century C.E. as well as vicious attacks by the 16th-century Protestant Reformer, Martin Luther, to justify the Holocaust and as a theological basis for anti-Jewish prejudice.[2]

ABOUT THIS SECTION

This section draws upon three major sources: *Zionism through Christian Lenses*, edited by Carol Monica Burnett; an essay by Dr. Carol Monica Burnett entitled "Eastern Orthodox Perspectives on Zionism and Christian Zionism…"; and an essay by Drs. Rosemary and Herman Reuther entitled "Roman Catholicism, Zionism and the Israeli-Palestinian Conflict," the last two in Wagner and Davis, eds., *Zionism and the Quest for Justice in the Holy Land*. Dr. Burnett is an editor with the Catholic University of America Press. Dr. Rosemary Ruether is Visiting Professor of Feminist Theology at Claremont School of Theology. The Ruethers are co-authors of two earlier books on the Israel-Palestine conflict.

Christianity arose in the first century C.E. as a reform movement within Judaism. In fact, the terms "Judaism" and "Christianity" originated about the same time in opposition to each other.[3] Each partially shaped and reshaped its self-identity in conflict and contrast with the other.

Sociologists have long recognized that dissent from within a homogeneous group is much more dangerous than opposition from without—heretics are treated much more harshly than infidels. Thus it is not surprising that early Christian writings depict the conflict between Christian communities and older Jewish communities as intense (as illustrated in the Acts of the Apostles). Sometimes, the literature claims the conflict was violent, as in the case of the stoning of Stephen (Acts 7). More frequently it gave rise to demonization of the other, all in the name of justifying one's own theological doctrines and cultic practices so as to maintain the unity and loyalty of members.

The Gospels depict an atmosphere of conflict between Jesus and a whole range of Jewish leaders including scribes, Pharisees, Sadducees, chief priests and others whose authority he challenged and threatened. Many of these leaders served the Judean temple-state that governed and collected taxes on behalf of the harshly oppressive Roman Empire. The Christian-Jewish conflict expanded during the next few centuries as Judaism and Christianity vied with each other throughout the Roman Empire. Christian leaders often used virulent anti-Jewish rhetoric in their competition with Judaism. These writings attacked differences in religious doctrine and practice and thus were *theological* in nature.

Many of these writings were addressed to Judaizing members of Christian congregations—members participating in both Christian and Jewish cultic practices. The writings reflect the high degree of threat that Christian leaders felt as they struggled to retain members and orthodoxy of beliefs and practices within their churches.

These attacks were not racial or ethnic. Christianity prided itself on including women and men of all races, classes, and cultures, declaring, as the apostle Paul put it, "there is neither Jew nor Greek, there is neither slave nor free, there is neither male nor female; for you are all one in Christ Jesus." (Galatians 3:28) At the same time however, *Adversus Judaeos* literature ("against the Jews" or "against the Judeans") created a tradition that would later become racial-ethnic in tone and provide a justification for the persecution of Jews in the centuries to come.

The aggressive, hostile tone of this anti-Jewish literature shocks us today. Scholars say it was the conventional rhetorical form known as "blame rhetoric" (Greek: *psogos*, meaning blame) and used to vilify opponents.

THE LITERARY GENRE *ADVERSUS JUDAEOS*

Four writings in the *Adversus Judaeos* tradition serve to illustrate this early Christian-Jewish conflict. Many of these accusations against Jews and Judaism have roots in New Testament texts.

1. The *Epistle of Barnabas*, written by an unknown author 130-140 C.E., addresses Judaizing Christians insisting on a complete separation of Gentile Christians and observant Jews. The central message of the epistle is that the Christians are the only true covenant people and that the Jewish people had never been in a covenant with God.

2. In his *Dialogue with Trypho*, written 155-161 C.E., the Christian philosopher Justin Martyr stages a fictitious two-day debate between himself and a Jewish veteran of the Bar Kokhba revolt of 132-135 C.E. The debate intends to answer Jewish and pagan criticisms of Christianity and to laud the superior qualities of Christianity while leveling the accusation of "Christ-killers" at Jews as a people. Again, the intended audience is Judaizing Christians, those participating in both Christian and Jewish cultic practices. Quoting Leviticus 26:40-41, Justin tells Trypho, the vanquished warrior, that the Jewish exile from Jerusalem and Judea is God's punishment "justly imposed upon you, for you have murdered the Just One, and His prophets before Him...."[4]

3. Mileto, Bishop of Sardis in Asia Minor, levels similar charges against Jews in his treatise "On the Passover" written between 160-170 C.E.:

> 72. This one was murdered. And where was he murdered? In the very center of Jerusalem! Why? Because he had healed their lame, and had cleansed their lepers, and had guided their blind with light, and had raised up their dead. For this reason he suffered.

> 73. Why, O Israel did you do this strange injustice? You dishonored the one who had honored you. You held in contempt the one who held you in esteem. You denied the one who publicly acknowledged you. You renounced the one who proclaimed you his own. You killed the one who made you to live. Why did you do this, O Israel?[5]

4. The homilies of John Chrysostom from the late fourth century (386-387) are perhaps the most egregious of the *Adversus Judaeos* literature. These were probably preached to Judaizing Christians in Chrysostom's own congregation in Antioch. In a series of eight anti-Jewish sermons Chrysostom described the synagogues as "homes of idolatry and devils" and declared that the Jews "do not worship God but devils" and that "all their feasts are unclean." God hates the Jews, said Chrysostom, and has always hated them. But since their murder of Jesus God allows them no possibility of repentance. Jews pretend that their misfortunes are due to Rome, but

> it was not by their own power that the Caesars did what they did to you: it was done by the wrath of God, and His absolute rejection of you.[6]

Such anti-Semitic theology did not disqualify Chrysostom from becoming Archbishop of Constantinople and, shortly after his death, a saint. In the 1930s James Parkes, a British Anglican priest, scholar,

Although contemporary Christians are not responsible for the sins of our spiritual ancestors, we are responsible for combating the perpetuation of those sins in our time.

and activist, described Chrysostom's homilies on Jews as the most horrible and violent denunciations of Judaism to be found in the writings of a Christian theologian.[7]

Although contemporary Christians are not responsible for the sins of our spiritual ancestors, we are responsible for combating the perpetuation of those sins in our time. Genuine reconciliation between Christians and Jews requires the recognition and vigorous renunciation of Christian anti-Jewish rhetoric and behavior. This task includes developing sensitivity to hearing some of the texts within the Bible itself as examples of anti-Jewish rhetoric and being careful in the congregation's worship and work to examine and correct how those texts are taught and understood.

THE VATICAN AND JUDAISM

In their essay entitled "Roman Catholicism, Zionism and the Israeli-Palestinian Conflict," Rosemary and Herman Ruether show how the Vatican's relation to Judaism has changed since the 1960s, although the Vatican has always and still does oppose the Zionist claim to all of the Holy Land.[8] At first the Vatican's opposition to Zionist land claims was *theological*. Now it is moral and humanitarian, based on the violation of Palestinian human rights, the suffering inflicted on Palestinians, and the Gospel ethic of love. The change in rationale is testimony to the sea change that has taken place since World War II in international law as well as in Jewish-Roman Catholic relations and the Vatican's teaching on interreligious relations in general. The same may be said for Eastern Orthodoxy. Contemporary opposition by Roman Catholic officialdom to the Zionist project is based on ethical, not theological grounds.

VATICAN RESPONSES TO THE ZIONIST POLITICAL AGENDA

In 1897, a year after publishing *The Jewish State*, Theodor Herzl announced the convening of a Zionist Congress in Basel, Switzerland, to begin the implementation of the Zionist project. In response, *La Civiltà Cattolica*, a Jesuit periodical published in Italy, rejected the Zionist project, reiterating the traditional teaching.

According to the sacred Scriptures, the Jewish people must always live dispersed and wandering among the nations, so that they may render witness to Christ not only by the Scriptures...but by their very existence. As for a rebuilt Jerusalem, which could become the center of a reconstituted state of Israel, we must add that this is contrary to the prediction of Christ himself.[10]

After repeated attempts to contact Vatican authorities to explain that Jewish settlement in Palestine would not harm Christian interests in the Holy Land, Herzl finally got an audience with Pope Pius X in January 1904. Pius X was blunt in his theological rejection of Jewish rule in Palestine:

Self-Determination Betrayed

Having fought alongside Britain in World War I for the mutual goal of defeating the Central Powers and ending Ottoman domination of the region, the Arabs of Palestine were not granted the independence they had been promised by their wartime allies, but instead made subject to a colonial mandate administered by Britain. Palestinians watched with justifiable alarm as British Mandate officials tolerated a massive population influx of Jews from Europe—an influx that created the demographic condition used only a few years later to justify partition of the land.

While many Jews thought of the Zionist migration to Palestine as a return to an ancient homeland or flight from European anti-Semitism, it was experienced as colonization by the indigenous Arab people of Palestine. And, like colonized people around the globe, they resisted their powerlessness and dispossession. As the colonial British Mandate was terminated in 1948, Palestinians did not gain sovereignty and self-determination as did other peoples emerging from colonialism; rather, the UN partition plan cast the Palestinians into yet another stage of externally-imposed subjugation.

During the Arab Revolt of 1916-1918, Arabs took up arms with the goal of ending the Ottoman Empire's domination of the region. As the Ottomans were allied during World War I with the Central Powers (Germany and Austria-Hungary), the Arab Revolt was incorporated into the larger strategic plan of the Allied Powers (Great Britain, France, Russia, Italy, and Japan). Arab nationalists received commitments (including, for instance, correspondence between the Grand Sharif Hussein and the British High Commissioner Henry McMahon) that their wartime military support of the Allied Powers would be rewarded with sovereignty and self-determination after the war. Those promises were not fulfilled.

We cannot encourage this movement. We cannot prevent the Jews from going to Jerusalem—but we could never sanction it. The ground of Jerusalem...has been sanctified by the life of Jesus Christ. As the head of the Church I cannot tell you otherwise. The Jews have not recognized our Lord, therefore we cannot recognize the Jewish people.[11]

When the British issued the Balfour Declaration in 1917 favoring "the establishment in Palestine of a national home for the Jewish people," the Vatican was hostile to the idea, fearing that a Jewish "national home" might lead to Jewish rule over the Holy Land and undermine Christian interests. For the next two decades the Vatican built many churches, schools, orphanages, and hospitals in Palestine and expanded its concern to include the well-being of local Palestinian Muslims as well as Christians and church properties.

During the 1930s Jewish immigration to Palestine increased dramatically as Nazi persecution intensified. Viewing this population influx as a major threat, Palestinians launched a a three-year revolt in 1936. The British government created the Peel Commission to study the matter. This commission recommended dividing Palestine between Jews and Arabs. Palestinian leaders protested strongly, and the Vatican joined them in objecting to the partition of the land. After World War II, the Vatican again joined with Palestinians and members of the Arab League in opposing UN resolution 181, which authorized the partition of Palestine into an Arab and a Jewish state.

In 1948 when war broke out between Jewish and Arab forces after partition and the departure of British forces, the Vatican began providing aid to Palestinian refugees, creating hundreds of social welfare centers and schools for Palestinian families and children. It also became a strong advocate for a "right of return" of the refugees and a just settlement to the conflict over land.[12]

A NEW INTERFAITH THEOLOGY

In a decisive shift from previous church teaching, on October 28, 1965, the Second Vatican Council (1962-65) issued *Nostra Aetate*, the Declaration on the Relationship of the Church to Non-Christian Religions, which altered Roman Catholic doctrine regarding other religions. Instead of mentioning the doctrinal failures of Hinduism, Buddhism, Islam, and Judaism, *Nostra Aetate* highlighted the strengths of each religion

Peace through Palestinian sovereignty

December 2012. Just weeks after the Vatican praised Palestine's boosted status as a non-member observer state at the United Nations, Pope Benedict XVI met with Palestinian President Mahmoud Abbas in a private audience at the Vatican (below). A month earlier, 138 member states voted to enhance Palestine's status from "entity" to "non-member state"—the same status held by the Vatican. Although the Vatican praised the United Nations vote, it called also for full recognition of Palestinian sovereignty as necessary for peace in the region. Canada, Israel, and the United States were among the nine states that voted against the motion.[13]

Since Benedict's resignation in February 2013, both the Palestinian President Mahmoud Abbas and Israeli Prime Minister Binyamin Netanyahu have traveled to the Vatican to meet the newly-installed Pope Francis. It is anticipated that Francis will travel to the Holy Land in 2014.

Catholic News Service/Maria Grazia Picciarella

in an ascending order, with Islam and Judaism seen as closest to Christianity....The strongest and the longest statement is reserved for Judaism.... Alluding to the idea that the Jews would repent at the end of history, the declaration says "the Church awaits the day, known only to God alone, on which all people will address the Lord in a single voice."[14]

In spite of this claim to salvation through Christ alone, *Nostra Aetate* insists that discrimination against Jews today cannot be justified by scripture or theology.

> Although the Church is the new people of God, the Jews should not be presented as rejected or accursed by God, as if this followed from the Holy Scriptures....[T]he Church, mindful of the patrimony she shares with the Jews and moved not by political reasons but by the Gospel's spiritual love, decries hatred, persecution, displays of anti-Semitism, directed against Jews at any time and by anyone.[15]

Nostra Aetate brought an end to Roman Catholic theological criticism of Judaism and consequently the state of Israel. After 1965, Vatican criticism of Israel would be grounded in ethical, not theological, objections, and the need for peace based on a just solution to sharing the land of Palestine between the two peoples. Ethical objections to Israeli policies and practices toward Palestinians prevented the Vatican from officially recognizing the state of Israel until 1993. The following year the Vatican also recognized the Palestinian Liberation Organization (PLO), signaling its commitment to the aspirations of both peoples. In 2012, when Pope Benedict XVI praised the United Nations for admitting Palestine as a non-member observer state with the same status in the UN as the Vatican, he reminded the world of Vatican support for peace in Israel-Palestine based on equal rights.

CHRISTIANITY AND OTHER RELIGIONS

The 1965 Declaration on the Relationship of the Church to Non-Christian Religions raises as many questions as it answers. By lifting up the virtues of other religions, the Second Vatican Council tried to avoid denigrating other religions. At the same time, the document uses Christian norms to measure the relative value of other religions by how closely those religions conform to Christian theological tenets and practices. Thus the presumption of Christian superiority remains, and that presumption continues to rankle members of other religions. Although Judaism is ranked second, it is still regarded as inferior to Christianity. In his article, "Reflections on the Holocaust," psychotherapist David Glick writes

> Despite what is welcome in this statement [the "Jewish Declaration" of Vatican II], there remains much that is disappointing. We see the perpetuation of the doctrine of supersessionism in the identification of the Church with "the new people of God." This hierarchy of righteousness leads to an arrogant Christian exclusivism and a religious imperialism which is sorely in need of being transmuted by genuine tolerance and appreciation for other religious paths. Moreover, what is glaringly missing in the Vatican II statement is any acknowledgment of the part which the Church's anti-Jewish teachings played in the discrimination and violence visited upon the Jews over many centuries in Christian lands. Especially with regard to the Holocaust, this [omission] is a profound disappointment.[16]

One phrase in *Nostra Aetate* that Glick draws attention to may account for the title of a paper presented in 2010 to the General Assembly of the Presbyterian Church (U.S.A.). Written by the Office of Theology and Worship in collaboration with a group of Presbyterian and Jewish theologians, "Christians and Jews: People of God" reads like a rebuttal to the Vatican II document definition of the Church as "*the* new people of God." (emphasis added)

Traditional Christian theology has often declared that the life, death, and resurrection of Christ is "the most complete revelation that God has yet granted to humankind."[17] Is there a way forward for interfaith dialogue that allows for each religion's uniqueness without claiming superiority for one's own religion and contempt for others'?

Referring to the concept of Jews as *The* Chosen People, Rabbi Brant Rosen writes

Is there a way forward for interfaith dialogue that allows for each religion's uniqueness without claiming superiority for one's own religion and contempt for others'?

To put it plainly, a voice that affirms claims of theological superiority in the name of *one people* cannot be the voice of God. A voice that asserts God's word to humanity was vouchsafed *exclusively* to the children of Abraham cannot be the voice of God. A voice that looks to the messianic day in which all nations will ultimately serve the *God of Israel* cannot be the voice of God.[18]

This is a much more modest claim to religious truth than has been the custom in the past. Similarly, many contemporary Christians choose to modify our traditional theology by saying that the life, death, and resurrection of Christ is the most complete revelation of God *that we know and that we have experienced*. This statement affirms the revelation of God in Christ while at the same time recognizing the limits of our knowledge and experience and honoring analogous claims by others which grow out of the knowledge and experience of their different faith traditions.

From a logical standpoint, only someone who had entered deeply into the faith and experience of every other religion could claim to know from an insider's perspective that God's revelation in Christ is "the most complete revelation of God." Perhaps stained-glass windows provide a metaphor to describe the conundrum of insider and outsider perspectives on religious experience. Looking at them from the outside, we see only a hint of their structure, but from the inside with light beaming through, we see splendid colors and ornate patterns, and are grasped by the stories they tell. Devoted followers of every religion are moved in this manner by their own holy narratives.

Indeed, there is Christian theological precedent for interfaith humility. It comes from classical Christian understandings of the relationship between faith and knowledge, belief and understanding. In the late eleventh and early twelfth centuries C.E., Anselm, Archbishop of Canterbury, developed an idea first suggested by Augustine in the late fourth century. Augustine had offered the following pastoral advice: *crede, ut intelligas*, "believe so that you may understand." Anselm then described the life of faith as *fides quaerens intellectum*, "faith seeking understanding" and declared "*credo, ut intelligam*, "I believe in order that I may understand." In other words, faith precedes understanding; without faith, there is no understanding. Ludwig Wittgenstein, one of the most important philosophers of the 20th century, said that immersion in a way of life is necessary for understanding its specific structures and guiding concepts.[19]

With Augustine's and Anselm's perspective in mind, the traditional view (that the life, death, and resurrection of Christ is "the most complete revelation that God has yet granted to humankind") claims more than any individual can know. Claims like this won't attract new members or keep existing members from falling away; in a pluralistic world any attempt to circle the wagons may alienate as many as it attracts. Humility can be both more honest and more enriching if it helps move interfaith dialogue to ever deeper levels.

Indeed, there is Christian theological precedent for interfaith humility.

REFLECTION

1. What questions arise for you from reading and reflecting on this section?

2. Many New Testament texts are perceived by Jews as anti-Jewish. These texts include Matthew 27:25, Luke 21:24, Acts 13:44-52, and many texts in the Gospel of John that criticize "the Jews." Do these texts or others in the New Testament sound anti-Semitic to you when you hear them read in worship? How should churches deal justly with biblical texts that appear to denigrate Jews?

3. When and how has the Church contributed to anti-Semitism?

4. "Classical Christianity saw the election of the Jews by God as having been superseded or replaced by the Church as the 'New Israel'" (see box, page 26). What have been the political consequences of this theological belief? Is it possible for Christians to affirm that the Old Testament covenants have been fulfilled in Christ without implying that God has replaced one people (the Jews) with another (the Christians)?

5. Critics of the ideology and practices of the state of Israel have been charged with anti-Semitism. How has this charge affected attempts at interfaith dialogue between Christians and Jews?

6. In today's globalized pluralistic society, can any religion claim uniqueness and truth without claiming superiority for itself and its believers? How do we deal with Peter's words in Acts 4:12, "There is salvation in no one else…," or with Jesus' words in John 14:6, "No one comes to the Father except through me."?

The Covenant

A particular interpretation of the biblical Abrahamic covenant has been instrumental in building Western Christian acceptance of the notion that the ancient Jewish claim to land is superior to the Palestinians' present-day, ongoing claim. As American journalist I.F. Stone wrote in 1969,

> there is a good deal of simplistic sophistry in the Zionist case. The whole earth would have to be reshuffled if claims 2,000 years old to *irredenta* [*i.e.*, a territory historically or ethnically related to one political unit but under the political control of another] were suddenly to be allowed.[1]

The Covenant-based case for a modern Jewish state in Palestine has been useful even for those with little other use for religious belief. Historian Ilan Pappe observes that "the secular Jews who founded the Zionist movement wanted paradoxically both to secularize Jewish life and to use the Bible as a justification for colonizing Palestine.... [I]n other words," Pappe notes, "they did not believe in God but He nonetheless promised them Palestine."[2]

Zionists understood that, in an era when European colonialism was beginning to wane, the secular political project of establishing a Jewish colony in Palestine might be viewed unfavorably. By linking the Zionist political project to prophetic "promises," many Jewish and Christian believers could be led to accept the Jewish state-building project as not emerging from the human mind, but God's. Pappe explains:

> [T]he Bible became both the justification for, and the map of, the Zionist colonization of Palestine....[P]ortraying the dispossession of Palestine as the fulfillment of a divine Christian scheme was priceless for galvanizing global Christian support behind Zionism.[3]

In the sacred texts of Judaism and Christianity, believers are granted special status. Like other communities, Jews and Christians believe the sacred texts in which they are described as partners in a special, privileged relationship with God (while, at the same time, unbelievers are not). Sacred texts, however, carry little weight with members of other faiths. It is not surprising, then, that Muslims do not accept the circular claim of Zionists that the Jews have been promised Palestine by God because Jewish sacred texts say so.

Regardless of whether one considers the creation of the modern Jewish state to be a perversion of prophecy or a fulfillment of it, Israel exists. This, writes Daniel Lazare, is its present-day reality for the Jews and Palestinians who cohabit the land:

> In what is supposedly the only real democracy in the Middle East, 97.5 percent of publicly held land in pre-1967 Israel is reserved exclusively for Jewish use; and a bizarre Law of Return allows any Jew immigrating to Israel from anywhere in the world to apply for a government-subsidized apartment in East Jerusalem, thereby displacing a Palestinian whose roots in the area go back generations. For Zionists, this is perfectly compatible with *Yahweh*'s supposed promise to Abraham some four thousand years ago; but for anybody committed to democratic principles, it is perfectly perverse.[4]

For many religious Zionists today, extremist and exceptionalist interpretations of Old Testament passages form a theological basis for considering Palestinians to be "foreigners" in the land that they and their ancestors have inhabited for generations. For these same Zionists, it is a natural progression from considering Palestinians foreigners and aliens to promoting their expulsion as appropriate and even necessary for the redemption of the land and restoration to its rightful owners, the Jews.

I.F. Stone's 1969 observations about the tragic consequences of Zionism's Jewish-centric beliefs hold true today, forty-four years after Stone originally wrote them:

> This moral myopia makes it possible for Zionists to dwell on the 1,900 years of Exile in which Jews have longed for Palestine but dismiss as nugatory the nineteen years in which Arab refugees have also longed for it."Homelessness" is the major theme of Zionism, but this [pathos-laden] passion is denied to Arab refugees.[5]

Portraying the dispossession of Palestine as the fulfillment of a divine Christian scheme was priceless for galvanizing global Christian support behind Zionism.

Zvi Yehuda Kook (1891-1982) was a leader of Religious Zionism and founder of the *Gush Emunim* settlement bloc. As head of the Mercaz HaRav yeshiva in Jerusalem, Rabbi Kook's ideology was influential in the development of the leading figures in the Religious Zionist settlement project. Following the 1973 Yom Kippur War, Rabbi Kook said, "I have said and written that there is to be war about the fate of Judea and Samaria, Jericho and the Golan Heights; no concession about these lands is permissible....These lands do not belong to *goyim* [non-Jews]; they have not been stolen from *goyim*....We must remind the government and people of the State of Israel that no concession of our land will be permitted." Gush Emunim faded in the 1980s, but its ideological heirs—including members of the Israeli Knesset—continue to promote a maximalist agenda that rejects territorial compromise.[6]

5 · A Jewish Theology of Liberation

If we deny or remain silent about the truth of these events, past and present, we remain complicit in this crime.

ABOUT THIS SECTION

This section is a condensed and edited version of an essay by Rabbi Brant Rosen entitled "Rising to the Challenge: A Jewish Theology of Liberation" in Wagner and Davis, eds., *Zionism and the Quest for Justice in the Holy Land.* The author is a Reconstructionist rabbi, Co-chair of the Rabbinical Council of Jewish Voice for Peace, and author of *Wrestling in the Daylight: a Rabbi's Path to Palestinian Solidarity,* 2012.

Rabbi Brant Rosen serves a Reconstructionist[1] congregation in Evanston, Illinois, and is co-chair of the Rabbinical Council of Jewish Voice for Peace. In his recent book, *Wrestling in the Daylight: A Rabbi's Path to Palestinian Solidarity,* Rosen recounts "a powerful and sacred experience." Jews and Palestinians met together in his home on May 14, 2009, the 61st anniversary of the Israeli declaration of independence. Their purpose was to remember the *Nakba* (Catastrophe), the displacement and dispossession from their land of hundreds of thousands of Palestinians before and after the creation of the state of Israel.

Similar commemorative events took place on the same night in four US cities, initiated by a new group, Rabbis Remembering the *Nakba,* who "believe it is crucial that the Jewish community find a way to honestly face the painful truth of this event—and in particular, Israel's role in it." These events took place just as Israel was talking of banning the commemoration of the *Nakba* in Israel. In 2011 the Knesset enacted a law cutting off funds to organizations and institutions where the *Nakba,* the Palestinian day of mourning, is commemorated.

The following statement was read to the groups assembled in each of the four cities:

> Rabbis Remembering the *Nakba*...are united in our common conviction that we cannot view *Yom Ha'atzmaut* [Israeli Independence Day]—or what is for Palestinians the *Nakba*—as an occasion for celebration. Guided by the values of Jewish tradition, we believe that this day is more appropriately an occasion for *zikaron* (memory), *cheshbon nefesh* (soul searching), and *teshuvah* (repentance).

These spiritual values compel us to acknowledge the following: that Israel's founding is inextricably bound up with the dispossession of hundreds of thousands of indigenous inhabitants of the land, that a moment so many Jews consider to be the occasion of national liberation is the occasion of tragedy and exile for another people, and that the violence begun in 1948 continues to this day. This is the truth of our common history—it cannot be denied, ignored, or wished away.

Jewish tradition teaches that peace and reconciliation can only be achieved after a process of repentance. And we can only repent after an honest accounting of our responsibility in the wronging of others. While it is true that none of the Jews present tonight were actively involved in the dispossession of Palestinians from their homes in 1948, it is also true that if we deny or remain silent about the truth of these events, past and present, we remain complicit in this crime. In the words of Rabbi Abraham Heschel, "In a free society some are guilty, but all are responsible."

Our gatherings this evening bring together Jews and Palestinians in this act of remembrance. This coming together is an essential, courageous choice. To choose to face this painful past together is to begin to give shape to a vision of the future where refugees go home, when the occupation is ended, when walls are torn down, and where reconciliation is underway.[2]

Here we have a rabbi, thoroughly immersed in the Zionist tradition and a veteran of Israeli *kibbutz* life, who comes to see the day of birth of the state of Israel as a day of memory, soul-searching, and repentance. It's a modern-day conversion story of a modest yet courageous rabbi wrestling with God about the meaning of Zionism in light of what he calls "the tragic story of Jewish political nationalism."[3]

The story began with Rosen's reaction to Operation Cast Lead, Israel's 22-day war on Gaza in 2008-2009. On December 28, 2008, he ended his blog post with these words:

> So, no more rationalizations. What Israel has been doing to the people of Gaza is an outrage. It has brought neither safety nor security to the people

January 9, 2009. A Palestinian woman and her child walk in front of the rubble of a building following an Israeli airstrike in the Rafah refugee camp, southern Gaza Strip, during Operation Cast Lead.

Khaled Omar/AP

In October 2013, Rabbi Brant Rosen (left) traveled with a delegation of American Jews and Palestinians to the West Bank and Israel. In the West Bank town of Bil'in, the delegates were hosted by Iyad Burnat (right), a leader in the Bil'in Popular Committee Against the Wall. Bil'in was one of the early West Bank villages to organize regular nonviolent demonstrations against the wall that was cutting the village off from a significant portion of its agricultural land in order to create a buffer around the nearby settlement of Mod'in Illit. By now, the weekly demonstrations have been ongoing for nine years. An Oscar-nominated documentary, *Five Broken Cameras*, documents Bil'in's ongoing struggle.

We inevitably witness religion at its very worst when faith becomes wedded to empire—when religion is used by powerful nations to justify the subjugation of others.

of Israel and it has wrought nothing but misery upon the people of Gaza. There, I've said it. Now what do I do?[4]

Rosen tells of reading a book shortly after writing this blog that shook his spiritual foundations. The book was entitled *Justice and Only Justice: A Palestinian Theology of Liberation*[5] by Anglican Canon Naim Ateek, founding director of Sabeel, the Jerusalem-based Ecumenical Center for Liberation Theology. Rosen recounts how it touched him deeply as a spiritual autobiography as well as a faithful theological statement. It caused him to look deeply at his own inherited religious tradition. In response to Ateek's challenge for theological dialogue, Rabbi Rosen began the journey of exploring what a Jewish liberation theology would look like.

THE CHALLENGE OF PALESTINIAN LIBERATION THEOLOGY[6]

In his important book, *Justice and Only Justice*, Canon Ateek, a Palestinian Israeli and 1948 refugee from his ancestral home in Beisan, Palestine (now northern Israel), identifies three ideological streams within the Hebrew Bible (the Old Testament). First, the tribal-nationalist-separatist tradition of the conquest of Canaan and the establishment of Israelite kingship so that Israel could become a military power like surrounding nations; second, the Torah-oriented tradition of the Pharisees which evolved into Rabbinic Judaism after the destruction of the Second Temple in 70 C.E.; and third, the prophetic tradition that rejected the idea of a tribal god in favor of *Yahweh* who not only ruled over the world but would eventually redeem *all* humanity.[7] Ateek writes:

What is quite clear from a Palestinian Christian point of view…is that the emergence of the Zionist movement in the twentieth century is a retrogression of the Jewish community into the history of its very distant past, with its most elementary and primitive forms of the concept of God. Zionism has succeeded in reanimating the nationalist tradition within Judaism. Its inspiration has been drawn not from the profound thoughts of the Hebrew Scriptures, but from those portions that betray a narrow and exclusive concept of a tribal god.[8]

Rosen reminds us that Ateek's criticism of Zionism is not all that different from the warnings of many prominent Jewish leaders, both secular and religious, long before the establishment of the state of Israel in 1948. Hannah Arendt warned of a Jewish Sparta.[9] Judah Magnes feared the rise of a terroristic nationalism patterned on Eastern European models.[10] Nonetheless, Ateek's accusation that Zionism today represents a retrogressive primitive tribalism earned him the charge of anti-Semitism from the Jewish establishment that today, says Rosen, "identifies Judaism as coterminous with Zionism."[11]

CONSTANTINIAN VS. PROPHETIC JUDAISM

Since the Holocaust and the rise of the state of Israel most Jewish theologians have turned a blind eye to the darker implications of the wedding of religion and state power in Israel. This marriage is now reflected in the liturgies of all four major American Jewish religious streams (Orthodox, Reform, Conservative, and Reconstructionist). Their prayer books all include the Prayer for the State of Israel, which begins: "Our Father Who are in Heaven, Protector and Redeemer of Israel, bless Thou the State of Israel which marks the dawn of our deliverance."[12] Rosen notes that even progressive theologians like Rabbis Arthur Waskow, Michael Lerner, and Arthur Green, who often criticize Israeli human rights abuses, are unwilling to deal with basic problems that arise with what Rosen calls the "merging of Judaism with idolatrous political nationalism."[13]

A rare exception to this trend is the Jewish theologian Marc Ellis. For Ellis, Zionism is a form of Constantinian Judaism, mirroring the empowerment of the Church in the fourth century when the Emperor Constantine established Christianity as the official religion of empire.[14] Rosen sees Ellis' framework as a reminder that religion has historically been at its best when it acts prophetically, when it holds power to account, and when it is leveraged on behalf of the powerless, the oppressed, and the voiceless. Conversely, we inevitably witness religion at its very worst when faith becomes wedded to empire—when religion is used by powerful nations to justify the subjugation of others.[15]

For Rosen and Ellis, the state of Israel has become "the living embodiment of Judaism as empire."[16] For centuries Rabbinic Judaism served as a spiritual alternative to the veneration of human power. Tragically, says Rosen, Zionism has traded this "unique spiritual vision in favor of idolatrous nation-statism and militarism." A Jewish theology of liberation would recover the insight of I Samuel 8—that the hunger for national power

> is in itself a kind of idolatry and a turning away from God....[And] it would affirm that when we put our faith in the power of empire, we may well be sowing the seeds of our own destruction.[17]

THE BIBLE AND LIBERATION

Rosen recognizes that the Bible contains texts that liberate and texts that oppress. A Jewish theology of liberation must lift up those texts that "help us to understand Jewish values as universal values and connect Jewish liberation with the liberation of *all* nations." Conversely, he asserts, we must recognize that

> ...those aspects of biblical and religious tradition that espouse triumphalism, xenophobia, and the extermination of indigenous peoples are not the voice of God at all, but are, as Rabbi Michael Lerner has suggested, "the voice of pain and cruelty masquerading as God."[18]

This means, among other things, that biblical texts cannot be used to justify claims for the expropriation of Palestinian land. As Rabbi Mordecai Kaplan, the founder of Reconstructionist Judaism, has written

> We cannot fail to recognize in the claims of Jewish superiority a kinship and resemblance to the similar claims of other national and racial groups which have been advanced to justify oppression and exploitation.[19]

In the past colonialism, slavery, European persecution of Jewry, as well as the Israelite conquest and expropriation of the Canaanites, all used similar justification. All claims "to the superiority of the one race, nation or caste... [are] essentially vicious."[20]

We must be prepared to read the story of the Exodus through the eyes of the Israelites and the story of the Eisodus through the eyes of the Canaanites.

Nasser Ishtayeh/AP

Israeli Rabbis Stand in Solidarity with Palestinians

October 2001, Haris, northern West Bank. Rabbi Arik Ascherman (left) co-founded the Israeli human rights organization, Rabbis for Human Rights (RHR), in 1988. Here, Ascherman joins a small group of Israelis providing the Palestinian residents of Haris with a Jewish human shield against violence from settlers during their olive harvest. RHR's positions are not popular with the Israeli public and the group has limited impact on Israeli public opinion. "Neither the public nor the religious community are receptive to their messages," observes Menachem Klein, a political scientist at Bar Ilan University in Tel Aviv.[19] The non-Orthodox streams of Judaism from which most of RHR's members are drawn have small followings in Israel and are widely viewed as foreign imports.

Referring to the concept of Jews as *The* Chosen People, Rosen writes

> To put it plainly, a voice that affirms claims of theological superiority in the name of *one people* cannot be the voice of God. A voice that asserts God's word to humanity was vouchsafed *exclusively* to the children of Abraham cannot be the voice of God. A voice that looks to the messianic day in which all nations will ultimately serve the *God of Israel* cannot be the voice of God.[21]

EXODUS (JOURNEY OUT), NOT EISODUS (JOURNEY IN)

The Exodus narrative resonates not only with Jews but also with all oppressed people who long for liberation. The story of going out, however, also contains a story of going in. This is the Eisodus, the journey into Canaan and God's command to Joshua and the Israelites to exterminate the indigenous peoples without pity. [Deut. 7:1-2; 20:16-18] The late English Roman Catholic scholar Michael Prior remarked that by modern standards of international law and human rights, the God of the Israelites appears to sanction ethnic cleansing, war crimes, and crimes against humanity.[22] History is, as they say, written by the victors.

Rosen contends that the Exodus tradition cannot be lifted up and honored without lifting up the Eisodus tradition.

> The insidious comparison of Palestinians to the nations of Canaan has become particularly ubiquitous in the words of Israeli politicians, settler leaders and ultra-religious rabbis alike. Statements such as these must not be dismissed as mere religious rhetoric. These theological linkages have enormous power, particularly when we consider the historical reality of the Zionist enterprise that includes the expulsion of Palestinians from their homes in 1947-48 and policies of displacement and transfer that continue to this very day....If we are to truly hear the God of liberation speaking to us through Biblical tradition, we must be prepared, quite simply, to read the story of the Exodus through the eyes of the Israelites and the story of the Eisodus through the eyes of the Canaanites.[23]

TOWARD A NEW INTERFAITH COVENANT

Rabbi Rosen closes his essay on a note of hope and challenge related to a new interfaith covenant that he sees unfolding today. The joint work of Jewish Voice for Peace (JVP)[24] with groups within the United Methodist, Presbyterian, and other denominations in the Boycott, Divestment, and Sanctions (BDS) movement to end the occupation is "challenging the American Jewish establishment's Constantinian hegemony on Israel."[25]

Interfaith cooperation is also advancing in the area of public advocacy. In 2012 American Christians published *Kairos USA*[26] in response to the 2009 Palestinian Christian declaration of faith entitled *Kairos Palestine*.[27] The Jewish Council for Public Affairs excoriated *Kairos USA* as "false witness."[28] The Jewish Voice for Peace Rabbinical Council defended Kairos USA, saying

> We are inspired by the confessional nature of the *Kairos* document for past sins against the Jewish people. Thank you for acknowledging your role in Jewish suffering. As Jews, the Christian confession awakens a responsibility to consider and confess our own sin, the sin of occupation....Our *vidui* (confession) must include ways in which we have privileged Jewish suffering over and against Palestinian suffering and the ways in which we use the claim of anti-Semitism to silence those who criticize Israel's violation of human rights. We share this perception with *Kairos USA*.[29]

Rabbi Rosen sees these events as indicative of "the emergence of a new kind of interfaith covenant," that neither avoids the tough issues nor "engages in emotional blackmail," but cooperates on issues of human rights in a land that is holy to all three Abrahamic faith traditions.[30]

REFLECTION

1. What issues or questions arise for you after reading and reflecting on this section?

2. What issues would a Christian Theology of Liberation focused on interfaith relationships need to address?

3. Read again Rabbi Rosen's confession in the first column on this page beginning, "To put it plainly, a voice that affirms claims of theological superiority in the name of *one people* cannot be the voice of God...." Rewrite this quotation so that each sentence becomes a Christian confession. Then discuss whether you and your congregation are prepared to make such a confession.

4. Discuss the exceptionalism (*i.e.*, the moral double standards) in the section on "Exodus, Not Eisodus." Compare the God of the Exodus (who delivers the Israelites from slavery) to the same God who commands the Israelites to exterminate the Canaanites and take over their land.

5. Rabbi Rosen writes that the state of Israel has become "the living embodiment of Judaism as empire." What evidence do you find to support this claim? How is Judaism as empire related to the US as empire?

6. What role do Palestinians have in the suffering of Israelis, and what do they owe Israelis? What role do Israelis have in the suffering of Palestinians, and what do they owe Palestinians? What role do Europe and the US have in the sufferings of both Israelis and Palestinians, and what do Europeans and Americans owe them?

Extremism and Intolerance in Israel

Israeli historian Simha Flapan, describing the years following the 1967 Six-Day War, writes,

> There always was an orthodox, fundamentalist current in Judaism, characterized by racial prejudice toward non-Jews in general and Arabs in particular. A substantial portion—perhaps even the overwhelming majority—of the religious movements, and a growing part of the population in general, came to conceive of the West Bank not as the homeland of the Palestinian people but as Judea and Samaria, the birthplace of the Jewish faith and homeland of the Jewish people. Many people not only became indifferent to the national rights of the Palestinians living there, *they did not even see the necessity of granting them civil rights*.2

New Yorker editor and veteran Israel-observer David Remnick presents a current snapshot of religious settler mentality and its relationship to the Israeli political power structure:

> Dov Lior, the head of an important West Bank rabbinical council, has called Baruch Goldstein—who, in 1994, machine-gunned twenty-nine Palestinians at the Cave of the Patriarchs in Hebron—"holier than all the martyrs of the Holocaust." Lior endorsed a book that discussed when it is right and proper to murder an Arab, and he and a group of kindred rabbis issued a proclamation proscribing Jews from selling or renting land to non-Jews. Men like [Avigdor] Lieberman [Israel's Minister of Foreign Affairs], [Elyakim] Levanon [chief rabbi of the Elon Moreh settlement, near Nablus], and Lior are scarcely embittered figures on the irrelevant margins: a hard-right base—the settlers, the ultra-Orthodox, Shas, the National Religious Party—is indispensable to Prime Minister Benjamin Netanyahu's governing coalition.3

Zvi Bar'el, a Middle Eastern affairs analyst for *Haaretz*, writes with apparent disgust about *The King's Torah*, a book written by two rabbis—Yitzhak Shapira and Yosef Elitzur—connected to a yeshiva in Yitzhar, a West Bank settlement known for its extremism. Rabbis Shapira and Elitzur, Bar'el reports,

> write that "the ban on killing a gentile does not stem from the intrinsic value of his life, which is not essentially legitimate as such." These are the rabbis of the occupation, the arbiters of Jewish law for those hooligans on the hilltops. They belong to a different country, one in which the laws of the State of Israel are deemed worthless.4

Racism and intolerance are in no way confined to Israel's religious extremists and settlers. Many observers who care deeply about Israel and Judaism express grave concern that a rising tide of racial prejudice and extremism is

becoming normalized not only among religious Jews but also among political figures and private citizens within Israel proper.

Israeli political scientist Neve Gordon reports on racially-charged political campaigns in Upper Nazareth5 and Omer6 (a Jewish town in the Negev), in which Jewish candidates seek votes by reassuring Jewish Israelis that the towns they inhabit shall remain Arab-free.

After describing a series of recent racist episodes in Israel, journalist and Israel-watcher Larry Derfner asks in the *Jewish Daily Forward*, "Does this mean all Israelis, or even most of them, are racists? No. Does it mean Israeli society, by commission and omission, encourages racism? Oh, yes."7

In an article analyzing why many liberal-minded Israelis are choosing to emigrate, *Haaretz* writers cite this trend among other reasons: "[In Israel] politically, the discourse is one of despair. It's a fanatic, illiberal discourse."8

Other observers see racism and intolerance as inextricably entwined with a political system that confers special privileges on Jews. Palestinians in particular are perceived as a perennial threat to Israel's Jewish character. It is inevitable, perhaps, that Palestinians are widely regarded with contempt and their marginalization is accepted as a state necessity. "Hatred of Arabs," admits Zvi Bar'el, 'is part of the test of loyalty and identity that the state gives its Jewish citizens. A good Jew hates Arabs."9

Anne Paq

"Kahane was right!" proclaims a sticker in Hebron, home to a population of Israeli settlers infamous for their extremism and anti-Palestinian violence. Such attitudes are not confined to Hebron: a 2010 poll of Israelis by the Israeli Democracy Institute suggested that "most Israelis [53%] might agree with the late rabbi and political leader [Kahane], who favored encouraging the emigration of Arabs from Israel."1

Anne Paq

Israeli settlers defaced this Palestinian school building in Hebron with the message "Death to the Arabs."

Anne Paq

"Gas the Arabs!" graffiti is a regular sight in Hebron's Old City. Israeli settlers in the area—many of them American-born—commit acts of harrassment, intimidation, vandalism, and violence on the local Palestinian population, often with the protection of Israeli military personnel.

6 · Mainline Liberal Protestants and Israel

MYTHS OF NATIONAL ORIGIN

Israeli and American myths of origin are similar and derived from the same biblical sources. Two American Jewish scholars, Todd Gitlin and Liel Leibovitz, have recently described these similarities in their book *The Chosen Peoples: America, Israel, and the Ordeals of Divine Election.*

Americans and Israelis have often thought that their nations were chosen, in perpetuity, to do God's work. This belief in divine election is a potent, living force, one that has guided and shaped both peoples and nations throughout their history and continues to do so to this day."[1]

The roots of American Protestant pro-Zionism lie in the ideology of the early Pilgrims whose beliefs were derived from the story of God's election of the ancient Israelites. On March 29, 1630, a boat carrying British Puritans left Southampton, England, carrying several important leaders including John Winthrop, who would become the first Governor of the Massachusetts Bay Colony. The departure sermon was delivered by John Cotton, who referred to their mission as a "divine calling." Cotton's sermon summarized many of the core beliefs that would inspire their perilous journey across the Atlantic. He turned to II Samuel 7:10 for his text: "And I will appoint a place for my people Israel and will plant them, so that they may live in their own place, and be disturbed no more." He drew a direct parallel between the Puritans' mission and that of ancient Israel in its journey from Sinai to the "Promised Land." For this group of Puritans, their mission and journey was no less important, nor was it any less divinely inspired than that of Moses and the Israelites. These "new Israelites" believed God would guide them and had in fact gone before them, preparing their way and granting a divinely ordained entitlement to a land that was, as it happened, already inhabited.

These "new Israelites" [the Puritans] believed God would guide them and had in fact gone before them, preparing their way and granting a divinely ordained entitlement to a land that was, as it happened, already inhabited.

American Progress (circa 1872), by John Gast, is an allegorical representation of the modernization of the new west. Columbia, a personification of the United States, leads civilization westward with American settlers, stringing telegraph wire and holding a schoolbook. The different stages of economic activity of the pioneers are highlighted, especially the changing forms of transportation.

Over the years other white colonizers would join the Pilgrims and embrace similar themes of what political scientists call "settler colonialism," *i.e.,* doctrines of racial superiority, divine entitlement to the land and its resources, and various systems of segregation, slavery, ethnic cleansing, genocide, and other forms of discrimination and violence against people of color and minority ethnic groups. During the wars with European powers and Mexico, and the 19th-century conquest of the frontier, the more the settlers' mission (which came to be identified as national Manifest Destiny) was challenged, the more the cycle of violence increased, often driven by their God-given sense of entitlement and conquest.

The slogan "the imperialism of righteousness" was coined to justify the Spanish-American War in 1898. President Woodrow Wilson rallied Congress to support the US entry into World War I by naming it a war to make the world "safe for democracy." During the Cold War (1947-1991) American leaders reiterated year after year the national mission to remain the "leader of the free world," often justifying the

ABOUT THIS SECTION

This section is a condensed and edited version of an essay by the Rev. Dr. Donald E. Wagner entitled "The Mainline Protestant Churches' Journey with Palestine and Israel" in Wagner and Davis, eds., *Zionism and the Quest for Justice in the Holy Land.* Dr. Wagner, the author of four books on the Israeli-Palestinian conflict, is the National Program Director of Friends of Sabeel-North America. He was a Professor of Middle Eastern Studies and Director of the Center for Middle Eastern Studies at North Park University from 1995 to 2010, and National Director of the Palestine Human Rights Campaign from 1980 to 1989.

covert or overt overthrow of democratically elected governments whose national interests conflicted with perceived US national interests. Now the US has become "the indispensable nation," fighting a "war on terror" as we attempt to control or—euphemistically—"stabilize" the entire Middle East. While there may be some truth to these slogans, they are half-truths that mask an ongoing imperial role in the world, while maintaining a self-righteous national image of acting solely from virtuous motivations. If the United States is "the indispensable nation," our nation's leaders present American interests as synonymous with the interests of the rest of the world.

The myths of entitlement, inequality, racial superiority, and conquest/dispossession have coexisted uncomfortably with constitutional guarantees of equality for all. It has taken generations to even begin to correct the moral and spiritual imperfections of these founding myths within the United States. In fact, the history and ideology of settler colonialism have been so central to the political history of the United States that it is not surprising the political and religious leadership in the US has been predisposed to uncritical support for the Zionist movement.

What is surprising is that some of the most influential and progressive American Protestant theologians of the twentieth century were also pro-Zionist, in spite of their denunciation of fundamentalism and dispensationalist "End Times" speculation. These include theologians who specialized in a prophetic critique of American foreign policy and the misuse of US power around the world. Some of their students who exercise influence in mainline denominations still cling to a form of liberal pro-Zionism that to this day turns a blind eye to more than 65 years of systemic violation of International law and human rights by Israel. In this section we will look at several mainstream theologians who may be called liberal pro-Zionists.

PAUL TILLICH AND REINHOLD NIEBUHR

In the 1930s a number of Jewish and Christian intellectuals with roots in Germany but subsequently teaching in New York City at institutions such as Columbia University, Jewish Theological Seminary, and Union Seminary formed a moral support group. Among the group were the philosopher and political theorist Herbert Marcuse, Rabbi Abraham Heschel, theologian Paul Tillich (1886-1965), and political ethicist Reinhold Niebuhr (1892-1971). As the Third Reich in Germany escalated its demonization and violence against Jews, the support group became a political think-tank, increasingly outspoken against the Nazi regime and demanding US intervention on behalf of European Jewry.

Tillich was already a strong critic of Nazism, having analyzed and condemned it in *The Socialist Decision*, a book on social theory, which he wrote in 1933. He noted that Nazi ideology was opposed to the spirit of Judaism, which was centered in the worship of God "who transcended blood, soil, and communal loyalties and demanded justice."[2] Thus it is not surprising that Tillich was not originally a supporter of the Zionist cause, questioning the concept of a nation-state "Israel" and arguing that the Jewish people should not be limited to an attachment to "space [land] and time." However, Tillich changed his position as conditions for Jews deteriorated in Germany. Once news of the concentration camps and corresponding genocide were confirmed, he became a supporter of the Zionist quest for Jewish statehood. He firmly believed that the only answer was to provide Jews with a safe haven in a state of their own.

Tillich found a close ally in fellow Union Seminary Professor Reinhold Niebuhr who would soon become a leading voice on US foreign policy and an outspoken advocate for Zionist causes. (President Barack Obama has called Niebuhr "my theologian" and one of the major influences on his political and ethical thought.) Unlike many of their theologian colleagues, Niebuhr and Tillich were not silent about what was occurring in Europe. Tillich, a German native, and Niebuhr, a second generation American of German descent, began to organize themselves with a goal of influencing US policy concerning the threat Germany posed to the Jews of Europe and the unity of Europe itself.

Tillich called upon all Christians and particularly the churches of the Reformation to join with Judaism in a prophetic critique of this highly distorted expression of German nationalism. He considered Nazism a false, secular alternative to prophetic Judaism and Christianity as it was based on pagan Teutonic myths of Aryan racial supremacy and was, in essence, a closed system with no room for the prophetic critique that the Hebrew Prophets and Jesus brought to humanity. In Tillich's view, the only just action by the church was to oppose Nazism in every conceivable way. Had Tillich anticipated that Zionism would become a closed system with little room for prophetic critique, might he perhaps have issued a similar prophetic critique against it?

Once news of the concentration camps and corresponding genocide were confirmed, [Tillich] became a supporter of the Zionist quest for Jewish statehood.

Paul Tillich

Reinhold Niebuhr

Kristallnacht, "the Night of Broken Glass," was a pogrom against Jews throughout Nazi Germany and parts of Austria that occurred on November 9-10, 1938, carried out by civilians and Nazi "brownshirt" paramilitary forces. Shards of broken glass littered the streets after Jewish-owned stores, homes, schools, and synagogues were ransacked (including the Berlin synagogue pictured above). More than 1,000 synagogues were burned (95 in Vienna alone) and over 7,000 Jewish businesses destroyed or damaged. At least 91 Jews were killed in the attacks, and 30,000 were arrested and incarcerated in concentration camps. The pretext for the attacks on Jews and Jewish property was the assassination in Paris of the German diplomat Ernst vom Rath by Herschel Grynszpan, a 17-year-old German-born Polish Jew.

After the turbulent but decisive decade of the 1940s, there was a gradual shift in the Protestant churches toward increased support for Israel.

KRISTALLNACHT

On November 9, 1938, *Kristallnacht* (the Night of Broken Glass) broke out—Nazi-organized pogroms targeting Jews in Germany and parts of Austria. Ten months later Germany invaded Poland and Europe was at war. Many Christian leaders opposed the US entering the war. Some, including the editors of the influential Protestant nondenominational *Christian Century*, called for caution and patience and for the US to stay out of the war. Niebuhr lost patience with this position, broke with the *Century*, and in 1941 founded a new liberal journal, *Christianity and Crisis*. He had described the *Century* in 1939 as "without question the most vital force in American theology,"[3] but by the early 1940s he came to believe that the *Century* and the segment of the church that stood with it were increasingly irrelevant. While a liberal Protestant himself, Niebuhr differed from traditional liberal Protestant theologians by advocating a theology of political realism where evil is given a prominent role. He wrote:"liberal Protestants who believe that Christianity will shame the enemy into goodness," are fooling themselves.[4] He was convinced that Christians had a moral obligation to fight Nazism and fascism if the Jews of Europe were to

be saved. In the first issue of *Christianity and Crisis*, Niebuhr wrote: "I think it is dangerous to allow Christian religious sensitivity about the imperfections of our own society to obscure the fact that Nazi tyranny intends to annihilate the Jewish race."[5]

THE BILTMORE PLATFORM

By 1939, if not before, most Zionist leaders were convinced the Nazis were committing genocide against the Jews in Poland and Germany. By the early 1940s, Zionism had taken a commanding role in the organized American Jewish community. With reports confirming the concentration camps and the Nazi genocide, the Zionist movement shifted its operational center from London to New York City and began to concentrate its political efforts on moving public opinion and policy in the United States. The conference held at New York's Biltmore Hotel in May 1942 and the resulting "Biltmore Platform" crystallized the Zionist movement's commitment to nothing less than the creation of a Jewish state in Palestine as the answer to Nazi atrocities. The Zionist leadership argued that only a Jewish state could provide Jews the security necessary to rise again from the ashes of the Holocaust.

The Biltmore conference united most major Jewish organizations and leadership behind a highly aggressive form of Zionism from this time forward. Membership in the major Zionist organizations grew rapidly as did the donations to underwrite their campaigns.

Also emerging from the Biltmore meetings was a proposal to establish and fund Christian organizations to support the call for Jewish statehood, mobilize Christians to support the Zionist cause, and lobby their members of Congress.[6]

Niebuhr supported the Zionist movement uncritically, with more vigor than did Tillich. Like his colleague, Niebuhr understood a Jewish state to be the necessary response to the Holocaust and Western anti-Semitism. He was adamant that the United States had a primary responsibility to protect Israel and the Jewish people for moral reasons and US national interests, particularly as a dimension of Cold War politics. He also believed that Israel deserved US political, military, and economic support.

Niebuhr's most revealing writing on Israel and Zionism is in his article "Our Stake in Israel,"that appeared in *The New Republic* on February 4, 1957. He states at the outset that one gains an appreciation for Israel by reviewing its beginnings as a state

> and the heroic battle which the nascent nation waged against the Arab nations, sworn to throttle Israel in its cradle. Thus the state's birth was both a gift from the world community and an achievement of the redoubtable army which the little nation was able to organize.

Discussion of the fate of Palestinians was taboo—a divisive hazard to be strenuously avoided for risk of derailing these interfaith dialogues.

Niebuhr's argument relied on the Israel-centric narrative of Israel's founding in which Palestinians are expunged from the story. Niebuhr embraced many of the popular Zionist myths that surrounded the creation of Israel, such as "making the desert bloom" and praising the vision of Theodor Herzl and Chaim Weitzmann without challenging their hardline goals. He adds that Israel became a melting pot for Jews, without mention of the resulting Palestinian loss of land and livelihood. Nor does Niebuhr express regret that half the population was driven into refugee status following Israel's creation. He ends the argument with the questionable mantra that the United States has an obligation to support Israel because "Israel is the only democracy in the Middle East."[7]

How ironic that Niebuhr, the exponent of a school of Christian social ethics named "Christian Realism," and the author of the famous aphorism, "Man's capacity for justice makes democracy possible, but man's inclination to injustice makes democracy necessary,"[8] would demonstrate moral blindness to the fact that the establishment of a "Jewish democracy" in Palestine was preconditioned on the exclusion of the native Palestinians. Niebuhr remains perhaps the most influential mainline American Protestant theologian of the 20th century, and his legacy continues in the 21st.

After the turbulent but decisive decade of the 1940s there was a gradual shift in the Protestant churches toward increased support for Israel. The primary Protestant organization was the American Christian Palestine Committee (ACPC), which received major financial support from Jewish Zionist organizations. One of its functions was to monitor and challenge any journal article or church statement that was sympathetic to the Palestinians.

An additional development that advanced the pro-Israel bias in Protestantism was the increased interest in Christian-Jewish dialogue and a multiplicity of Jewish and Christian organizations that emerged to facilitate it. The National Conference of Christians and Jews played an important role for many decades, as did the B'nai B'rith-Anti-Defamation League (ADL), and eventually most major Zionist organizations. Dialogue programs seemed to be a significant instrument to promote healing as Christians grappled with the anti-Semitism that had plagued the Church for centuries culminating in the Nazi Holocaust. Discussion of the fate of Palestinians was taboo—a divisive hazard to be strenuously avoided for risk of derailing these interfaith dialogues.

Jewish-Christian dialogue would continue for decades following the rules of the Ecumenical

Krister Stendhahl

Deal: Christian silence on Israel as expiation for guilt incurred during centuries of anti-Semitism. It was Jewish theologian Marc Ellis who named this price-tag rule for Christians over 25 years ago. When 15 Protestant and Roman Catholic leaders broke these rules for the first time on September 15, 2012, by writing a letter to Congress asking for sanctions against Israel, Ellis celebrated by announcing, "The interfaith ecumenical deal is dead." He continued,

> Strange, looking on the internet for commentary on the Church leaders' letter, one site had the letter opposite a quotation from the Holocaust survivor, Elie Wiesel: "Neutrality helps the oppressor, never the victim. Silence encourages the tormentor, never the tormented." It seems that the Church leaders have finally learned the central lesson of Christian complicity in the Holocaust. It was taught to them by Jews in the personal witness of Elie Wiesel. The lesson: The ultimate sin is silence in the face of injustice.[9]

KRISTER STENDAHL

One of the influential biblical theologians of the 1950s-1990s was the Swedish New Testament scholar and Harvard Divinity School professor, Krister Stendahl. As a Swedish teenager in the late 1930s, Stendahl sought relief for an arthritic spine at a German spa. There he met Swedish missionaries who told him about Nazi persecution of Jews and rescue operations. These experiences were to have a life-long impact on him.

Stendahl earned his doctorate from Uppsala University in Sweden and wrote his dissertation on the newly discovered Dead Sea Scrolls. In 1954 he began a long and illustrious ecclesiastical and academic career, first at Harvard Divinity School where he gained recognition for his scholarly writings on Pauline theology.

One of Stendahl's radical claims was his argument that Paul's letter to the Romans was not primarily a discussion of "justification by faith," which had been the traditional interpretation since St. Augustine and was reinforced by both Martin Luther and John Calvin. Instead, Stendahl asserted that Paul's thesis in Romans was a discussion of God's mysterious plan for the Jews, an argument he found especially in Romans 9-11. Stendahl claimed that Paul's argument demonstrates that God desires harmonious coexistence between Judaism and Christianity, thus paving the way for deeper and more open relationships between Christians and Jews. Christians should no longer follow Paul's example of attempting to convert Jews, nor should they practice any form of anti-Semitism or claim superiority with such arguments as "replacement theology," which

Krister Stendahl and Rabbi David Hartman: A Wounded Friendship

A new study by Paul Verduin describes Stendahl's relationship with his close friend, the influential late Rabbi David Hartman. As the founder and President of the Shalom Hartman Institute in Jerusalem, Hartman distinguished himself as a liberal Jewish defender of Zionism. Hartman and Stendahl became friends during the latter's scholarly career at Harvard and later when he moved to Brandeis University. Once Stendahl retired, Hartman offered him the position of co-chair of the Hartman Institute. Stendahl served in this capacity from 1994 to 1998, taking the opportunity to visit the West Bank where he saw for himself the ugly face of military occupation. There he met Palestinian Christian leaders, including Lutheran Bishop Munib Younan and the Rev. Dr. Mitri Raheb, pastor of the Christmas Lutheran Church in Bethlehem. He

also reconnected with the Revs. Susan and Michael Thomas who were serving as co-pastors of the Lutheran Church of the Redeemer in the Old City of Jerusalem. Michael had been one of Stendahl's students at Harvard Divinity School and Susan had served as a pastor at the Lutheran church the Stendahls attended in Cambridge, MA.

In early March 2002 Stendahl received a disturbing email from the Thomases. As he read down the page, he was directed to an article incorporated in the email that had appeared in the *International Herald Tribune* and the *Washington Post*. The article described a Palestinian suicide bombing in Jerusalem and the terrible suffering it brought to Israeli families. As Stendahl came to the end of the article he read the concluding statement by his friend, Rabbi Hartman, who

said: "What nation in the world would allow itself to be intimidated and terrified as this whole [Israeli] population is, where you can't send your kid out for a pizza at night without fear he'll be blown up?" Then came Hartman's conclusion: "Let's really let them understand what the implication of their actions is," he said of the Palestinians. "Very simply, wipe them out. Level them."[12]

Stendahl must have been stunned by his friend's words. A copy of a handwritten letter from Stendahl to Hartman dated March 4, 2002, is preserved in the collection of Stendahl's papers. It reads: "Dear, dear David: How to answer this e-mail we received?" Then Stendahl pasted the text of the interview into his message, followed by an obviously troubled plea for clarity: "If this is true, it puts much stress

and pain on one of the most precious friendships I have been given. We will be in Sweden [contact phone number supplied] March 9–13. Then back in C–e [Cambridge, MA]. Yours Krister."[13] There is no record that Stendahl ever received an answer to his letter. Stendahl died in 2008.

This experience near the end of his life seems to be the closest Krister Stendahl came to articulating a single criticism or even questioning Israel's intentions, and it remained entirely private. He was obviously stunned by Hartman's phrase, "Wipe them out," but other than the letter to Hartman, he did nothing. Was he immobilized by his life-long commitment to never criticize Israel? Did his residual guilt over the Holocaust or his belief in Jewish exceptionalism lead him to give Rabbi Hartman and Israel "a pass"? We will never

Rabbi David Hartman

know, but here is the case of a brilliant New Testament scholar and author of many scholarly volumes, who could not reconcile his belief system and commitment to the Zionist "narrative" with this problematic statement by his progressive friend, Rabbi David Hartman.

Note: For a perspective on Rabbi Hartman's views on Religious Zionism and contemporary Israel, read the interview, "Religion now more dangerous than Arabs,"[14] published in YNet News a year before his death in February 2013.

Paul van Buren

God's promises to Israel include... possession of the Land. In Jesus Christ...God said Yes also to that promise.

PAUL VAN BUREN

asserts on the basis of New Testament texts that the old covenant of God with the Jews has been replaced by the new covenant in Christ. His exegesis and interpretation of Romans transformed New Testament scholarship in terms of Christian-Jewish dialogue and interfaith relationships.

In the same volume, Stendahl made a remarkable statement about Jewish-Christian relationships by adding that Jews are not only equal to Christians in the eyes of God, but that Christians are "honorary Jews."[10] This statement raises several theological concerns. Stendahl implies that Christians should adopt a theology of Jewish "chosenness," a choice by God that means superiority and exclusive privileges for the Jewish people. Christians can be called "honorary Jews" because Jews are God's first, and by implication, God's primary "chosen" people. Certainly the arguments made by Stendahl are theological. Nonetheless, they can be harnessed to support Israeli political goals.

Is Stendahl suggesting that Christians should adopt a form of Jewish exceptionalism?[11] Given the implied and overt theological exceptionalism that one finds in several theologians of this era, there is certainly no cautionary note from Stendahl to resolve this theological dilemma. One of the many negative consequences of this tendency toward Jewish exceptionalism in liberal Protestant theology is its failure to hold the state of Israel to the same standard of international law and human rights as that to which every other nation should be held.

Stendahl's views on the modern state of Israel are similar to Niebuhr's and Tillich's, viewing Israel as the answer to the Holocaust and necessary for Jewish survival. But Stendahl seems to go beyond both of them, not only in his "honorary Jews" comment, but also in his claims that the Jewish people are intimately tied to this particular land, the land of Palestine, to which he gives a theological value. These claims clearly place Stendahl in the liberal pro-Zionist category, and his writings and public statements supported the Zionist agenda throughout his career. Any reservations Stendahl may have had as a result of his personal witnessing of the Israeli military occupation in the West Bank during his 1994-1998 tenure as co-chair of the Hartman Institute in Jerusalem remained private.

PAUL VAN BUREN

Paul van Buren (1934-1998) was an Episcopal priest who for over two decades taught theology at Temple University in Philadelphia. In the 1980s he served as an associate of the Shalom Hartman Institute in Jerusalem. He is popularly remembered as a "Death of God" theologian and for his advocacy of "Secular Christianity." But van Buren's *magnum opus* was his post-Holocaust theology, a three-volume work entitled *Theology of the Jewish-Christian Reality*. Here van Buren struggles against the anti-Semitic theology of the Christian tradition and stresses the continuity rather than the discontinuity between Jewish and Christian faith.

Van Buren thought that even the terms that Christians use for the scriptures—Old Testament/ New Testament—send a message that the new (Christianity) has replaced the old (Judaism). To avoid this linguistic trap, van Buren substitutes the term "Scriptures" for Old Testament and "Apostolic Writings" for New Testament.

In Volume 2, which carries the subtitle *A Christian Theology of the People Israel*, van Buren's pro-Zionist theology is stated in clear terms with clear *political* implications:

> God's promises to Israel include, for example, possession of the Land. In Jesus Christ, if we are to believe the apostle Paul, God said Yes also to that promise. The church of Jesus Christ, therefore, cannot coherently do other than confirm and support the promise of the Land to the Jewish people. It cannot twist this promise to the Jews into a spiritualized promise to the church, for to do so would be to witness to Jesus Christ as God's No to this particular and by no means peripheral promise of his....[I]t seems to us to be clear that God's church cannot be itself without confirming his choice of, covenant with, and promises to his people Israel.[15]

Since van Buren was in Jerusalem during the 1980s it is reasonable to assume that he visited the West Bank and must have seen some of the effects of the Israeli occupation of Palestine. Evidently the Holocaust and his dialogue with Jewish Holocaust theologians had so touched him that he was unable to question Israel's confiscation of Palestinian land and the pauperization of the Palestinian people underway during his time of residency in the country.

However, in one area—the activity of God in all religions—he was more open than many theologians of his time. Van Buren wrote,

> One of the more difficult challenges which they [Christians and Jews] will do well to face together is that of our understanding of the way in which the God of Abraham, Isaac, and Jacob has been and is at work in the People of the Book (Islam),

After the Holocaust of World War II, it would appear that mainstream liberal Protestants... have replaced the error of anti-Jewish bigotry with another.

Bad Arabs

The "crude, essentialized caricatures" Edward Said wrote of in his 1980 article "Islam through Western Eyes" (see page 43) are alive and well in popular media. Is there a double standard that tolerates negative stereotypes of Arabs while appropriately rejecting them as racist when Jews, African Americans, and other groups are caricatured?

Art Malik (right) as Palestinian terrorist Salim Abu Aziz in the 1994 movie "True Lies," starring Arnold Schwarzenegger.

John Turturro as Fatoush "The Phantom" Hakbarah, in the 2008 movie "You Don't Mess with the Zohan."

Rob Schneider (in brownface) as Salim, a Palestinian cab driver, in "You Don't Mess with the Zohan."

Sacha Baron Cohen as Admiral General Aladeen in the 2012 movie, "The Dictator."

and in the many peoples of many books (Hindus and Buddhists, and others).[16]

Niebuhr, Stendahl, and van Buren stand in a long line of liberal pro-Zionist Protestant and Jewish clergy, theologians, and politicians who influenced successive generations of religious leaders and US policy-makers on the Middle East by their uncritical support for Israel and their silence about the plight of the Palestinians. Among the Christian theologians who often excuse Israel while remaining quiet about the plight of Palestinians are John Bright, James Carroll, Clark Williamson, Karl and Marcus Barth, Robert Osborn, and many scholars in the W. F. Albright Institute of Archeological Research, and Jewish writers such as Michael Wyschograd, Arthur Hertzberg, Michael Waltzer, Franz Rosenzweig, Irving Greenberg, and—while not a theologian—Elie Wiesel, to name but a few. Regrettably the *Christian Century* since 2004 has also avoided criticism of Israeli violations of international law and human rights while defending Israel against its critics, thus muting the voice of justice.

IS ORIENTALISM THE CULPRIT?

Edward Said was a Columbia University professor of English and Comparative Literature and a founder of the critical theory of post-colonialism. His highly acclaimed 1978 publication, *Orientalism*, describes the persistence in Western scholarship, from the 19th century on, of stereotypes of the native peoples in the Middle East and elsewhere reflecting Western colonial views and ambitions. Said, who was born into a Palestinian Christian family in Jerusalem in 1935, became a scholar equally at home in both the Arab and the Western world. From that unique vantage point he was able to recognize and analyze the use of modern/backward, superior/inferior categories that frame Western understandings of the Muslim world and the Israel/Palestine conflict and shape Western foreign policies toward the Middle East. Said demonstrated how Islamic cultures and societies were depicted as having values at odds with the Western values of rationality, equality, and individuality. Such caricatures helped the British and French legitimize their regional interventions from the early 19th century onwards.

In a 1980 article entitled "Islam through Western Eyes," Said wrote:

> So far as the United States seems to be concerned, it is only a slight overstatement to say that Muslims and Arabs are essentially seen as either oil suppliers or terrorists. Very little of the detail,

REFLECTION

1. What issues arise for you after reading and reflecting on this section?

2. What evidence do you find that the myth of divine election is still at work in American and Israeli national life? Is it hypocritical for Americans to criticize Israeli policies today for the same abuse of human rights that our "settler colonial" American ancestors committed?

3. Why do you think that Niebuhr, Stendahl, van Buren, and other liberal Protestant theologians were either blind to or silent about the suffering inflicted upon Palestinians by the state of Israel from 1948 on? How does one reconcile their position with support for a Jewish-only state that is ethnically cleansing Palestinians from their homeland?

4. Reflect on the story of the relationship between Krister Stendahl and Rabbi David Hartman (see box on page 41). Does Rabbi Hartman's response to the suicide bombing reflect the level of fear that Israelis live under? In what ways does Zionism and the forced segregation between Israelis and Palestinians exacerbate this fear and make reconciliation more difficult?

5. Should US Christian and Jewish organizations that promote a pro-Zionist US foreign policy be held accountable for promoting violence and oppression toward the Palestinian people?

6. How does exceptionalism relate to the concept of chosenness? Can you think of instances in which Americans apply one standard to US actions abroad and a different standard to actions of other nations?

the human density, the passion of Arab-Moslem life has entered the awareness of even those people whose profession it is to report on the Arab world. What we have is a series of crude, essentialized caricatures of the Islamic world presented in such a way as to make that world vulnerable to military aggression.[17]

As a new theology and language emerged after World War II, the work of liberal Protestant theologians was grounded in an unconscious Orientalist framework. Niebuhr, Stendahl, and van Buren stood on a "Western shore" that defined itself as "Judeo-Christian" and by default treated anything outside that framework as alien "other," rendering it susceptible to criticism, assumptions of cultural inferiority, and ultimately to aggression and war. After the Holocaust of World War II, it would appear that mainstream liberal Protestants—like Western evangelical and fundamentalist Christians—have replaced the error of anti-Jewish bigotry with another. This is to say, Western Christianity has arrived at a place where the "other" is no longer Jews, but Islam and its 1.5 billion adherents. Arab Christians have been largely ignored and left out of the discussion.

Why then, it must be asked, are we comfortable with Orientalism, while we find anti-Semitism abhorrent and unacceptable? Are not both prejudiced thinking that lead to hatred and violence?

Why are we comfortable with Orientalism, while we find anti-Semitism abhorrent and unacceptable?

Israel's "Image Problem"

Hasbara Goes to College

Campuses are hotly contested battlefields for hearts and minds in the *hasbara* project. Numerous organizations, including Hillel, Stand-WithUs, and Campus Watch employ a variety of strategies for shutting down campus activities and academic inquiry that promote criticism of Israeli policy, including blackballing professors who dissent from the dominant Zionist narrative, pressuring university administrators, and, in the case of Hillel, enforcing a closed-door policy to Jewish student activities that deviate from the mainstream party line.

Hasbara Handbook: Promoting Israel on Campus was produced in 2002 by the World Union of Jewish Students to provide Israel's college-age supporters with advocacy tools. [*Available online*1]

"Israel's advocacy effort has become one of the world's most efficient and productive," writes journalist Barak Ravid, "but Israel nevertheless suffers from an image problem."2 The Hebrew term for the Israeli advocacy effort to which Ravid refers is *hasbara*. Depending on the context, *hasbara* can mean "explanation," "public relations," "media spin," or "propaganda."

Ravid reports that multiple government bodies are involved in Israel's *hasbara* initiatives, including the National Information Directorate, the Prime Minister's Office, the Foreign Ministry, the Public Diplomacy and Diaspora Affairs Ministry, the IDF Spokesman's Office, the Tourism Ministry, and the Jewish Agency. The Foreign Ministry alone, Ravid reports,

> invests an unprecedented annual sum of NIS 100 million [$28.4 million] in branding Israel; in bringing over experts, academics and opinion makers; and in organizing pro-Israel events around the globe (including the annual Salute to Israel parade in New York City and the Israeli film festival in Paris).3

The Jewish Agency for Israel is planning to spend $300 million annually for pro-Israel public relations programs with a focus on US campuses—where some fear Israel is losing ground in the public opinion war. $100 million of this fund would be supplied by the Israeli government.4

Writing in the *Forward*, Nathaniel Popper explains,

> The new approach to Israeli image control first began... with the founding of Israel21c, a small California-based group that has worked with public relations experts to place news stories about Israel that do not focus on the conflict with the Palestinians. The organization...posts articles about...medical and technological advances in Israeli laboratories.5

Volunteers complement the work of consultants. The Israeli government, Ravid writes, "conducts an unofficial advocacy effort involving hundreds of Israelis and overseas activists, organizations and NGOs, along with non-Jewish supporters;...delivering Israel's messages mainly in the United States and the EU."6

In the United States, Peter Beinart reports, "Groups like AIPAC and the Presidents' Conference patrol public discourse, scolding people who contradict their vision of Israel...."7 He continues, "Not only does the organized American Jewish community mostly avoid public criticism of the Israeli government, it tries to prevent others from leveling such criticism as well."8

Like Beinart, UK journalist Seth Freedman sees an "other, darker side of Israeli *hasbara*...,the relentless pursuit of anyone deemed a danger to the state, whether domestic dissidents or external critics."9 More often than not, he writes, "the campaigns are based more on witch-hunts and whitewashes than honest debate over the most thorny issues surrounding the state."

Despite the massive resources employed to burnish Israel's standing in the eyes of the international community, many supporters of the Jewish state complain that Israel suffers from a poor international image and is losing the public relations war.

Increasingly, analysts are suggesting that Israel's "image problem" is not a result of a poor public relations strategy but, as Ravid puts it, "a product of the Israeli government's policies." Seth Freedman, not mincing words, declares that "Israel's image problem will only disappear when the core crimes committed in the name of the state cease, and the Palestinians are dealt with equitably."10

Swarthmore College campus, Swarthmore, Pennsylvania

Swarthmore Says, "Open Hillel!"

In December 2013, the student board of the Swarthmore College campus Hillel issued a press release announcing their decision to be an "Open Hillel," an organization

> whose purpose is not to advocate for one single political view, but rather to open up space that encourages dialogue within the diverse and pluralistic Jewish student body and the larger community....11

The Swarthmore students' statement affirmed that "all are welcome to walk through our doors and speak with our name and under our roof, be they Zionist, anti-Zionist, post-Zionist, or non-Zionist."12

The Open Hillel movement emerged in 2012, mobilizing against the Hillel Foundation's "standards of partnership," which explicitly disallow events critical of Israel. Hillel rules have forced controversial cancellations at several universities—including Avraham Burg (former speaker of the Israeli Knesset and author of the 2009 book *The Holocaust Is Over*) and Breaking the Silence, an Israeli veterans' group that relates personal testimonies of human rights abuses perpetrated while in uniform.13

Meanwhile, the Hillel Foundation and the American Israel Public Affairs Committee (AIPAC) have pledged their commitment to "working together to expand support for Israel on campus."14

7 · Evangelicals and Christian Zionism

Rev. John Hagee is the founder of Christians United for Israel (CUFI), which describes itself as "the largest pro-Israel organization in the United States with over one million members."[3]

For decades The Presbyterian Church (U.S.A.) has opposed the evangelical blend of dispensationalism and Christian Zionism because it fuses religion with politics, distorts faith, and imperils peace in the Middle East.[1] A major segment of the pro-Israel lobby in the US consists not of Jews but of evangelical Christians who are Zionists and claim that Christian Zionism is an essential component of their faith. In his essay, "Evangelicals and Christian Zionism," Gary Burge, an evangelical Presbyterian and Professor of New Testament at Wheaton College, takes pains to distinguish between "mainline evangelicals" and evangelicals who are also Christians Zionists. In this section we present Burge's critique of contemporary evangelical Christian Zionism as espoused by its most visible contemporary advocate, Rev. John Hagee. Hagee, a dispensationalist, is pastor of Cornerstone Church in San Antonio, Texas, a Pentecostal mega-church with 19,000 members. He is also the founder of Christians United for Israel (CUFI), a major player in the pro-Israel lobby in Washington, DC, which seeks to foster unwavering support for Israel among members of the US government.

Dispensationalism developed in the mid-19th century among the Plymouth Brethren and was popularized by the Scofield Reference Bible first published by Oxford University Press in 1909. This translation of the Bible contains the text of the King James version along with a commentary that divides history between the creation and the final judgment into seven different time periods—or dispensations—in which God's covenants with humanity operate differently. Republished in 1917, it captured the spirit of the times, namely, a deep pessimism brought on by the catastrophic brutality of World War I. Updated versions of this Bible are still best sellers in the UK and Ireland, and it has been translated into several European languages. Millions of

Christians believe that the last dispensation—the Second Coming of Christ, the great battle of Armageddon, and Christ's one-thousand-year rule of the world from its center, Jerusalem—is about to arrive.

Instead of engaging in the work of building society as part of heeding Christ's call to share the Gospel, this pessimistic worldview encourages Christians to set themselves apart from society to prepare for judgment day. In contrast, mainline evangelical theology that is shaped by the Reformed Tradition is more hopeful, teaching that Christians are called to transform society and enjoy the goodness of the creation, including the secular arts.

Dispensationalist evangelicals adopted a Christian version of Zionism during the 20th century, claiming that

> the catalyst of the end of time was the reestablishment of the secular State of Israel—which thrilled them in 1948 when Israel announced its nationhood. Israel's various military victories in 1967 and 1973 were confirmations of a divine hand on Israel's future.[2]

The corollary of this belief is that evangelical Christian Zionists now have a divine mandate to support the modern state of Israel because they

A major segment of the pro-Israel lobby in the US consists not of Jews but of evangelical Christians who are Zionists and claim that Christian Zionism is an essential component of their faith.

ABOUT THIS SECTION

This section is a condensed and edited version of an essay of the same name by Professor Gary Burge in Wagner and Davis, eds., *Zionism and the Quest for Justice in the Holy Land*. Dr. Burge, an Evangelical and Reformed (Presbyterian) biblical scholar, is Professor of New Testament Studies at Wheaton College and Graduate School. His 2010 book, *Jesus and the Land*, challenges Zionist land theology.

believe that 1) modern-day Israel is the heir of the Old Testament promises of land to Abraham and his descendants; and 2) by supporting Israel they help usher in the return of Christ and His one-thousand-year reign.

In his 2010 book, *Jesus and the Land: The New Testament Challenge to "Holy Land" Theology*, Burge undercuts the Christian Zionists' uncritical endorsement of Israel's occupation and settlement of Palestinian lands by stressing the ethical preconditions that God places on the promise of land in the Old Testament. He also describes the way in which the New Testament spiritualizes these land promises. In this essay he challenges the *theological exceptionalism* of Christian Zionists "that sets it [the state of Israel] apart from the requirements of behavior expected of other nations."[4]

Burge examines five problematic theological convictions of evangelical Christian Zionists. First, he questions the evangelical Christian Zionist claim that God's promises of land to Abraham in Genesis 12, 15, and 17 are valid today. Burge writes:

> To think in Christian terms about land and promise is to think differently than Judaism thinks. *In short, the New Testament changes the spiritual geography of God's people.* The Kingdom of God is tied neither to an ethnicity nor to a place. Because the early Christians understood this truth, they carried their missionary efforts to the entire world. ...The point is this: many evangelical theologians are not convinced that the promises to Abraham, much less those to Moses, are still theologically significant today. The work of Christ is definitive. There is one covenant. And it is with Christ.[5]

Second, evangelical Christian Zionists believe that biblical prophecy has been fulfilled because *Israel has been restored to the land*. For these Christian Zionists the establishment of the state of Israel in 1948 was a *theological*, not just a political, event (as was the restoration following the Babylonian exile).

Third, a corollary of this belief is *fidelity to Israel*. Any criticism of the state of Israel is not only anti-Semitic but also against God's will. "God blesses those who bless Israel and curses those who curse Israel."[6] (Genesis 12:2-3) "Stand with Israel!" is one of John Hagee's favorite crowd-rousing slogans.

A fourth evangelical Christian Zionist belief is that *history is coming to its close*. There's nothing new here—apocalyptic doomsday prophets have appeared repeatedly in times of crisis and change. What distresses Burge and other Reformed evangelicals is how this zeal for the Second Coming of Christ has distorted the ethics of Christian Zionists and eclipsed any concern for justice in Israel-Palestine.

Finally, the "crown jewel" in the worldview of evangelical Christian Zionism, *Jesus' Second Coming*, is contingent upon the fulfillment of God's promise to bless Israel with land, security, and prosperity. Evangelical Christian Zionists regard the withdrawal of Jewish settlements from the West Bank and the establishment of a Palestinian state as contrary to God's will because it would weaken or diminish Israel's control of the land and thereby jeopardize Jesus' return. Evangelicals of the Reformed Tradition like Burge believe that Christ has already come and, through the work of the Holy Spirit, Christ is already at work in the world transforming it. Therefore they engage in the work of justice and peace rather than seeking an escape from history and God's final blockbuster, the destruction of all unbelievers.

Burge writes that he joins a host of Jewish leaders in sounding an alarm: the alliance between evangelical Christian Zionists and Jewish Zionists is dangerous. He and these Jewish leaders condemn Pastor Hagee's call for the United States "to join Israel in a pre-emptive military strike against Iran to fulfill God's plan for both Israel and the West."[7]

THE PROBLEM OF REPLACEMENT THEOLOGY

Burge believes most Reformed theologians, including evangelicals, hold to a "one-covenant" theology (fig. 2, below). This means that with the coming of Christ and the founding of the Church, the covenant with Abraham and the Israelites has been

Zeal for the Second Coming of Christ has distorted the ethics of Christian Zionists and eclipsed any concern for justice in Israel-Palestine.

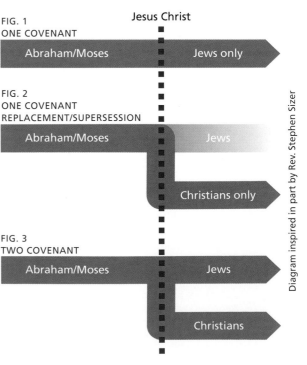

FIG. 1
ONE COVENANT
Jesus Christ
Abraham/Moses — Jews only

FIG. 2
ONE COVENANT
REPLACEMENT/SUPERSESSION
Abraham/Moses — Jews
Christians only

FIG. 3
TWO COVENANT
Abraham/Moses — Jews
Christians

Diagram inspired in part by Rev. Stephen Sizer

Using Words As a Weapon

LIBERATION AND CONFLICT

In the history of colonial wars and anti-colonial resistance, especially in the context of settler-colonies, the struggles of natives against European colonists have always been named "liberation" struggles. Examples include the Algerian liberation struggle against French colonialism and colonists, the Zimbabwean people's liberation struggle against British colonialism and colonists, and the anti-apartheid struggle for liberation in South Africa against the racial privileges of white colonists.

In none of these cases was the struggle for liberation from colonialism referred to primarily or secondarily as a "conflict." Indeed there has never been such a technical term as the Algerian-French "conflict," a White-Black Rhodesian or South African "conflict," not even for the colonists themselves. In these cases, both the settler-colonists and those resisting them were not shy in naming their struggle as a struggle for colonial and racial supremacist privilege or for liberation from racism and settler-colonialism respectively. This nomenclature would also apply to Zionist settler-colonialism in Palestine and to Palestinian resistance.[8]

ANTI-COLONIALISM AND ANTI-SEMITISM

In the period between 1944 and 1948...Zionism would begin to call its terrorist war against Britain a "war of independence," casting itself as an anti-colonial movement,...Zionists began to recode their colonial project as "anti-colonial" while proceeding with colonization....As the Palestinian people mounted their resistance to Jewish colonization year after year, and decade after decade, Zionism began to fight them by labeling them anti-Semites.[9]

—JOSEPH MASSAD

transformed and opened to all humanity, Jews and Gentiles. Thus in some sense the old covenant has been replaced or superseded by the new covenant in Christ.

The primary theological fault that Burge finds in dispensationalist Christian Zionism is its belief in two covenants, one with Israel, the other with the Church, both of which are still equally valid.

The "two-covenant" view (fig. 3, left) presents two problems, says Burge. First, it validates the Zionist claim to Palestinian land based on Old Testament passages and rejects the New Testament teaching that spiritualizes and universalizes the Old Testament land promises by treating them as spiritual metaphor, not literal land grants in perpetuity. Second, and more important for Burge, two-covenant theology diminishes the importance of what God has done in Christ and negates biblical texts that claim salvation is through Christ alone.[10]

In spite of Burge's commitment to a one-covenant and some form of replacement theology, he agrees with the historians who claim that replacement theology has been the cause of much Christian anti-Semitism. If God has chosen a new people in Christ, has not God abandoned the old people of Moses? Burge wrestles with this dilemma. On the one hand,

> *Burge agrees with the historians who claim that replacement theology has been the cause of much Christian anti-Semitism.*

the New Testament is indeed announcing the replacement of one thing with another. Christianity did not arise as a rival religion to Judaism. Christian faith was a religious movement *within Judaism* announcing that what Jewish faith sought had been found in the arrival of the Messiah, Jesus of Nazareth....The church was not seen as something 'Gentile.' The church was the community of believers (both Jewish and Gentile) that now represented the people of God....[11]

On the other hand, "when this replacement motif denigrates any valid place for Judaism as a legitimate religious faith,"[12] it can lead to anti-Jewish attitudes that, at their most extreme, lead to atrocities. Burge finds a solution to this problem in Romans 11:

> God continues to hold a place for Judaism in history. However this is a 'suspended blessing' for they are 'branches...broken off' (Rom 11:17, RSV) that will be restored at the end of history when Christ returns, when 'all Israel will be saved' (Rom 11:26, RSV). This understanding of Romans 11 means that we should not tolerate anti-Semitism and that church and synagogue should share mutual respect.[13]

[For a personal view of these issues by a Palestinian Evangelical New Testament scholar, Munther Isaac, see bonus episode of the DVD.]

REFLECTION

1. What questions arise for you after reading and reflecting on this section?

2. How does Prof. Burge's "suspended blessing" which he derives from Romans 11 differ from the ultimate fate of Jews according to Christian Zionism? What are the implications of the suspended blessing for the Christian attitude toward Jews between now and the return of Christ? How might Jews view the dilemma of one-covenant and two-covenant theology found in Christianity?

3. Does the Bible justify the modern-day land dispossession of Palestinians or any other people?

4. What happens when the doctrines of Christian Zionism are applied to modern day politics?

5. Why has the Presbyterian Church (U.S.A.) rejected Christian Zionism?

6. One basis for Zionism's claim to Palestine is the Abrahamic covenant described in the Old Testament. Christians like Burge reject these Old Testament claims, saying that in the New Testament land promises are spiritualized and universalized—*i.e.*, promised to all people in Christ. Are these two conflicting claims, both based on the Bible, relevant to contemporary politics, and if so, how can they be adjudicated?

What Diaspora?

GLOSSARY OF
HEBREW TERMS[1]

- *Aliyah* ascent;
immigration to Israel

- *Yerida* descent;
emigration from Israel

- *Galut* exile; a nation
uprooted from its
homeland and subject
to alien rule

The Hebrew terms used to describe the physical relationship of Jews to Israel are mirrored in Zionism, the political movement. Jewish existence outside Israel, according to Zionism, is a *diaspora* (a Greek term meaning "scattering") from the spiritual and ancestral homeland.

Galut notwithstanding, more than half of the world's Jews choose to live outside Israel. And in doing so, Micah Goodman writes, they are contributing to Jewish—and global—culture in a way that, across the span of 2,000 years, has been thoroughly and essentially Jewish.

> Indeed, the great achievement of the Diaspora was precisely the formation of a living, meaningful Judaism in the absence of a political or territorial base. To deny the worth of Jewish life outside the land of Israel is thus essentially to deny millennia of Jewish creativity.[5]

Millions of Jews are not only "voting with their feet" on Zionism, they are living richly diverse Jewish lives around the globe despite the scolding voices telling them they can't. Recent opinion polls of American Jews "do not include even one question about their attitude toward *aliyah* or about Israel as a place to live," writes Israeli journalist Shlomo Shamir. A veteran American Jewish activist explains to Shamir that "It is better not to ask," because "the disgrace to the community and to Israel would be great if they were to reveal the depth of alienation among American Jews from the idea of making *aliyah*."[6]

Many—perhaps most—Jews embrace an identity and culture that rejects the Israel-or-exile perspective on Jewish life. Caryn Aviv and David Shneer

> envision a new map for the Jewish world, one that has multiple homelands, that does not break the Jewish world into a dichotomous relationship between "diaspora" and "Israel," and that suggests a positive vision of the Jewish future....[7]

Aviv and Shneer note the enormous resources expended "to cultivate among Jews a sense of connection and

Jewish life is alive and well in the Islamic Republic of Iran.[2,3,4] Estimates of the current Jewish Iranian population range from 10,000 to 30,000. The Jewish presence in Persia/Iran is ancient, stretching 2,700 years to the Assyrian and Babylonian conquests of the Israelites. Middle Eastern Jews, also called *Mizrahi* Jews, share a history of largely harmonious integration and acculturation in their host countries. Sadly, this model of coexistence was destabilized by the regional penetration of Zionism beginning in the late 19th century.

Each year in the US capital, *Hanukkah* is ceremonially launched by the lighting of an immense menorah on the lawn of the White House. The US is home to approximately 6.8 million[8] Jews, and the vitality and diversity of the community leads some Jewish scholars to locate the US, not Israel, as the global center of Jewish life. Given the number of Israeli emigres to the US (somewhere between 600,000 and a million), the US is an increasingly important center for Israeli life as well.

belonging to Israel and, through Israel, to one another."[9] They see the diversity of Jewish culture and religious/nonreligious practice around the world as something to celebrate. There is no diaspora; Jewish life is alive and well in many expressions both inside and outside Israel.

Some Jewish communal organizations, however, see a crisis in assimilation and diversity of practice. Lacking an answer to the question "Who is a Jew?" expansive enough to describe the many ways Jews relate to their history, identity, and culture, Jewish communal institutions have "made support for Israel a civic religion around which to build a modern secular Jewish identity."[10]

British historian Eric Hobsbawm describes the Jewish state as "the new segregation of a separate ethnic-genetic state-community" and warns that this historical development is not "good either for the Jews or for the world."[11]

Mizrahi Jews—that is, Jews who descend from the centuries-old Jewish communities throughout the Middle East, have a different sense of diaspora from that of their European counterparts. Ella Shohat points out that the Jews "who had lived in the Middle East and North Africa for millennia ...cannot be seen as simply eager to settle in Palestine and in many ways had to be 'lured' to Zion." These Jews, she writes, "did not exactly share the European-Zionist desire to 'end the diaspora' by creating an independent state peopled by a new archetype of Jew."[12]

Jewish life is poorer for the near-extinction of the ancient Middle Eastern Jewish communities, as is the cultural life of the Middle Eastern countries that were home to those deeply-rooted communities. "In many respects," Shohat writes,

> European Zionism has been an immense confidence trick played on Sephardim, a cultural massacre of immense proportions, an attempt, partially successful, to wipe out, in a generation or two, millennia of rooted Oriental civilization, unified even in its diversity.[13]

David Shasha, director of the Brooklyn-based Center for Sephardic Heritage, laments the loss:

> The Judeo-Arab cultural world of Maimonides and Judah Halevi has been sacrificed on the Ashkenazi-Zionist altar, and along with it the deep and rich historic culture of Mediterranean Judaism.[14]

8 · A Palestinian Muslim Experience with Zionism

Abu Sway contrasts what he calls the inclusive theology of the Qur'an with the exclusive theology of Zionism.

AN ISLAMIC THEOLOGY OF THE HOLOCAUST

When Professor Abu Sway was invited to give two lectures at Yad Vashem, the Holocaust museum in Jerusalem, he entitled his presentations "An Islamic Theology of the Holocaust." Such an evil as the Holocaust, he said, should never again be inflicted upon Jews or any other group of human beings. According to both the *Qur'an* and the Bible, all human beings are made of one blood, descendants of one father, Adam, and are of equal value in the eyes of God.

In like manner, the *Nakba* (Catastrophe) that befell the Palestinian people in the late 1940s at the time of Israeli independence should never have taken place. The Palestinian story is one of suffering at the hands of the international community, which authorized the division of Palestine in 1947, and at the hands of the Zionists who planned, organized, and implemented systematic ethnic cleansing that resulted in the exodus of over half of the Palestinian population in 1947-1948 and prevented those refugees' return to their homes after the end of the war. The Zionists destroyed over 500 Palestinian villages. They slaughtered untold numbers of Palestinian men, women, and children. And they drove over 750,000 refugees from their homes and land.

The *Nakba* is not only an historical event; it is an ongoing process that has continued since 1948 as Israel, with the help of its overseas supporters, continues to inflict pain and humiliation upon Palestinians. Zionists deny this ongoing *Nakba*, blaming Palestinians themselves while excusing all violations of Palestinian rights on the basis of necessity ("security").

In the light of this tragic history, Abu Sway asks, as have many others: Why would the international community, led by Europe and America, make Palestinians pay for the sins committed by European Christians against Jews, sins that culminated in the Holocaust? And how could Zionists, past and present, condemn the suffering inflicted on Jews through the ages while inflicting so much suffering today on Palestinians?

Abu Sway contrasts what he calls the inclusive theology of the *Qur'an* with the exclusive theology of Zionism, which makes use of certain texts of the Old Testament to justify separatism, domination, and ethnic cleansing. It is generally accepted that scriptures from any religion can be misused by misguided believers. Muslims, like Jews and Christians, may act unjustly, but when the followers of Islam commit injustice, says Abu Sway, they are misinterpreting or choosing not to obey the teaching of the *Qur'an*.

For contrast, he questions the influence of biblical texts sacred to Christians and Jews, such as Psalm 137:9 (crushing babies against rocks) and Joshua 6 (the slaughter of all living creatures in Jericho). What, Abu Sway asks, is the connection between these ancient texts and the ongoing killing of Palestinian and other Arab children? How can these texts be divinely inspired or have any authority today when they contradict the image of God as a source of love and justice—and at the same time contradict international law and human rights conventions? As for the use of violence by Muslims, Abu Sway writes: "Children as well as adults in the Middle East and

United Nationa Refugee Relief and Works Agency

Untold numbers of Palestinians were murdered during the 1948 *Nakba*. Many of those who survived fled with only what they could carry on their backs; they lost homes, farms, and family.

ABOUT THIS SECTION

This section is a condensed and edited version of an essay by Dr. Mustafa Abu Sway, entitled "Zionism: A Different Memory" in Wagner and Davis, eds., *Zionism and the Quest for Justice in the Holy Land*. Dr. Abu Sway, a Palestinian Muslim, is Associate Professor of Philosophy and Islamic Studies at Hussein College, Al Quds University in Jerusalem. For the past 25 years he has been engaged in interfaith dialogue among the Abrahamic faiths.

Just another racist?

August 2013. As part of his re-election campaign, Upper Nazareth's incumbent mayor Shimon Gapso posted signs promising his (Jewish) constituents: "I will not allow the city's Jewish character to be changed. I will block the establishment of an Arab school and will build neighbourhoods for Jewish residents....Upper Nazareth is a Jewish city!" Responding in *Haaretz* to critics of his campaign messaging, Gaspo explained defiantly, "If that makes me a racist, then I'm a proud offshoot of a glorious dynasty of 'racists' that started with...the explicitly racist promise: 'To your seed I have given this land' [Genesis 15:38]."[2]

elsewhere are sometimes killed by Muslims who act in violation of the message of Islam....Islam allows self-defense...[but] no civilians of any age, group, or background should be targeted."[1]

THE INCLUSIVE NATURE OF ISLAM

There are many texts in the *Qur'an* that affirm God's love for all people, demand that humans act justly toward others, and condemn any form of discrimination. The *Qur'an* insists that Muslims demonstrate God's special respect for Jews and Christians because God is revealed in all three Abrahamic faiths. For example,

> We have believed in God and what has been revealed to us and what has been revealed to Abraham and Ishmael and Isaac and Jacob and the Descendants and what was given to Moses and Jesus and what was given to the prophets from their Lord. We make no distinction between any of them, and we are Muslims [in submission] to Him. (The Holy *Qur'an* 2:136).[3]

This respect and acceptance was embodied in the Constitution of Medina, which the Prophet Muhammad drafted in the first quarter of the 7th century C.E. The constitution offered equal rights—including freedom of religion—to Muslims, Jews, Christians, and pagans.[4] The inclusivity of God's love for all peoples also explains the peaceful acceptance by Muslims of Jewish and Christian minorities living in their midst across western Asia and northern Africa throughout much of history as long as Jews and Christians act justly toward Muslims.

Abu Sway has developed an "Islamic Theology of Soft Otherness" to teach the *Qur'an*'s message of respectful and peaceful relationships among members of the three Abrahamic faiths. He writes,

> The *Qur'an* prevents the total *othering* [classifying as total outsiders] of Jews and Christians and names them 'People of the Book' because their prophets received revealed books. Islam promotes *conviventia*[5] between Muslims and members of these two other faiths based on sharing commonalities in theology, law, and ethics, despite some serious differences that are mostly post-revelational. In practice, Jews and Christians enjoy a special status in the Holy *Qur'an* and the Prophetic traditions, permitting intermarriage with the chaste women of the People of the Book without their conversion, sharing a meal (literally, "the food of the People of the Book is lawful to Muslims"),[6] and doing business transactions and having partnership with them as the Prophet himself did. These practices lead to a healthy social fabric, in which a religious community has a larger place where it feels at home.[7]

Zionism, however, has not reciprocated this respect for all peoples. Instead, says Abu Sway, Zionism is by nature a system of discrimination and exclusion.

THE ZIONIST PROJECT

"Racism is the cornerstone of the Zionist project," says Abu Sway.[8] Instead of equal rights for all, Zionism has created a system of domination and subservience. As evidence for this charge he cites a recent article by Shimon Gapso, Mayor of Upper

"If that makes me a racist, then I'm a proud offshoot of a glorious dynasty of 'racists'."[11]

SHIMON GAPSO, MAYOR, UPPER NAZARETH, ISRAEL

Nazareth, entitled "If you think I'm a racist, then Israel is a racist State." Responding to charges from other Israeli Jews that he is a racist, Gapso reminds his accusers that Zionist leaders all the way back to Theodor Herzl have worked for a Jewish state, which is "a state for the Jews." God is the author of the Zionist plan, having warned the Israelites that if they failed to seize the land and cleanse it of its local inhabitants, God would remove the Israelites from the land.

"Yes, the racist Joshua conquered the land in a racist manner," Gapso explains to his critics.

More than 3,000 years later, the Jewish people stood bruised and bleeding on the threshold of their land, seeking once again to take possession of it from the wild tribes that had seized the land in its absence. And then an outbreak of racism flooded the country. [9]

Gapso's Jewish-centric view of Israeli society is a familiar one to Palestinians who live within Israel. Systematic discrimination that guarantees preferential status to Jews is a feature of Israeli law. The Legal Center for Arab Minority Rights in Israel (Adalah) has compiled a database documenting over fifty Israeli laws that discriminate in all areas of life against Palestinian citizens of Israel. [10]

Islam teaches that

all peoples are equal in the divine plan for humanity, and God's oneness should be reflected in the unity of humanity. To elevate a people unconditionally as the 'chosen' and to use the state apparatus to discriminate against others while crediting God as the source of the injustices is idolatrous in nature. [12]

Abu Sway understands that many Jews and Christians agree with this principle and cites as an example the title of a recent book by Jewish theologian Marc Ellis, *Judaism Does Not Equal Israel*.[13] At the heart of Judaism, says Ellis, is prophetic justice, especially for the vulnerable, the poor, and the oppressed, and a love for all people. More recently, Ellis has referred to today's establishment Judaism as "Constantinian Judaism," because it is now inside the halls of power within empire. Ellis says that like "Constantinian Christianity," today's "Constantinian Judaism" has been greatly affected and changed by its acquisition of power.

THE PALESTINIAN REALITY: THE ONGOING *NAKBA*

Not much has changed in Zionism's purpose since Israel was born: to maximize the amount of Palestinian land and minimize the number of Palestinian people falling within the borders of the state. What has changed over the course of Israel's history is the modality used to achieve these goals: the crude brutal force at the beginning continues and is now supplemented by laws that promote the same ends.[14] Abu Sway sees the centerpiece of Zionism as it affects Palestinians as ethnic cleansing.

Since 1948, Abu Sway explains, Israel has used three forms of ethnic cleansing: hard cleansing, soft cleansing, and stealth cleansing.

HARD ETHNIC CLEANSING

Israeli historian Ilan Pappe has written a detailed analysis of the force that was used to kill and expel Palestinians from their land and homes in 1947-1948. An ethnic cleansing program, code-named *Plan Dalet*, was designed upon the orders of David Ben-Gurion, head of the Jewish community in Palestine, and discussed and finalized in his home two months before Israel's independence in May 1948.[15]

The most infamous of the massacres took place on April 9, 1948, in the village of Deir Yassin, a few miles west of Jerusalem. This Palestinian village had made a non-aggression pact with the *Hagana* (the "official" Jewish militia) in Jerusalem. To distance itself of any responsibility for the actions in Deir Yassin, *Hagana* commanders dispatched two other Jewish militias noted for their violence, the Stern

Not much has changed in Zionism's purpose since Israel was born: to maximize the amount of Palestinian land and minimize the number of Palestinian people falling within the borders of the state.

Noga Kadman

Arabic-language place names have been defaced by vandals on this directional sign in Jerusalem's Sacher Park.

July 2009. Jewish immigrants to Israel from Britain pose at the Western Wall in Jerusalem with their new Israeli ID cards, issued by the Jewish Agency. While Jews are free to enter and leave Israel without restrictions and many Israelis live outside the country for extended periods, a discriminatory Israeli policy has revoked the residency rights of 250,000 Palestinian residents of Gaza, East Jerusalem, and the West Bank since 1967.

A Modern Wave of Palestinian Exiles

In response to a freedom-of-information request filed by Hamoked, the Center for the Defense of the Individual, the Israel Defense Ministry's Coordinator of Government Activities in the Territories (COGAT) was forced in June 2012 to release statistics revealing the number of Gaza and West Bank residents stripped of their residency rights. Nearly 250,000 Palestinians who left the territories between 1967 and 1994—primarily for education and employment opportunities elsewhere—were barred from ever returning. Of these, 100,000 were residents of Gaza and approximately 140,000, residents of the West Bank.

According to *Haaretz*, which exposed the secret procedure in May 2011,

> Palestinians who went abroad were required to leave their identity card at the border crossing. Unlike those from Gaza, who were allowed to leave for seven years, [West Bank] Palestinians received a special permit valid for three years. The permit could be renewed three times, each time for one year. But any Palestinian who failed to return within six months after his permit expired would be stripped of his residency with no prior notice.[16]

Many of the Palestinians who lost their residency rights and became permanent exiles were students or young professionals, whose descendants presumably number in the hundreds of thousands today.

Gang and the *Irgun*, to carry out the killings.[17]

"As they burst into the village," Abu Sway relates, quoting Israeli historian Ilan Pappe,

> the Jewish soldiers sprayed the houses with machine-gun fire, killing many of the inhabitants. The remaining villagers were then gathered in one place and murdered in cold blood, their bodies abused while a number of the women were raped and then killed.[18]

The Jewish leadership then broadcast an exaggerated number of deaths as a warning to other Palestinian villages that the same fate awaited them if they refused to leave all behind and run for their lives.

Since that time, Israel has conducted numerous other military campaigns to discourage any kind of resistance and to frighten Palestinians into submission and flight. Abu Sway cites as an extreme example the December 2008-January 2009 war on Gaza in which 1,400 Palestinians were killed, including 850 civilians, 350 children, and 110 women.

SOFT ETHNIC CLEANSING

The Israeli government has continuously promoted ethnic cleansing since the founding of the Jewish state. Laws rather than guns are now used to promote the exodus of Palestinians. In 1967 when Israel occupied Palestinian territories, administrative rules were set in place on how long a Palestinian from the occupied territories could live abroad. Between 1967 and 1994, almost a quarter of a million Palestinians from the West Bank and Gaza were rendered stateless as a result of studying or working outside the country too long, or for failing to register with the annual census.[19] Abu Sway comments:

Now,...
Palestinian "former" residents of Jerusalem need a tourist visa to visit Jerusalem, the city of their birth.

As for Palestinian Jerusalemites, the revocation of residency continues unabated. The only thing that differs from year to year is the number of Palestinians who lose their IDs and get expelled from the city of their birth simply because their center of life is not Israel anymore.

B'Tselem, the respected Israeli Human Rights watch group, reports that the highest number in any given year was 2008, when the Israeli Ministry of the Interior revoked the IDs of 4,577 Palestinians from East Jerusalem.[20] Now, those Palestinian 'former' residents of Jerusalem "need a tourist visa to visit Jerusalem, the city of their birth," writes Abu Sway,

> and to see their extended families, who are indigenous to this city. The irony is that the revocation of the ID could well be enforced by an Israeli immigrant with no personal, historical roots in Jerusalem.[21]

These statistics translate into personal, painful real-life stories affecting almost every Palestinian family, including Dr. Abu Sway's.[22] By contrast, Israeli citizenship for Jews is not predicated on uninterrupted physical residency. More than 750,000 Israeli Jews live outside Israel. They can come and go as they wish. Why this double standard? For Abu Sway, the answer is obvious: it is ongoing, unpublicized ethnic cleansing of Palestinians by the Israeli state.[23]

A series of absentee property laws was created in the first three decades after Israel's establishment as a state, rescinding ownership rights of Palestinian refugees who had fled or been expelled during the conflict. The Palestinians who fled their homes but remained within the borders of the new state became a class of Palestinian Israeli citizens whose land was confiscated even though they were present to claim it. These Palestinians continue to be mired in a Kafkaesque tangle of unfulfilled hopes. Even now, 65 years after the 1948 war, they are called "present absentees," meaning they are present in Israel, but considered absent for the purposes of the law and, therefore, unable to legally reclaim their land, homes, and possessions.[24]

ETHNIC CLEANSING BY STEALTH

Theodor Herzl, founder of the World Zionist organization, set the tone that most Zionist leaders would later follow. In an 1895 entry in his diary, Herzl described the process of ethnic cleansing that would be necessary: "Both the process of expropriation and the removal of the poor [Arabs] must be carried out discretely and circumspectly."[25] Otherwise, Herzl knew, Zionist activity in Palestine would risk drawing international condemnation. Both the Balfour Declaration of 1917 and the Israeli Declaration of Independence promised equal rights for all. However, because equal rights for all would compromise the concept of a Jewish state, a dual legal system had to be created to ensure Jewish supremacy.

Even memory is selective. While Israelis hold a somber annual commemoration of *Yom HaShoah*, Holocaust Remembrance Day, commemoration of the historical event of the Palestinian *Nakba* in Israel is suppressed. A *"Nakba* Law" was passed by the Israeli Knesset in March 2011 which authorizes the Ministry of Finance to withhold support from schools and other institutions and organizations where Independence Day is commemorated by Palestinians living in Israel as a day of mourning for the losses they suffered during the *Nakba* of 1947-48. Such mourning is described by the law as "an activity that is contrary to the principles of the state."[26] This law aims to suppress awareness of Palestinian history from public life.

This process of psychological and cultural erasure continues the process of physical erasure begun with the destruction of Palestinian villages in 1947-48, the replacement of Palestinian place names with Hebrew place names, and the alteration of maps to eliminate present-day Palestinian communities in Israel. This kind of erasure has been referred to as "cultural genocide" when referring to specific examples in the history of Native Americans under European settlement, Armenians under the

Israel's Absentee Property Law: One Man's Story

Absentee property laws, widely applied in Israel proper since 1948, are now applied to property owned by Palestinians living between Jerusalem and the Jordan River (occupied East Jerusalem and the West Bank). Israel's confiscation of land for the development of Jewish settlements continues unabated, even though this is not recognized as a legal part of Israel by any nation.

The home of Ali Ayyad, a Palestinian resident of the West Bank who lives in Abu Dis, just outside East Jerusalem, is a mere 300 meters from the ancestral home in East Jerusalem that his father converted into the Cliff Hotel in the 1960s.

Ali Ayyad is fighting the Israeli government to regain ownership of his ancestral home (visible in photo) in East Jerusalem, confiscated in 2003 under "absentee" property laws.

Israel "annexed" East Jerusalem in 1967, and, contrary to international covenants and UN resolutions, absorbed it into "Greater Jerusalem" by passing laws removing it from Palestinian territory, *i.e.*, the West Bank.

In 2003 Israel confiscated the Cliff Hotel from the Ayyad family. It remained empty until recently when the state began remodeling it for use by the Israeli Border Police. In response to legal action by the Ayyad family, the Israeli Supreme Court held a hearing in May 2013 to consider whether Mr. Ayyad and his family should be declared absentee owners or whether the 2003 takeover by the state should be reversed.[27]

In late August 2013, in response to much publicity and legal action taken by Palestinian families, the state reversed its decision to confiscate the Cliff Hotel and four other Palestinian properties.

This reprieve may only be temporary, since over the years, depending upon the political climate at the time, the state has repeatedly switched positions on using or not using the Absentee Property Laws to take Palestinian property.[28]

Stories like Ayyad's are repeated with numbing repetition. Palestinians see it as a type of gradual, incremental ethnic cleansing—one person and one family at a time.

In the West, the process is mostly unseen and unknown. The routine legal mechanism of a series of seemingly unrelated property expropriations is rarely reported in the western media or identified for what it is—bureaucratic ethnic cleansing.

Mamilla Cemetery contains the tombs of prominent Muslims, Jews, and Christians, some dating to the seventh century. In an open letter addressed to the Wiesenthal Center and the mayor of Jerusalem, 84 American, European, Arab, and Israeli archeologists protested the project, saying "Such insensitivity towards religious rites, towards cultural, national and religious patrimony, and towards families whose ancestors lay buried there causes grave concern from a scientific and humanitarian standpoint."

Ottoman Turks, and Koreans under the Japanese Occupation.

Meanwhile, Israeli leaders continue to insist that Israel is both democratic and Jewish. They have mounted an expensive propaganda (*hasbara*) campaign to buttress a litany of myths exonerating Israel and vilifying critics of Israel. The Jewish Agency for Israel has established an annual fund of $300 million for pro-Israel public relations programs, with heavy focus on US campuses where the boycott, divestment, and sanctions movement has gained traction. $100 million of this fund has been supplied by the Israeli government.[29]

In August 2013 *Haaretz* reported a covert social media "public diplomacy" (*hasbara*) program involving Israeli university students. During the next academic year, *Haaretz* reveals, Prime Minister Netanyahu's office will recruit and organize up to 550 students who will receive scholarships to make pro-Israel Facebook posts and tweets to foreign audiences. These student-diplomats are instructed to conceal the fact that they are paid government propagandists. The program is designed to include a team of "covert units" at seven of Israel's top educational institutions.[30]

HYPOCRISY, BLINDNESS, OR INTENTIONAL DECEIT?

The desecration and removal of Palestinian cemeteries is another dimension of the suppression of Palestinian history. In 2005 Rabbi Martin Hier, Dean and founder of the Simon Wiesenthal Center (SWC) in Los Angeles, announced the plan to build a Museum of Tolerance in Jerusalem on the site of the historic Muslim cemetery Mamilla, which dates back to the seventh century C.E. The idea of a Jewish museum promoting tolerance while desecrating an historic Muslim cemetery in the holy city of Jerusalem was so outrageous that it has backfired, prompting world-renowned architect Frank Gehry to withdraw from the project,[31] and creating an international opposition movement that includes many rabbis and other Jewish leaders.[32]

In spite of an international campaign to halt construction of the museum, however, Israeli authorities in July 2011 granted final approval for the project, estimated to cost $100 million. Already the remains and markers of hundreds of tombs have been removed. The mayor of Jerusalem wrote a congratulatory letter to Rabbi Hier declaring that the Museum of Tolerance in Jerusalem is rooted in Jewish values that advance human dignity and social justice. Not to be outdone, Prime Minister Binyamin Netanyahu wrote a letter saying that the Museum gives visitors a better understanding of Jewish history and the promotion of universal tolerance and respect. One must ask, is the practice of ethnic cleansing an aspect of Israeli history that the Prime Minister wants to have memorialized?

Dr. Abu Sway concludes with this summary: Zionism claims that God promised the land of Palestine exclusively to the Jews. In contrast, the *Qur'an* claims that God has blessed the land *"for the nations."* (The Holy *Qur'an* 21:71) The "conflict" between Israel and the Muslim world will not end without justice. God's love for all peoples must be translated into justice between Israelis and Palestinians.

In spite of an international campaign to halt construction of the museum, in July 2011 Israeli authorities granted final approval for the project, estimated to cost $100 million.

REFLECTION

1. What questions arise for you after reading and reflecting on this section?

2. Discuss Abu Sway's claim that racism is the cornerstone of Zionism. What examples does he cite to back up his claim?

3. If, as Abu Sway claims, racism is the dark side of Zionism, what is the dark side of Islam? of Christianity?

4. Chapter 3, verse 85, of the *Qur'an* says: "And whoever desires other than Islam as religion—never will it be accepted from him, and he, in the Hereafter, will be among the losers." [http://quran.com/3/85] Is this similar to or different from John 14:6 in which Jesus says "No one comes to the Father but through me"? Since there is no separation of church and state in Islam, what are the social and political consequences of this belief in situations where Islam is allied with state power?

5. We have seen that all three Abrahamic religions contain elements of theological exceptionalism. How do these elements hinder conflict resolution and reconciliation?

6. International law allows resistance to military occupation and dispossession. What kinds of Palestinian resistance to Jewish expansionism and oppression do you feel are justified?

Memoricide

Official signs in Canada Park educate about the history of the area but omit the hundreds of years of Palestinian settlement.

Numerous Palestinian and Israeli scholars use the term "memoricide" to describe the Israeli encounter with Palestinian history. Nur Masalha defines memoricide as "the systematic erasure of the expelled Palestinians and their mini-holocaust from Israeli collective memory."[1]

Several strategies have been used to erase consciousness of the Palestinian historical presence in the land. The depopulated Palestinian villages of Imwas, Yalu, and Beit Nuba, for instance, are now the site of Canada Park, a reforestation project funded by $15 million in charitable donations from Canadian Jews.[2] The remains of some 86 Palestinian villages today lie buried beneath such reforested "parks" established by the Jewish National Fund.

In a similar way, place names have been a means for erasing the Palestinian presence on the land. Meron Benvenisti, an Israeli political scientist and former deputy mayor of Jerusalem, describes his personal childhood experience of this transformation of the Palestinian landscape in his book, *Sacred Landscape*. Benvenisti's father, a distinguished geographer, was tasked with the project of renaming Palestinian sites with Hebrew names linked to Israel's ancestral homeland. In all, Benvenisti relates, more than 9,000 natural features, villages, and ruins in Palestine were renamed.[3]

Zochrot's installation of informational signs (like these in Canada Park) is exposing Israelis to the Palestinian history of the region.

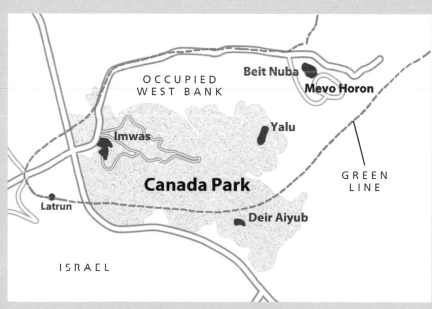

Canada Park is controversial not only because it is an example of reforestation as memoricide, but also because most of the park's land is on the east side of the Green Line—outside Israel's internationally recognized borders. A smaller portion of the park land lies on the west side of the Green Line and includes Deir Aiyub, a village that was ethnically cleansed of its 370 Palestinian residents in 1948 and destroyed except for the remains of a few houses and the village cemetery. Before 1967, Imwas was home to 2,000 residents, Yalu 1,700, and Beit Nuba 1,400.

Zochrot: Israelis Remember the *Nakba* in Hebrew

Nineteen years after the upheaval and dislocation of the 1948 *Nakba*, a second wave of Palestinian refugees and village demolitions occurred in the wake of the Six-Day war. Three villages—Imwas, Yalu, and Beit Nuba—a short distance northwest of Jerusalem, were overrun in 1967 by the Israeli military. The residents were expelled and their houses razed. Most of the villages' former residents now live as refugees in Baythunia (West Bank), al-Bireh (West Bank), and Jordan.

On the site of Imwas and Yalu and surrounding terrain, the Jewish National Fund (JNF) in 1975 established Canada Park (also called Ayalon Park) with funds donated by Canadian Jews.

According to the Israeli human rights organization *Zochrot* [Hebrew for "Remembering"], 86 Palestinian villages lie buried and obscured by JNF parks. *Zochrot* was founded in 2002 to create an alternative to "memoricide" in Israeli society. *Zochrot*'s projects promote acknowledgment of and accountability for the *Nakba* and foster the conditions for the return of Palestinian refugees to Israel. The organization has drawn attention for its pioneering work in transforming Israeli consciousness.

9 · A Palestinian Christian Postscript

We in Sabeel welcome this study of Zionism because we agree with its fundamental premise as articulated in 2009 by the Jewish writer Ben Ehrenreich: *Zionism is the problem.*[1]

Zionism is a doctrine that provides the state of Israel with a firm—even dogmatic—religio-national identity justified by an appeal to God's will, to historical memory, and to mythical racial ancestry. It provides many Jews in Israel and around the world with a deep-seated, emotionally compelling, personal and social identity. As such, Zionism is a theologically infused ideology of Jewish identity that has changed the course of Jewish life in the twentieth and twenty-first centuries.

Section 2 of this booklet declares that there is a positive side to the Zionist dream of creating "A New Jew." At the same time it also recognizes what Palestinians uniformly claim: Zionism and the creation of "A New Jew" has a dark side that has resulted in almost a century of Palestinian humiliation, dispossession, and death.

The recent creation of a new Israeli government bureau entitled the "Jewish identity administration" appears to be an attempt to strengthen the dark side of Zionism at a time when Zionism is once again under attack by the international supporters of human rights as well as by thousands of Jews of conscience.[2]

For Palestinians and a growing number of internationals around the world it is clear that Zionism is a false theology. It drives our ongoing humiliation and dispossession by the Israeli government, with the active cooperation of the US government and mainstream American Jewish communal organizations. Israel simply could not continue its mistreatment of the Palestinians without the support, encouragement, or silent acquiescence of the majority of Jewish Israelis and their Zionist supporters abroad.

> *Any theology... that legitimizes the occupation is far from Christian teachings, because it calls for violence and holy war in the name of God Almighty.*
>
> KAIROS PALESTINE 2.5

ABOUT THE AUTHOR

The Rev. Dr. Naim Ateek, is an Anglican priest and Founder/Director of Sabeel Ecumenical Liberation Center in East Jerusalem. He was one of the authors of *Kairos Palestine: A Moment of Truth*. His book *Justice and Only Justice* (1989) was influential in Rabbi Rosen's "Path to Palestinian Solidarity."

Jews of conscience in the US, Israel, and elsewhere around the world are at the front lines in the struggle for equality for all inhabitants of the area Palestinians and Israelis both call home.

In its fundamentalist Christian manifestation, Zionism functions to justify and support this ongoing humiliation and dispossession, not primarily for the sake of Jews, but for hastening the return of Christ and the apocalyptic "End Times" in which Jews will be given their last opportunity to convert to Christ and be saved, or be condemned to Hell.

In its liberal Christian manifestations, Zionism serves as a "price-tag" theology providing Christians a vehicle of repentance for the guilt accrued during centuries of European Christian anti-Semitism culminating in the Holocaust. It is the "price-tag" Christians need to pay.

Kairos Palestine-A Moment of Truth, the 2009 document of faith and call to action of Palestinian Christians, states,

> We...declare that the Israeli occupation of Palestinian land is a sin against God and humanity because it deprives the Palestinians of their basic human rights, bestowed by God. It distorts the image of God in the Israeli who has become an occupier just as it distorts this image in the Palestinian living under occupation. (*Kairos Palestine*, section 2.5)[3]

This word of faith is unique among Christian confessions in that its central theme, from start to finish, is Christ's command to love our enemies even while resisting the evil they visit upon us.

The tone of this document is simple, direct, and uncompromising. It declares the truth in stark terms, reflecting the Palestinian experience of it in our daily lives. We know how constant humiliation and deprivation distort the image of God in us. And just as certain, we see daily how the image of God is distorted in our oppressors who often experience perverse pleasure and even humor in cruelty.

Kairos Palestine does not stop with the declaration of the Israeli occupation as a sin against God and humanity. It raises the stakes by proclaiming,

> We declare that any theology, seemingly based on the Bible or on faith or on history, that legitimizes the occupation, is far from Christian teachings, because it calls for violence and holy war in the name of God Almighty, subordinating God to temporary human interests, and distorting the divine image in the human beings living under both political and theological injustice. (*Kairos Palestine*, section 2.5)

Zionism commits theological injustice by its appeal to God, history, and race. Zionism claims the right to *Eretz Yisrael* on the basis of Yahweh's promises to the ancient Hebrew tribes in the Torah;

the age-long dreams of religious Jews to return to Zion; and the erroneous claim that all Jews are racial descendants of the Israelites of biblical times. Thus, Zionism is considered "far from Christian teachings."

> Therefore, we declare that any use of the Bible to legitimize or support political options and positions that are based upon injustice, imposed by one person on another, or by one people on another, transforms religion into human ideology and strips the Word of God of its holiness, its universality and truth. (*KP*, 2.4)

The casual reader may miss the severity of these charges. It is the equivalent of declaring Zionism heretical, a doctrine that fosters both political and theological injustice. This is the strongest condemnation that a Christian confession can make against any doctrine that promotes death rather than life.

Of course Christian theological statements have little merit in the eyes of non-Christians, Jews included. However, such theological statements, made in the context of a confession of faith, commit the Christian Churches to oppose the ideology in

Will Palestinians and Israelis—victims of the twin catastrophes, *Nakba* and *Shoah*—find a shared future that provides for the well being of both peoples? Peaceful coexistence cannot be established within the current system of inequality, oppression, and ethnic exceptionalism.

Anne Paq

*When those
of other religions
fall prey to...
theological
injustice,
opposition such
as boycotts and
divestment are
warranted.*

KAIROS PALESTINE 4.2.6

December 2013. Activists gather outside the Target store in Chicago's Loop district to urge holiday shoppers to not buy SodaStream products. SodaStream's principal manufacturing facility is located in Mishor Adumim, the industrial zone of the West Bank settlement of Maale Adumim. The Palestinian-led boycott, divestment, and sanctions (BDS) movement employs the classic nonviolent strategy of economic pressure and exposes corporations that profit from occupation. The SodaStream international boycott campaign has already seen dozens of actions in six countries and is growing rapidly.

question as a matter of faithfulness to the Gospel. In the Christian Church such condemnations carry the weight of a charge of heresy. When fellow Christians fall prey to theological injustice, the punishment of exclusion is warranted, as was the case with the white Dutch Reformed Church in South Africa during the 1980s and 1990s.[4] When those of other religions fall prey to similar theological injustice, opposition such as boycotts and divestment are warranted. (*KP*, 4.2.6)

The implications of this condemnation are clear in the major sections dealing with faith, hope, and love. In *Kairos Palestine* these cardinal Christian virtues are regarded as both personal and social, requiring Christians to oppose that which is evil and to carry out that opposition in a spirit of faith, hope, and love. Faith in God means "it is our duty to liberate (this land) from the evil of injustice and war. It is God's land and therefore it must be a land of reconciliation, peace, and love." (*KP*, 2.3.1) "Hope means not giving in to evil but rather standing up to it and continuing to resist it." (*KP*, 3.2)

Love is the commandment of Christ our Lord to us and it includes both friends and enemies…. Resistance is a right and duty for the Christian. But it is resistance with love as its logic. It is thus a creative resistance for it must find human ways that engage the humanity of the enemy….Christ our Lord has left us an example we must imitate. We must resist evil but he has taught us that we cannot resist evil with evil. (*KP*, 4.2; 4.2.3; 4.2.4)

This is, therefore, the challenge at hand. It is a challenge that is addressed directly to Christians around the world, their churches and denominations, as well as to people of all faiths or no faith. It is a challenge that should face all those who are concerned about a just peace in Israel-Palestine. It is a call for courage and action to take a clear and uncompromising stand for justice. It is a call to use all the nonviolent means available to stop the injustice and oppression perpetrated under the mantle of Zionism by the government of Israel against the Palestinian people. It is a call to do everything we can to end Israel's occupation of Palestine and implement the requirement of international law so that the God-given human dignity can be restored to the Palestinian people, and justice will be done. The words of the prophet Isaiah of long ago can then assume new meaning and relevance "… and justice will produce lasting peace and security." (32:17 NEV)

REFLECTION

1. What questions arise for you from this essay by Canon Ateek?

2. What preparatory steps are needed before meeting with your church's pastoral leadership and worship committee to discuss how your congregation can "make explicit what is implicit" in the Zionist language of Christian worship? (See the activity recommended in the Leaders' Guide on page 66.)

3. What can you and your congregation do to walk with Palestinian and Israeli peacemakers? What, if any, do you anticipate to be the costs of truth-telling and peacemaking? What might be the benefits?

Emerging from the American Jewish "Cocoon"

"**E**ven after fifty years of living the Palestinian exile," Palestinian American scholar Edward Said wrote in 2000, "I still find myself astonished at the lengths to which official Israel and its supporters will go to suppress the fact that a half century has gone by without Israeli restitution, recognition, or acknowledgment of Palestinian human rights and without, as the facts undoubtedly show, connecting that suspension of rights to Israel's official policies."[2]

Given the liberal values shared by many American Jews and the long, proud tradition of Jewish participation in the struggle for human rights worldwide, why has there been so little outrage expressed at Israel's human rights abuses of Palestinians in the decades since Israel's founding?

Paul Krugman, Princeton economist and *New York Times* columnist, offers a personal answer: "The truth is that like many liberal American Jews—and most American Jews are still liberal—I basically avoid thinking about where Israel is going."[3]

Why, then, do so many liberal American Jews avoid thinking about where Israel is going? Krugman points to the high price for speaking out, which is "to bring yourself under intense attack from organized groups that try to make any criticism of Israeli policies tantamount to anti-Semitism."

Peter Beinart, in whose defense Krugman wrote the remarks above, makes the connection between the "*de facto* restrictions that exist in many establishment American Jewish groups" and their dismal consequence: The organized American Jewish community is "a closed intellectual space, isolated from the experiences and perspectives of roughly half the people under Israeli control." Beinart continues, "American Jewish leaders, even those who harbor no animosity toward Palestinians, know little about the reality of [the Palestinians'] lives."[4]

This, then, is what Peter Beinart calls the American Jewish "cocoon." Beinart explains that the high-profile individuals who are accepted as spokespersons for the American Jewish community, (Beinart lists Abe Foxman and Elie Wiesel) are "unfamiliar with the realities of ordinary Palestinian life because they live inside the cocoon the organized American Jewish community has built for itself."

Beinart lists two consequences of the American Jewish "cocoon." One is "a lack of information, the other is a lack of empathy." And without empathy, Beinart writes, it is easy for American Jews "to minimize the human toll of living...without the basic rights that your Jewish neighbors take for granted."

The ignorance and passivity of many liberal American Jews have left the way open for insular Jewish organizations to speak, unchallenged, as representatives of US Jews.

Jewish Voice for Peace and a host of interfaith and non-religious groups are magnets for Jewish Americans who choose to speak out against Israeli policies. Activists at this 2013 protest at the TIAA-CREF headquarters in Chicago demanded that the pension fund divest from corporations that profit from violence and injustice in Israel/Palestine.

I got really into claiming Judaism as my own and finding the religious parts and practice that really speak to me as a political activist.[1]

JACOB ROSENBLUM
BIRTHRIGHT UNPLUGGED
2005 PARTICIPANT

Unfortunately for both Israel and the Palestinians, the Jewish organizations that dominate the public discourse are the ones for whom defending Israel's image and silencing Israel's critics are top priorities.

Even at this late date, however, Beinart identifies a hopeful trend:

Particularly in the younger generations, fewer and fewer American Jewish liberals are Zionists; fewer and fewer American Jewish Zionists are liberal. One reason is that the leading institutions of American Jewry have refused to foster—indeed, have actively opposed—a Zionism that challenges Israel's behavior in the West Bank and Gaza Strip and toward its own Arab citizens. For several decades, the Jewish establishment has asked American Jews to check their liberalism at Zionism's door, and now, to their horror, they are finding that many young Jews have checked their Zionism instead.[5]

From out of the cocoon, one hopes, a beautiful moth may yet emerge.

Birthright Israel has provided free ten-day trips to Israel for 350,000 young Jewish people from 64 countries since its founding in 1994. Birthright's annual capacity is 37,000 participants and its annual operating budget exceeds $660 million due largely to support from wealthy American donors. No travel is permitted to the West Bank, Gaza, or East Jerusalem, other than the Jewish quarter of the Old City. Participants report that critical examination of Israeli policy and encounters with non-Jews in Israel are avoided and discouraged.

Birthright Unplugged was founded in 2004 as a response to fully-funded, Jewish-only trips to Israel and a rejection of the notion of a "birthright" for Jewish people to the land of Israel/Palestine. Participants are encouraged to use the knowledge they gain through first-hand experience to make positive change in the world. Although participation numbers are tiny in comparison to the Birthright Israel program, Unplugged alumni/ae speak of being moved and changed by the experience.

"Judaizing" the Land

Historically, many Jews have chosen to settle in the Central District, Israel's mid-section. The Israeli government has identified "at risk" regions of the country with relatively high Palestinian populations concentrations—Galilee, in Israel's northern section, the Negev, in Israel's south, and East Jerusalem. Despite the fact that Palestinians have centuries-old roots in the entire land area of modern-day Israel, and although the present Palestinian population is a decimated remnant of the population that was exiled in 1948 and 1967, many Israelis characterize them as trespassers, squatters, and invaders. Government policies have been implemented to "Judaize" the land, that is, to reduce the "demographic threat" to the character of the state posed by its non-Jewish population.

While they're investing in new communities, it would be appropriate to strengthen the nearby Arab ones. Our situation is very bad, terrible.[1]

SALAH SULEIMAN
HEAD, BUEINA-NUDIJAT
ARAB REGIONAL
COUNCIL, GALILEE

Israel's regional "Arab Problem" is highlighted in this map based on population data from 2000. State planners have responded to the perceived demographic threat to Jewish sovereignty by implementing long-range planning projects targeting "at risk" regions—particularly Galilee, East Jerusalem, and Negev. These projects stimulate Jewish settlement while containing Arab populations in enclaves with little or no room for expansion.

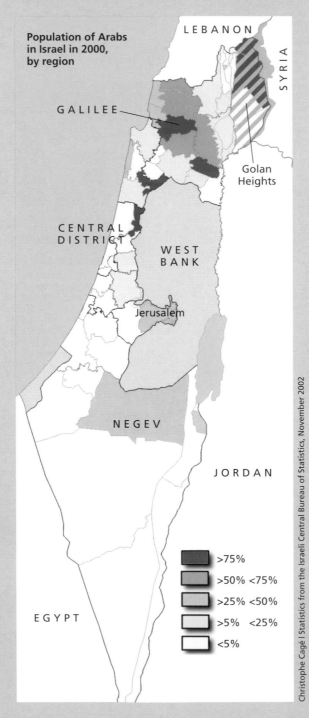

Population of Arabs in Israel in 2000, by region

LEBANON

SYRIA

GALILEE

Golan Heights

CENTRAL DISTRICT

WEST BANK

Jerusalem

NEGEV

JORDAN

EGYPT

>75%
>50% <75%
>25% <50%
>5% <25%
<5%

Christophe Cagé | Statistics from the Israeli Central Bureau of Statistics, November 2002

Arabs are buying and/or squatting all over Galilee (Northern Israel) Lands. Help save Jewish Sovereignty in the Galilee.

Be a partner in the mitzvah:

"One who purchases 4 cubits (amot) in the Land of Israel is assured a portion in the World to Come"

from Midrash Zuta on Megilat Ruth (4:5)

All land we purchase is planted with olive trees which are managed by our **Avoda Ivrit (Jewish Labor)** team. The more land that is managed by Jewish Labor the greater chance of maintaining Jewish control of the Galilee.

B'Ahavat Yisrael: "Because I am a Jew!"

Copyright © 2012 B'Ahavat Yisrael. All Rights Reserved.

Jerusalem Post online edition, 2013

Galilee

The Settlement Division of the World Zionist Organization (an executive branch of the Israeli government) has implemented a plan to "Judaize the Galilee" by attracting 100,000 new Jewish residents to the area. According to the Settlement Division, the plan will create housing options "that will attract a stable Jewish population and create a meaningful demographic balance."[2]

A *Haaretz* editorial from December 2013 explains that

Since 1948, Israel has blocked the establishment of new Arab communities in the Galilee, even though the older communities are bursting at the seams for lack of land reserves, while it has expropriated huge tracts of Arab land. It has developed industrial zones almost exclusively in the Jewish communities.[3]

Negev

The campaign to "Judaize" the Negev dates back six-plus decades to the Bedouin expulsions and land seizures committed by the Israeli government in 1948.[4] Today, 35 Bedouin villages in the Negev—home to nearly 90,000 inhabitants—are "unrecognized" by the state. Without municipal jurisdiction, the villages are deprived of access to basic services and infrastructure such as electricity and running water.[5, 6]

The Prawer-Begin Plan, approved in draft by the Israeli Knesset in May 2013, proposes to displace thousands of Bedouins in the Negev. According to the Association for Civil Rights in Israel (ACRI), the plan would forcibly evict nearly 40,000 Bedouins, destroying the social fabric of their communities and intensifying the poverty and unemployment endemic to their current precarious existence as citizens without status.

The Prawer-Begin Plan was frozen in December 2013, due partly to domestic and international outrage over its provisions. The reprieve may be temporary; Prawer-Begin mirrors the territorial acquisition scheme that has historically been applied within Israel's internationally accepted borders and is currently underway in the territories occupied by Israel in East Jerusalem and the West Bank. The goal: to achieve "maximum land with minimum Palestinians."

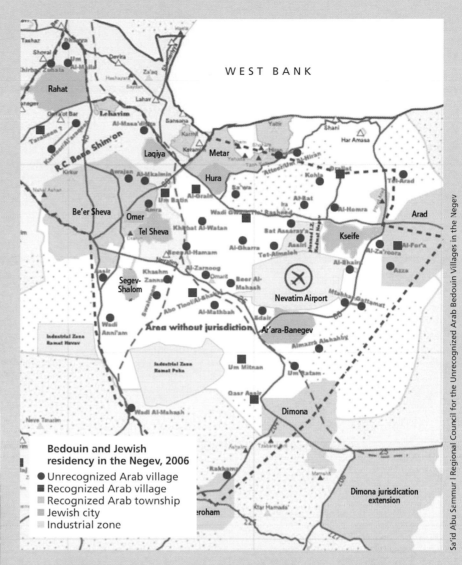

Sa'id Abu Sammur | Regional Council for the Unrecognized Arab Bedouin Villages in the Negev

Bedouin and Jewish residency in the Negev, 2006
- ● Unrecognized Arab village
- ■ Recognized Arab village
- ▨ Recognized Arab township
- ▨ Jewish city
- ▨ Industrial zone

Ilana Curiel

On November 21, 2010, representatives from the Israel Land Administration and security forces demolished the Bedouin village of al-Arakib in the Negev for the seventh time.

"Omer Post Office – For Omer Residents Only!" pledges an election pamphlet distributed by a party running for local office in an affluent suburb of Be'er Sheva (see yellow highlight in map, above right). Omer's unwelcome visitors are the Bedouins from the nearby townships of Tel-Sheva and Laqiya and the unrecognized village of Abu Kaff.[7]

IKHWANiWeb

September 2012. Demonstrators in Jerusalem protest Israeli government land policies in the Negev. Palestinian Bedouins and human rights advocates in Israel and around the world mobilized to fight implementation of the controversial Prawer-Begin dislocation plan. The public backlash caused the government to shelve the plan in December 2013.

The municipality of Be'er Sheva had an organized archive during the British Mandate period which contained all the agreed ownership arrangements for Bedouins in the province. Following the occupation of the city by Israeli forces in the 1948 War, the archive was transferred to the State Archive where it was "lost." This is one of the reasons why the ownership claims to 800,000 dunams (200,000 acres) in the northern Negev is disputed.[9]

Palestinian Bedouins, ca. 1910

I have citizenship, but they still destroyed my house. Now I have only the shirt on my back. It's like they're saying to me, "Just leave and go to hell."[8]

KHADER ABU AL-KIAN, AGE 70, RESIDENT OF ATIR, AN "UNRECOGNIZED" NEGEV BEDOUIN VILLAGE

Timeline

1882-1903
First *Aliya* (35,000 Jews immigrate to Palestine)

1896
Theodor Herzl writes *The Jewish State*

1897
Herzl convenes first Zionist Conference in Basel, Switzerland

1904-1914
Second *Aliya* (40,000 Jews immigrate to Palestine)

1914
Ottoman Empire enters World War I allied with Germany

1917
Balfour Declaration promises "establishment in Palestine of a national home for the Jewish people"

1937
Irgun paramilitary terrorist group founded

1938
Kristallnacht pogrom throughout Germany and parts of Austria. Anti-Jewish climate intensifies in Europe

1942
Biltmore Platform unites most American Jewish leaders and organizations behind Zionism

1945
World War II ends with German, Japanese surrender. Auschwitz, Buchenwald, and other Nazi concentration camps liberated by Allied forces

1947
UN General Assembly passes Resolution 181 recommending partition of Palestine. Arabs reject it. Six months before Israeli independence, 250,000 Palestinians displaced by Jewish paramilitary groups

1964
Palestine Liberation Organization (PLO) established

1967
Third Arab-Israeli War, the "Six-Day" War. American Zionism consolidates

1973
Fourth Arab-Israeli War, the "*Yom Kippur*" War

1974
Gush Emunim begins to establish Jewish religious settlements in occupied Palestinian territories

1974
Arab League declares PLO to be "the only legitimate representative of the Palestinian people." UN recognizes Palestinians' right to sovereignty; grants PLO observer status

1985
Israeli troops withdraw from most of Lebanon

1987
First Palestinian *Intifada* (uprising) against Israeli military occupation

1988
PLO accepts UN Security Council Resolutions 242 and 338, implicitly recognizing Israel. US opens dialogue with PLO

1992
President George H. W. Bush's administration holds up ten billion dollars in US loan guarantees in attempt to limit Israeli settlement building

1993
Oslo Peace accords signed by Prime Minister Yitzhak Rabin and PLO Chairman Yasser Arafat

1994
Hebron settler massacres 29 Palestinians. First Palestinian suicide bombing in Israel

2002
Arab League proposes normal relations with Israel in exchange for end to the occupation and "just solution" to refugee problem. Israel rejects offer, begins construction of Wall

2002-2003
"Quartet" (US, UN, EU, Russia) develops "Roadmap." Palestinians pledge support; Israel agrees, but raises 14 objections that render it ineffective

2004
Yasser Arafat dies

2005
Israel unilaterally removes Jewish settlers from Gaza, escalates West Bank settlement

2006
Hamas wins democratic legislative elections

1918
WWI ends; Ottoman Empire defeated

1923
League of Nations grants Palestine Mandate to Britain. Palestinians protest Zionist immigration. Vladimir Jabotinsky writes *The Iron Wall*

1933-1945
HaShoah

1935-1948
David Ben-Gurion leads Jewish Agency. Jewish immigration to Palestine escalates in response to Nazi atrocities. Zionists fight British restrictions on Jewish immigration to Palestine

1936-1939
Arab revolt against Jewish immigration

1947-1949
Palestinians' *al-Nakba* ("Catastrophe"). 750,000 Palestinians flee Israel's "war of liberation"

1948
March. Ben-Gurion and advisors adopt *Plan Dalet*
April 9. Massacre at Deir Yassin
May 14. British troops withdraw; Mandate ends; Israeli Declaration of Independence; first Arab-Israeli War begins
December. UN adopts Universal Declaration of Human Rights and Resolution 194

1949
Armistice with Arab countries and establishment of "Green Line." West Bank and Gaza come under Jordanian and Egyptian control, respectively

1956
Second Arab-Israeli War (Suez Canal Crisis and Sinai War)

1977
Labor Party defeated by Menachem Begin and Likud (right-wing Revisionist party)

1978
Camp David Accords signed by Israeli Prime Minister Begin and Egyptian President Anwar Sadat

1980
Knesset passes Basic Law, declaring Jerusalem Israel's "eternal, undivided capital"

1981
Israel annexes Golan Heights

1982
Israel invades Lebanon. Massacre in Sabra-Shatila Palestinian refugee camps

1983
Israel and Lebanon end war. Arafat and PLO forced to leave Lebanon, go to Tunis until 1994

1994
Palestinian National Authority (PNA) established in Gaza and West Bank. Yasser Arafat and PLO arrive in Gaza. Jordan and Israel sign peace treaty

1995
Prime Minister Rabin assassinated in Tel Aviv by Israeli fundamentalist

1996-1999
Binyamin Netanyahu's first term as Prime Minister

1997
Israel builds Har Homa settlement in East Jerusalem; widespread protests result. Israel imposes closures in West Bank and Gaza

2000
Al-Aqsa or Second Palestinian *Intifada* erupts during provocative visit of Defense Minister Ariel Sharon to Temple Mount

2007
Hamas and Fatah militants fight for control of Gaza

2008-2009
"Operation Cast Lead" (three-week War on Gaza)

2009
Likud party leader Binyamin Netanyahu reelected Prime Minister

2011
January-February. Egyptian Revolution

2012
UN General Assembly recognizes Palestine as non-member observer state

2013
Israel frames controversial Bedouin relocation plan. Boycott, divestment, and sanctions (BDS) campaign builds momentum

A Leader's Guide

Martha Reese

GET READY

- Because of the volume of material provided, the eight-week format described in the box on page 65 is highly recommended. Your group will want to process what they experience during the sessions and to discern what it is God may be calling them to do after the series is completed.

- Before the series begins, acquaint yourself with the entire resource, including the free DVD.

- Purchase a quantity of the resource so each session participant has his/her own copy. (See inside back cover for ordering information.)

- Make sure your class is held in a comfortable space where all can see and hear.

- Display a large post-1967 map of Israel/Palestine to help in identifying the places discussed in the materials.

- Test your DVD player and screen ahead of each class.

- This resource is not only a stand-alone curriculum but also a study guide to the book of essays entitled *Zionism and the Quest for Justice in the Holy Land,* released in 2014. Have on hand at least one or two copies of the book for class members who want to go deeper into the issues. Order the book at Amazon.com/books or visit the publisher's website, wipfandstock.com.

GET STARTED

- The first encounter sets the tone for those that follow. Create a space for open, safe conversation by being a non-anxious presence and example for those present.

- Make sure that everyone gets to speak before others share for a second time.

- Act as a moderator if participants too quickly take sides in the conversation. Present ground rules for honorable speech when discussing controversial or emotional topics.

FOLLOW UP

- Circulate a survey at the last session to collect feedback, then share the results with us at info@ theIPMN.org so we may continue to improve our resources and outreach.

- Direct your class participants to the website of the Israel/Palestine Mission Network of the PC(USA), www.theIPMN.org, where they will find a list of resources for further study.

- Encourage class members to join an alternative study tour or human rights delegation that offers first-hand encounters with the Palestinians and Israelis who live there. Upcoming tours are listed under the Travel tab at www.theIPMN.org.

One-Week Exploratory

If your church is unsure about whether to dedicate several weeks to the study of this resource, a one-week encounter with some of the material can help stimulate interest for a multi-week series. To begin, select topics that you think will be of immediate interest to your congregation. In preparation for the class, view the DVD episode and read the corresponding booklet section, then select two or three topics to present. Using the three-part meeting format described on this page, give an introduction and watch the first few minutes of the DVD episode. Encourage class members to engage one another in discussing both the episode and the related issues you have selected for group exploration.

Leading difficult conversations: a three-part format

1. Recognize God's presence in your midst with an opening prayer. Then, begin by providing a 15- to 20-minute overview of the range of materials. You may want to screen DVD episode excerpts in class and a give a spoken overview of the assigned reading.

2. Next, ask the participants to share aloud what was new or surprising to them. This will help you determine where the participants are in their understanding of the issues. Help the more introverted participants feel safe in sharing their thoughts with the group.

3. Offer some "digging deeper" questions and draw out differing responses from the members of your group. Avoid the temptation to answer questions yourself. Finish with the assignment for the following week and a closing prayer.

As with other topics of exploration, the Israeli-Palestinian conflict can bring out strong feelings and reactions. The PC(USA) Peacemaking Program has resources to help congregations with such conversations, including "To Strengthen Christ's Body: Tools for Talking about Tough Issues." (PDS Item #2435808001).

Eight-Week Series

Week	Theme	Booklet	In-class viewing of DVD	Pre-class preparation
1	• Introduction	Pages 5-10	• Episode 1: The Rocks of Judea – 21 mins. – stop at 12:44 mins.	Booklet: Section 1 DVD: Episode 1 (21 mins.)
2	• Political Zionism	Pages 11-16	• Episode 2: Historical Myths – 23 mins. – stop at 10:30 mins.	Booklet: Section 2 DVD: Episode 2 (23 mins.)
3	• A Jewish State	Pages 17-24	• Episode 3: The Triumph of Zionism – 21 mins. – stop at 13 mins.	Booklet: Section 3 DVD: Episode 3 (21 mins.)
4	• Christian Views of Jews and Judaism	Pages 25-31	• Episode 4: Anti-Semitism and Evolving Jewish Identity – 26 mins. – stop at 13:30	Booklet: Section 4 DVD: Episode 4 (26 mins.)
5	• A Jewish Theology of Liberation	Pages 32-36	• Episode 5: Wrestling in the Daylight – 26 mins. – stop at 12 mins.	Booklet: Section 5 DVD: Episode 5 (25 mins.)
6	• Mainline Protestant Pro-Zionism	Pages 37-44	• Episode 6: Mainline Protestant Theology – 23 mins. – stop at 12 mins.	Booklet: Section 6 DVD: Episode 6 (23 mins.)
7	• Evangelicals and Christian Zionism	Pages 45-48	• Episode 7: Onward Christian Zionists – 23 mins. – stop at 11:30 mins.	Booklet: Section 7 DVD: Episode 7 (23 mins.)
8	• A Palestinian Muslim Experience of Zionism • A Palestinian Christian Postscript	Pages 49-61	• Episode 8: Zionism, the Shadow Side – 20 mins. – stop at 11:30 mins. • Bonus Episode – The Living Stones Speak Out – 16 mins.	Booklet: Sections 8 and 9 DVD: Episode 8 (20 mins.) Bonus Episode: Living Stones Speak Out (16 mins.)

Follow-up class action: meet with Pastoral Staff and Worship Committee to discuss the group exercise on page 66

Four-Week Series

Week	Theme	Booklet	In-class viewing of DVD	Pre-class preparation
1	• Introduction • Political Zionism • A Jewish State	Pages 5-24	• Episode 1: The Rocks of Judea – 21 mins. – stop at 12:44 mins. • Episode 3: The Triumph of Zionism – 21 mins. – stop at 13 mins	Booklet: Sections 1, 2, and 3 DVD: Episode 1 (21 mins.) Episode 3 (21 mins.)
2	• Christian Views of Jews and Judaism • A Jewish Theology of Liberation	Pages 25-36	• Episode 4: Anti-Semitism and Evolving Jewish Identity – 26 mins. – stop at 13:30. • Episode 5: Wrestling in the Daylight – 26 mins. – stop at 12 mins.	Booklet: Sections 4 and 5 DVD: Episode 4 (26 mins.) Episode 5 (26 mins.)
3	• Mainline Protestant Pro-Zionism • Evangelicals and Christian Zionism	Pages 37-48	• Episode 6: Mainline Protestant Theology – 23 mins. – stop at 12 mins. • Episode 7: Onward Christian Zionists – 23 mins. – stop at 11:30 mins.	Booklet: Read Sections 6 and 7 DVD: Episode 6 (23 mins.) Episode 7 (23 mins.)

4	• A Palestinian Muslim Experience of Zionism
	• A Palestinian Christian Postscript
		Pages 49-61	• Episode 2: Historical Myths – 23 mins. – stop at 10:30 mins.
			• Episode 8: Zionism, the Shadow Side – 20 mins. – stop at 11:30 mins.
				Booklet: Sections 8 and 9
				DVD: Episode 2 (23 mins.)
				    Episode 8 (20 mins.)
				    Bonus Episode: Living Stones Speak Out (16 mins.)

Follow-up class action: meet with Pastoral Staff and Worship Committee to discuss the group exercise on page 66

Making Explicit That Which Is Implicit

Do you get uneasy singing "O Come, O Come, Emmanuel, and ransom captive Israel...that mourns in lowly exile here" during Advent? How about "We're marching, to Zion...."? There are a number of terms commonly used in Christian liturgy that are used to "brand" biblical Israel as today's political State of Israel. How do we deal with them?

Consider the terms: exile; exodus; covenant; return; blossoming of the desert; promised land; zion; Zionism; Zionist; Israel. What are your associations with them? Is there any acknowledgement by worship leaders that there is confusion over biblical terms and current political terms related to the State of Israel?

Why is this a problem?

Palestinian theologian Mitri Raheb observes that "The establishment of the State of Israel created...an intended confusion....Huge efforts were put by the State of Israel and Jewish organizations in branding the new State of Israel as a 'biblical entity.'"[1] While many worship leaders recognize the truth in Raheb's observation, they hesitate to tread the political minefields involved in exploring what is meant by the words we use in liturgy related to ancient, Biblical Israel and the confusion that exists about the applicability of those scriptures and terms to the modern, political State of Israel.

Words shape our reality. Groups that are unnamed in our liturgy remain invisible, unnoticed, unheeded. That's why Presbyterians revised the sexist language in the Hymnal to be inclusive. Sexism is similar to racism as it assumes a preference for one group over another. In the words of Jesmyn Ward:

> There is power in naming racism for what it is, in shining a bright light on it, brighter than any torch or flashlight. A thing as simple as naming it allows us to root it out of the darkness and hushed conversation where it likes to breed like roaches. It makes us acknowledge it. Confront it. And in confronting it, we rob it of some of its dark pull. Its senseless, cold drag. When we speak, we assert our human dignity. That is the worth of a word.[2]

Palestinian liberation theologians also speak from the context of exile, displacement, dispersion, and captivity. They argue with any passage of the Bible that does not portray a compassionate God who wants us to reconcile

AN UNBRANDING EXERCISE FOR LITURGISTS

Make a difference!
Your class group can take practical steps to help shape the language used during worship in your faith community. Reflecting thoughtfully on the traditional language we Christians have previously taken for granted is an excellent place to start. By choosing language that promotes justice in Israel-Palestine and other struggles for freedom, equality, and self-determination, we are empowering ourselves and our congregations to make a difference locally.

How to get started?
First, read and discuss the accompanying article "Making Explicit That Which Is Implicit" as a group. Next, provide a copy of this article to your pastoral staff and committee on worship. Finally, meet with them to discuss the implications of this approach for liturgy and worship in your congregation.

Ignored?

Palestinian Christians tell us they feel ignored by the debate over supersessionism and whether or not the covenant gives Jews the right to the land. Be sure to view the discussion of this point by Munther Isaac, a Palestinian theologian at Bethlehem Bible College in Bethlehem, Palestine, in the bonus episode of the DVD that accompanies this study guide.

with our neighbor. Refusing to be marginalized, Palestinian theologians have learned to identify the words that now brand the political State of Israel and to name them and bring them into the light.

Consider this: "zion" = fortress, or refuge, the holy hill, one section of Jerusalem. "Zionism" is a modern movement to resettle Jews and to make Israel a modern state. The term for "Promised land" is now translated by biblical scholars as "Land of Promise," a land that is available to all God's creation, not promised exclusively to one group.

Unfortunately, the new Presbyterian hymnbook, *Glory to God*, [PC(USA), 2013] includes one section of hymns within the category "God's covenant with Israel." Yes, the Bible tells us of God's activity in covenanting with Israel, but it was ancient Israel, not the modern political State.

Christians who reject a doctrine of supersessionism (the belief that Jesus Christ made God's covenant with Israel null and void by replacing it) embrace the words of Paul that make us "heirs of God's promise to Abraham and his offspring" [Ga. 3:16]. There are different interpretations of this doctrine, as this study guide indicates (see page 46). It is important to remember that Palestinian Christians are *part of the story*. Our seminary biblical studies departments can help us wade through the doctrine; what is required is to acknowledge the distinction between ancient Israel and the modern political state of Israel.

We who advocate for a just peace for both Israel and Palestine must raise our voices to point out language that eliminates Palestinian Christians from full presence in our liturgy and our understanding. We ask worship leaders, Christian educators, and seminaries to take up this calling and enlighten these crucial distinctions.

ABOUT THIS SECTION

This exercise was developed by Dr. Pauline Coffman as a transformational congregational tool. Dr. Coffman is Professor and Director (retired) of the School of Adult Learning, North Park University in Chicago and an author/editor of *Steadfast Hope: The Palestinian Quest for Just Peace* (2009, 2011).

Endnotes

INSIDE FRONT COVER
PAGE 2

1 Gavriel Fiske and Elie Leshem, "'What occupation?' Bennett asks, rejecting Palestinian state," *Times of Israel*, June 17, 2013, timesofisrael.com/what-occupation-asks-bennett-rejecting-two-state-solution

2 Noah Browning, "Opposition mounts to Israel's Arab Bedouin transfer plan" (Reuters), December 11, 2013, news.yahoo.com/opposition-mounts-israel-39-arab-bedouin-transfer-plan-172844120.html

1: TOWARD A NEW FRAMEWORK
PAGES 5-9

1 Ian S. Lustick, "Two-State Illusion," *New York Times*, September 14, 2013

2 Rashid Khalidi, "Is Any Hope Left for Mideast Peace?" *New York Times*, March 12, 2013

3 Nur Masalha, *The Palestine Nakba: Decolonising History*, 2012, 5

4 Adam Shatz (ed.), *Prophets Outcast: A Century of Dissident Jewish Writing about Zionism and Israel*, 2004, xi

5 *Ibid.*, xii

6 Ben Ehrenreich, "Zionism is the Problem," *Los Angeles Times*, March 15, 2009

7 Paul Krugman, "The Crisis of Zionism," *New York Times*, "The Conscience of a Liberal" (blogpost), April 24, 2012

8 Philip Weiss, "It's time for the media to talk about Zionism," *Mondoweiss*, December 4, 2012

9 Transcript of a talk and Q&A given by Ilan Pappe to a visiting group from Friends of Sabeel North America, Holy Land Hotel, Jerusalem, January 9, 2013

10 "Israel Needs a New Map," remarks by Ian Lustick, February 26, 2013, at the Carnegie Endowment for International Peace, Washington, DC, www.sas.upenn.edu/polisci/sites/www.sas.upenn.polisci/files/Israel%20Needs%20a%20New%20Map_MEP_0.pdf

11 Caryn Aviv and David Shneer, *New Jews: The End of the Jewish Diaspora*, 2005, xv

12 Adam Shatz (ed.), *op. cit.*, 202

13 *Ibid.*, 206

14 See Orientalism, p. 43.

15 See Taner Akcam, *A Shameful Act: The Armenian Genocide and Question of Turkish Responsibility*, 2007

16 Edward W. Said, *The End of the Peace Process: Oslo and After*, 2000, 208

17 Akiva Eldar, "Israel is fighting a losing battle over victimhood," *Haaretz*, March 19, 2012

18 Said, *op. cit.*, 209

19 Avraham Burg, *The Holocaust Is Over: We Must Rise from Its Ashes*, 2008, 172

20 Nadia Abu El-Haj, *Facts on the Ground: Archaeological Practice and Territorial Self-Fashioning in Israeli Society*, 2001, 2, 162

PALESTINE, ISRAEL, AND THE UNITED STATES
PAGE 10

1 Israeli Violations of UN Security Council Resolutions, 1948-2009, foreignpolicyjournal.com/2010/01/27/rogue-state-israeli-violations-of-u-n-security-council-resolutions

2 List of UN resolutions passed and disregarded (through 1990) Paul Findley, *Deliberate Deceptions: Facing the Facts About the U.S.-Israeli Relationship*, 1995, 188 -192; also available at guardian.150m.com/palestine/UN-condemnation-of-israel.htm

3 Arab High Committee address to United Nations Palestine Commission February 16, 1948, unispal.un.org/UNISPAL.NSF/0/B9EE848FD989E7AF85256FB00075C092

4 ICJ advisory opinion on the Wall: icj-cij.org/docket/files/131/1677.pdf

5 List of UN resolutions vetoed by US, as well as resolutions passed and disregarded (through 1990) Paul Findley, *Deliberate Deceptions: Facing the Facts About the U.S.-Israeli Relationship*, 1995, 188 -192; see also guardian.150m.com/palestine/UN-condemnation-of-israel.htm

6 jewishvirtuallibrary.org/jsource/UN/usvetoes.html

7 "Palestinians cast first vote at UN General Assembly, angering Israel, US," *Deutsche Welle*, November 18, 2013, dw.de/palestinians-cast-first-vote-at-un-general-assembly-angering-israel-us/a-17238312

2: POLITICAL ZIONISM
PAGES 11-15

1 Benny Morris, *The Birth of the Palestinian Refugee Problem*, Cambridge University Press, 2004, 597

2 The phrase "Jewish and democratic" has been used repeatedly by Zionist leaders over the years.

3 Balfour Declaration, 1917

4 jewishvirtuallibrary.org/jsource/Judaism/ispray.html. This religious definition comes from Jewish messianism. It is included in the Prayer for the State of Israel written by Israel's Chief Rabbinate in 1948. Now it is included in the prayer books of the four major American Jewish "denominations."

5 Brant Rosen, *Wrestling in the Daylight*, 2012, 293

6 jewishvirtuallibrary.org/jsource/Zionism/zionism.html

7 Mark Braverman, *Fatal Embrace,* 2010, 96

8 A common view among human rights groups opposed to 1) Israel's discriminatory laws against Palestinian Israeli citizens and 2) Israel's occupation of Palestinian territories.

9 A host of Jewish scholars and political leaders have contributed to Zionist thought. In his classic anthology of Zionist writings from 1843 to 1944 entitled *The Zionist Idea*, Arthur Hertzberg includes excerpts from 37 major Zionist thinkers. In the space available, we can only summarize the principal contributions of five of those thinkers.

10 Benny Morris, *Righteous Victims*, 2001, 76

11 Arthur Hertzberg, *The Zionist Idea*, 1997, 268

12 In I Samuel 8, God tells the prophet to warn the people of the consequences of their desire to become "like all the nations."

13 *Aliyah* means ascent (to Zion). Departure from Palestine is called *yerida* (descent from Zion)

14 Charles D. Smith, *Palestine and the Arab-Israeli Conflict: A History with Documents*, 2004, 37

15 Benjamin Beit-Hallahmi, *Original Sins*, 1993, 103

16 *Ibid.*

17 Herzl had reserved his thoughts about ethnic cleansing to a diary entry of 1895 where he wrote: "We must expropriate gently the private property on the state assigned to us. We shall try to spirit the penniless population across the border by procuring employment for it in transit countries, while denying it employment in our country."

18 Ilan Pappe, *The Ethnic Cleansing of Palestine*, 2007, xi

19 Nahum Goldmann, *The Jewish Paradox*, 1978, 99-100

20 Sephardic Jews are those descended from Spanish and Portuguese Jews. Today the term is often used to refer to almost any Jew who is not Ashkenazi (from northern Europe). This includes the Mizrahim (Jews from Arab countries) and as well as Jews from North Africa and elsewhere.

21 Paul Schemm, "Morocco film searches out Jews who left for Israel," Associated Press, Feb. 26, 2013, bigstory.ap.org/article/morocco-film-searches-out-jews-who-left-israel

22 Charles Dahan, "The Moroccan-Jewish experience and why I have hope for peace in the Middle East," *Washington Post*, June 24, 2013, washingtonpost.com/blogs/on-faith/wp/2013/06/24/the-moroccan-jewish-experience-and-why-i-have-hope-for-peace-in-the-middle-east/

23 Idith Zertal, *Israel's Holocaust and the Politics of Nationhood*, 2005, 34

24 Ilan Pappe, *The Forgotten Palestinians*, 2011, 119

25 Paul Merkley, *American Presidents, Religion, and Israel*, 2004, 64

26 Ben-Gurion, *Israel*, 1971, 745. Cited by Jacqueline Rose in *The Question of Zion*, 2005, 45

27 In the Preface to the German edition of *Fatal Embrace: Christians, Jews, and the Search for Peace in the Holy Land*, 2013, the Jewish American psychologist Mark Braverman observes that the civil religions of Nazi Germany and Apartheid South Africa were both supported by state churches. "The civil religion of Zionism developed in the late 19th century, albeit non-theistic in origin, was ultimately embraced by the Orthodox Jewish establishment in Israel, and has now become a part of the religious identity and sensibility of Jews worldwide along a broad continuum of theology and practice, from progressive to conservative."

CONSTANTINIAN RELIGION
PAGE 16

1 Samuel Hayim Brody, "Martin Buber's Bi-Nationalism," *Sh'ma: A Journal of Jewish Ideas*, May 2, 2011, shma.com/2011/05/martin-bubers-bi-nationalism

2 Jews Not Zionists, "The Difference Between Judaism and Zionism," G. Neuburger, jewsnotzionists.org/differencejudzion.html

3 Rabbi Brant Rosen, rabbibrant.com (blog post), September 24, 2013

4 Rebecca Shimoni Shoil, "J Street, New Israel Fund slam ADL for Top 10 anti-Israel list," *The Times of Israel*, October 23, 2013, timesofisrael.com/j-street-new-israel-fund-slam-adl-for-top-10-anti-israel-list

5 Marc Ellis, "The Palestinian Uprising and the Future of the Jewish People," from *Towards a Jewish Theology of Liberation: the Uprising and the Future* (1988), as reprinted in *Prophets Outcast: A Century of Dissident Jewish Writing about Zionism and Israel*, ed. Adam Shatz, 2004, 333

6 Marc H. Ellis, "Exile and the Prophetic: The interfaith ecumenical deal is dead," *Mondoweiss*, Nov. 12, 2012, mondoweiss.net/2012/11/exile-and-the-prophetic-the-interfaith-ecumenical-deal-is-dead.html

7 James Carroll, *Constantine's Sword: The Church and the Jews*, 2001, 599

8 *Ibid.*, 171

9 Marc Ellis, "Exile and the Prophetic..." *op. cit.* Here Ellis is paraphrasing a statement by Elie Wiesel.

3: THE CONCEPT AND PRACTICE OF A JEWISH STATE
PAGES 17-23

1 William Rogers Louis and Avi Shlaim, *The 1967 Arab-Israeli War*, 2012, 46

2 "The Gush Emunim settlers movement is established," *Haaretz*, February 10, 2011, haaretz.com/print-edition/features/the-gush-emunim-settlers-movement-is-established-1.342378

3 Ethan Bronner, "Hanan Porat, Jewish Settlement Leader, Dies at 67," *New York Times*, October 4, 2011. nytimes.com/2011/10/05/world/middleeast/hanan-porat-jewish-settlement-leader-dies-at-67.html?_r=0

4 Todd Gitlin and Liel Liebovitz, *Chosen Peoples*, 2010, 2

5 J.J. Goldberg, "Jews Now Minority in Israel and Territories," *Jewish Daily Forward*, September 19, 2013, blogs.forward.com/jj-goldberg/184245/jews-now-minority-in-israel-and-territories

6 Abba Solomon, *The Speech and Its Content*, 2011, 127. See also the 2008 film, *Defamation*, by Israeli filmmaker Yoav Shamir

7 Jack Ross, *Rabbi Outcast*, 2011, 89

8 Marc Ellis, *Judaism Does Not Equal Israel*, 2009, 119

9 For a list of these organizations, see jewishvirtuallibrary.org/jsource/judaica/ejud_0002_0005_0_04563.html

10 Menachem Begin, *The Revolt*, [1948], 1972, xi, as cited in Bernard Avishai, *The Tragedy of Zionism*, 1985, 167-68

11 Sadat refused to go to Oslo to receive the Nobel Peace Prize alongside Begin.

12 Bernard Avishai, "Begin vs. Begin," *New York Review of Books*, May 31, 1979, nybooks.com/articles/archives/1979/may/31/begin-vs-begin/?pagination=false

13 Benjamin Netanyahu, Early Political Career, Focus On Israel–Radio, www.facebook.com/focusonisrael.radio/posts/552751658120431

14 Tovah Lararoff, "PM: Ariel will remain under Israeli sovereignty," *Jerusalem Post*, January 9, 2013. jpost.com/Diplomacy-and-Politics/PM-Ariel-will-remain-under-Israeli-sovereignty

15 Peace Now: peacenow.org.il/eng/8monthsreport. Full report here: peacenow.org/Bibis%20Settlements%20Boom%20-%20March-November%202013%20-%20FINAL.pdf

16 In July 1980, the Knesset passed the Jerusalem Law, which declared that "Jerusalem, complete and united, is the capital of Israel." This law formalized Israel's unilateral annexation. Resolution 478, which the United Nations Security Council adopted in August

1980, declared the Jerusalem Law to be "null and void."

17 Benjamin Netanyahu biographical profile, *Haaretz*, haaretz.com/misc/tags/Benjamin%20Netanyahu-1.476753

18 Douglas Martin, "Benzion Netanyahu, hawkish scholar, dies at 102," *New York Times*, April 30, 2012, nytimes.com/2012/05/01/world/middleeast/benzion-netanyahu-dies-at-102.html?_r=0

19 *Ibid.*

20 David Myers, "Benzion Netanyahu: In life and death," *Jewish Journal*, May 15, 2012, jewishjournal.com/opinion/article/benzion_netanyahu_in_life_and_death_20120515

21 The Amalekite view of Jewish history includes the mitzvah (commandment) of genocide. As reflected in I Samuel 15:3, it requires the elimination of the enemy, including men, women, children, cattle, etc. For an overview of Jewish debate over the mitzvah of genocide, see myjewishlearning.com/beliefs/Issues/War_and_Peace/Combat_and_Conflict/Types_of_War/Genocide.shtml

22 The Association for Civil Rights in Israel: Anti-democratic initiatives, acri.org.il/en/category/democracy-and-civil-liberties/anti-democratic-legislation

23 Adalah, the Legal Center for Arab Minority Rights in Israel: New discriminatory laws and bills in Israel, June 2011, adalah.org/upfiles/2011/New_Discriminatory_Laws.pdf. Also the Association for Civil Rights in Israel, *op. cit.*

24 Glenn Kessler, "Defining 'Jewish state': For many, term has different meanings," *Washington Post*, October 2, 2010, washingtonpost.com/wp-dyn/content/article/2010/10/01/AR2010100104177.html?sid=ST2010100106889

25 President Barack Obama's remarks to the United Nations General Assembly, September 23, 2010, un.org/en/ga/65/meetings/generaldebate/Portals/1/statements/634209239344218750US_en.pdf

26 Glenn Kessler, "Defining 'Jewish state': For many, term has different meanings," *Washington Post*, October 2, 2010, washingtonpost.com/wp-dyn/content/article/2010/10/01/AR2010100104177.html

27 "Israel plans 16,000 more illegal settlement units in West Bank and Jerusalem," *Middle East Monitor*, Mar 21, 2013, middleeastmonitor.com/news/middle-east/5546-israel-plans-16000-more-illegal-settlement-units-in-west-bank-and-jerusalem

28 Philip Podolsky, "Bennett promises to prevent capitulation to Palestinians," *The Times of Israel*, March 30, 2013, timesofisrael.com/bennett-says-hell-do-everything-to-prevent-capitulation-to-palestinians

29 Herb Keinon, "Reporter's Notebook: Studying Bible with Bibi," *Jerusalem Post*, May 25, 2012, jpost.com/Features/In-Thespotlight/Reporters-Notebook-Studying-Bible-with-Bibi

30 Mitri Raheb, "Displacement Theopolitics," *The Invention of History: A Century of Interplay between Theology and Politics in Palestine*, 2011

31 Nurit Peled-Elhanan, *Palestine in Israeli School Books: Ideology and Propaganda in Education*, 2012, as cited in Max Blumenthal, "Why the Israeli Elections Were a Victory for the Right," *Nation*, January 23, 2013

32 Uri Misgav, "Religion now more dangerous than Arabs," *YNet News*, December 11, 2011, ynetnews.com/articles/0,7340,L-4159477,00.html

33 Rami G. Khouri, "Consolidating Its Center or Its Criminality?" *Beirut Daily Star*, January 26, 2013

34 Mark Karlin, "A Rabbi's Path to Palestinian Solidarity, *Truthout*, October 10, 2012, truth-out.org/opinion/item/12009-a-rabbis-path-to-palestinian-solidarity

35 For a list of these organizations, see jcwishvirtuallibrary.org/jsource/judaica/ejud_0002_0005_0_04563.html

36 In his 2012 book *The Crisis of Zionism*, Peter Beinart discusses the role of American Jewish organizations that began their work on the left of the political spectrum but are now on the far right because of their hawkish support of the far-right Israeli government. Organizations like the American Jewish Congress and the American Jewish Committee were tasked with providing access to power for American Jews. By the 1970s when Jews were well assimilated and were elected to the US Congress in large numbers, the *raison d'être* of such groups began to disappear. Rather than declare victory and fold, these organizations with multi-million dollar budgets changed their purpose to one of unconditional support for Israel and its government, even as it trended further and further to the right, which is cultural anathema for most of the American Jewish community who are traditionally social justice Democrats.

37 Fouzi El-Asmar, *To Be an Arab in Israel*, 1975, preface

38 Donald W. Shriver, Jr., President Emeritus of Union Theological Seminary, is one of the few social ethicists who has examined the complex process of reconciliation between nations and groups within nations with a history of enmity. In his groundbreaking work, *An Ethic for Enemies: Forgiveness in Politics*, Shriver uses three case studies to illustrate four elements required to restore relationships between nations and other collectivities with a history of enmity. These are moral truth, forbearance, empathy, and commitment to repair fractured human relationships. "Forgiveness in a political context...calls for a collective turning from the past that neither ignores past evil nor excuses it, that neither overlooks justice nor reduces justice to revenge, that insists on the humanity of enemies even in their commission of de-humanizing deeds, and that values the justice that restores political community above the justice that destroys it," 9

39 Mark Karlin, *op.cit.*

A TALE OF TWO VILLAGES
PAGE 24

1 Moshe Gilad, "From Al-Tantura to Ein Hod: a journey past Palestinian buildings and villages that once lay along the Mediterranean coast," *Haaretz*, November 24, 2012. (Translation by Charles Kamen posted online at zochrot.org/en/content/searching-lost-palestinian-villages)

2 Nur Masalha, *The Palestine Nakba: Decolonizing History*, 2012, 6

3 Gabriel Piterberg, "Erasures," *New Left Review*, July-August 2001, as reprinted in *Prophets Outcast: A Century of Dissident Jewish Writing about Zionism and Israel*, ed. Adam Shatz, 2004, 157

4 Ein Hod municipal website, en.ein-hod.org/about-ein-hod

4: CHRISTIAN VIEWS OF JEWS AND JUDAISM
PAGES 25-30

1 nunraw.blogspot.com/2013/03/melito-of-sardis-easter-homily-36-3739.html

2 Walter Laqueur, *The Changing Face of Antisemitism…*, 2006, 48; Eric Metaxas, *Bonhoeffer*, 2010, 91-94

3 Carol Monica Burnett, *Zionism Through Christian Lenses*, 2013, 73

4 Justin Martyr, Dialogue with Trypho, 16, p. 172 in *The Fathers of the Church: Saint Justin Martyr*, ed. Thomas B. Falls, 1947, 172

5 kerux.com/documents/keruxv4n1a1.asp

6 Saint John Chrysostom, Eight Homilies Against the Jews, *Patrologia Greaca*, vol. 98, cited in James Parkes: *The Conflict of the Church and the Synagogue: a Study in the Origins of Antisemitism*, 1934, 163-166

7 See two books by James Parkes, *The Jew and his Neighbor…*, 1930 and *The Conflict of the Church…*, 1934

8 Rosemary and Herman Ruether in Wagner and Davis, 16-19, citing four sources: 1) *Fundamental Agreement between the Holy See and the State of Israel* (1993), mfa.gov.il/MFA/MFA-Archive/1993/Pages/Fundamental%20Agreement%20-%20Israel-Holy%20See.aspx 2) "The PLO-Vatican Agreement."

jerusalemquarterly.org/ViewArticle.aspx?id=233 3) George E. Irani, *The Papacy and the Middle East: The Role of the Holy See in the Arab-Israeli Conflict, 1962–1984*, 1986, 38. 4) subsequent actions taken by Popes John Paul II and Benedict XVI

9 Rosemary Ruether, *Faith and Fatricide*, 1996, 144-49

10 *La Civiltà Cattolica*, May 1, 1897: cited in Sergio I. Minerbi, *The Vatican and Zionism*, 1990, 96

11 Entry of January 26, 1904, Herzl's Diaries, cited in *Ibid.*, 100

12 "Vatican cardinal: Palestinians have right to return to homeland" (Reuters), November 28, 2007, imra.org.il/story.php3?id=37021

13 Carol Glatz, "Solution to Israeli-Palestinian conflict requires talks, Pope says," *Catholic Register*, December 17, 2012. catholicregister.org/news/international/item/15574-solution-to-israeli-palestinian-conflict-requires-talks-pope-says

14 Donald E. Wagner and Walter T. Davis, *Zionism and the Quest for Justice in the Holy Land*, forthcoming, 13-14

15 *Nostra Aetate*, vatican.va/archive/hist_councils/ii_vatican_council/documents/vat-ii_decl_19651028_nostra-aetate_en.html

16 David Glick, "Reflections on the Holocaust," *Pastoral Psychology*, Vol. 44, No. 1., 1995, 26

17 Burnett, *op. cit.*, 73

18 See Section 5 in this publication, "A Jewish Theology of Liberation," 34

19 answers.com/topic/credo-ut-intelligam-1

THE COVENANT
PAGE 31

1 I.F. Stone, "Holy War," Polemics and Prophecies, 1969, as reprinted in *Prophets Outcast: A Century of Dissident Jewish Writing about Zionism and Israel*, ed. Adam Shatz, 2004, 198

2 Ilan Pappe, "Reclaiming Judaism from Zionism," *The Electronic Intifada*, October 18, 2013 (electronicintifada.net/content/reclaiming-judaism-zionism/12859?utm_source=EI+readers&utm_campaign=9d-25e77d47-RSS_EMAIL_CAMPAIGN&utm_medium=email&utm_term=0_e802a7602d-9d25e77d47-260782657)

3 Pappe, *ibid.*

4 Daniel Lazare, "Estranged Brothers: Reconsidering Jewish History," *Harpers Magazine*, April 2003, as reprinted in *Prophets Outcast: A Century of Dissident Jewish Writing about Zionism and Israel*, ed. Adam Shatz, 2004, 27

5 I.F. Stone, *op.cit.*, 200

6 Chaim Levinson and Yair Ettinger, "Rabbi Kook's followers are still debating his legacy," *Haaretz*, March 11, 2012, haaretz.com/print-edition/features/rabbi-kook-s-followers-are-still-debating-his-legacy-1.417753

5: A JEWISH THEOLOGY OF LIBERATION
PAGES 32-35

1 Together with Orthodox, Reform, and Conservative "denominations," Reconstructionism is one of the four major streams of Judaism in the United States.

2 Brant Rosen, *Wrestling in the Daylight: A Rabbi's's Path to Palestinian Solidarity*, 2012, 75-82

3 Brant Rosen, "A Jewish Theology of Liberation…", essay in Donald E. Wagner and Walter T. Davis, eds., *Zionism and the Quest for Justice in the Holy Land*, 2014, 6

4 Rosen, 2012, *op. cit.*, 24

5 Naim Ateek, *Justice and Only Justice; A Palestinian Theology of Liberation*, 1989

6 Liberation theology interprets scripture and other disciplines to elucidate the call of God to freedom, hope, justice, and transformation for a people, country, or culture that has been oppressed or marginalized.

7 Rosen, 2014, *op. cit.*, 3

8 Ateek, *op. cit.*, 101

9 Rosen, 2014, *op. cit.*, 5

10 *Ibid.*

11 *Ibid.*, 4-5

12 internationalwallofprayer.org/IWOP-014-Prayer-for-the-Welfare-of-the-State-of-Israel.html

13 Rosen, 2014, *op. cit.*, 9

14 Ellis, *Toward a Jewish Theology of Liberation*, 206

15 Rosen, 2014, *op. cit.*, 12

16 *Ibid.*, 32

17 *Ibid.*, 32-33

18 *Ibid.*, 14

19 Mordecai M. Kaplan, *The Meaning of God in Modern Jewish Religion*, 1994, 95

20 *Ibid.*

21 Rosen, 2012, *op. cit.*, 16

22 Michael Prior, *Zionism and the State of Israel*, 1999, 4-5

23 Rosen, 2014, *op. cit.*, 23-24

24 Jewish Voice for Peace is a progressive, grassroots-based American Jewish organization founded in 2006. According to its mission, JVP is "inspired by Jewish tradition to work together for peace, social justice, equality, human rights, respect for international law, and a US foreign policy based on these ideals," jewishvoiceforpeace.org

25 Rosen, 2014, *op. cit.*, 34

26 www.kairosusa.org

27 To review *Kairos Palestine* or order a copy, go to theIPMN.org, then click on study resources, then publications.

28 Jewish Council for Public Affairs, "Jewish Council for Public Affairs Shocked by Extreme Rhetoric of Kairos USA Document," engage.jewishpublicaffairs.org/blog/comments.jsp?blog_entry_KEY=6389

29 Jewish Voice for Peace Rabbinical Council, "Honor the Courage, Clarity, and Sensitivity of Kairos USA," kairosusa.org/?q=node/53

30 Rosen, 2014, *op. cit.*, 36

31 *Ibid.*, 36

EXTREMISM AND INTOLERANCE IN ISRAEL
PAGE 36

1 Gil Ronen, "Kahane was Right? Most Jews Think it's OK to Prod Arabs to Go," *Arutz Sheva Israel National News*, November 30, 2010, www.israelnationalnews.com/News/News.aspx/140920#.UzzPGaWRjfM

2 Simha Flapan, "The Birth of Israel," as reprinted in *Prophets Outcast: A Century of Dissident Jewish Writing about Zionism and Israel*, ed. Adam Shatz, 2004, 140

3 David Remnick, "Threatened," *New Yorker*, March 12, 2012, newyorker.com/talk/comment/2012/03/12/120312taco_talk_remnick

4 Zvi Bar'el, "A Good Jew Hates Arabs," *Haaretz*, Aug. 22, 2012, haaretz.com/opinion/a-good-jew-hates-arabs-1.459832

5 Neve Gordon, "Being honest about the dominant Zionist narrative," *Al Jazeera*, August 13, 2013 (aljazeera.com/indepth/opinion/2013/08/2013811131034480853.html)

6 Neve Gordon, "Residents Only," *London Review of Books* (blogpost) October 22, 2013, lrb.co.uk/blog/2013/10/22/neve-gordon/residents-only

7 Larry Derfner, "Israel's Everyday Racism - and How American Jews Turn a Blind Eye to It," *Jewish Daily Forward*, August 12, 2013, forward.com/articles/182171/israels-everyday-racism-and-how-american-jews-tu/

8 Sivan Klingbail and Shanee Shiloh, "Bye, the beloved country - why almost 40 percent of Israelis are thinking of emigrating," *Haaretz*, December 15, 2012, haaretz.com/news/features/bye-the-beloved-country-why-almost-40-percent-of-israelis-are-thinking-of-emigrating.premium-1.484945

9 Zvi Bar'el, *op.cit.*

6: MAINLINE LIBERAL PROTESTANTS AND ISRAEL
PAGES 37-43

1 Todd Gitlin and Liel Leibovitz, *The Chosen Peoples: America, Israel, and the Ordeals of Divine Election*, 2010, inside front flap

2 Ronald H. Stone, *Politics and Faith*, 2012, 201

3 Caitlin Carenen, *The Fervent Embrace* (Kindle version), 2012, Chapter 1

4 *Ibid.*, Chapter 2

5 *Ibid.*

6 Charles D. Smith, *Palestine and the Arab-Israeli Conflict*, 2004, 167

7 Reinhold Niebuhr, "Our Stake In Israel," *The New Republic*, February 3, 1957. www.newrepublic.org

8 Reinhold Niebuhr, *The Children of Light and the Children of Darkness*, 1944. Cited in nytimes.com/2005/09/18/books/review/18schlesinger.html?pagewanted=all&_r=0

9 Here Ellis is paraphrasing a statement by Elie Wiesel. Marc Ellis, "Exile and the Prophetic: The interfaith ecumenical deal is dead," *Mondoweiss*, Nov. 12, 2012, mondoweiss.net/2012/11/exile-and-the-prophetic-the-interfaith-ecumenical-deal-is-dead.html

10 Krister Stendahl, *Paul Among Jews and Gentiles*, 1976, 37

11 See page 8 for a discussion of ethical exceptionalism that flows from theological exceptionalism.

12 Verduin, in Burnett, *Zionism Through Christian Lenses*, 2013, 156-157

13 *Ibid.*, 157. (Verduin reports that the Krister Stendahl letter to David Hartman was probably faxed on March 4, 2002. The letter was accessed in the Stendahl Papers, Andover Newton Theological Seminary, box 7.)

14 Uri Misgav, "Religion now more dangerous than Arabs," *YNet News*, December 11, 2011, ynetnews.com/articles/0,7340,L-4159477,00.html

15 Paul van Buren, *A Christian Theology of the People Israel: Part II, A Theology of Jewish-Christian Reality*, 1983, 30

16 *Ibid.*, 262-263

17 Edward Said, "Islam through Western Eyes," *Nation*, April 26, 1980

ISRAEL'S "IMAGE PROBLEM"
PAGE 44

1 *Hasbara Handbook: Promoting Israel on Campus*, World Union of Jewish Students, March 2002, 8, middle-east-info.org/take/wujshasbara.pdf

2 Barak Ravid, "Think tank: Israel's poor international image not the fault of failed hasbara, *Haaretz*, Dec. 30, 2012

3 *Ibid.*

4 Josh Nathan-Kazis, "Jewish Agency Plans $300M-a-Year Push for Israel, *Forward*, August 15, 2013, forward.com/articles/182354/jewish-agency-plans-m-a-year-push-for-israel/?p=all

5 Nathaniel Popper, "Israel Aims to Improve Its Public Image," *Forward*, October 14, 2005, forward.com/articles/2070/israel-aims-to-improve-its-public-image/

6 Ravid, *op. cit.*

7 Peter Beinart, "The failure of the American Jewish establishment," *New York Review of Books*, June 10, 2010

8 *Ibid.*

9 Seth Freedman, "Israel's smiling PR drive," *Guardian*, February 22, 2010

10 *Ibid.*

11 Philip Weiss, "Defying Hillel rules, Swarthmore chapter invites anti-Zionists to come on in," *Mondoweiss*, December 9, 2013, mondoweiss.net/2013/12/swarthmore-chapter-zionists.html/comment-page-1

12 *Ibid.*

13 Derek Kwait, "Swarthmore Hillel Defies Headquarters on Boycott Israel Program Restrictions," *Forward*, December 9, 2013, forward.com/articles/189013/swarthmore-hillel-defies-headquarters-on-boycott-i/

14 Eric Fingerhut and Jonathan Kessler, "Working Together to Expand Support for Israel on Campus," *Jewish Week*, November 13, 2013, thejewishweek.com/editorial-opinion/opinion/working-together-expand-support-israel-campus

EVANGELICALS AND CHRISTIAN ZIONISM
PAGES 45-47

1 See presbyterianmission.org/ministries/global/resolution-confronting-christian-zionism/

2 Gary Burge, "Evangelicals and Christian Zionism," in Wagner and Davis, eds., *Zionism and the Quest for Justice in the Holy Land*, 2014, 4-5

3 www.cufi.org

4 *Ibid.*, 6

5 *Ibid.*, 10-11

6 *Ibid.*, 13

7 Laurie Zimmerman, "A Night to Honor Israel? Christian Zionism and Jewish Community," jewsonfirst.org/07b/zimmerman.pdf

8 Joseph Massad, "Peace is war: After the Oslo Accords," *Al Jazeera*, November 3, 2013, aljazeera.com/indepth/opinion/2013/10/peace-war-after-oslo-accords-20131031124827574136.html

9 Joseph Massad, "Zionism, anti-Semitism, and Colonialism," *Al Jazeera*, December 24, 2012, aljazeera.com/indepth/opinion/2012/12/201212249122912381.html

10 For example, John 14:6 ("I am the way, the truth, and the life. No one comes to the Father except through me") and Acts 4:12 ("There is salvation in no one else, for there is no other name under heaven given among mortals by which we must be saved.")

11 Burge, *op. cit.*, 18

12 *Ibid.*

13 *Ibid.*, 20

WHAT DIASPORA?
PAGE 48

1 Jewish Virtual Library, .jewishvirtuallibrary.org/jsource/judaica/ejud_0002_0007_0_07029.html

2 Robert Tait, "Iran's Jews spurn cash lure to emigrate to Israel," *The Guardian*, July 12, 2007, theguardian.com/world/2007/jul/13/iran.israel

3 Adiv Sterman and Elhanan Miller, "Jewish Iranian MP lauds country's religious freedom," *The Times of Israel*, September 29, 2013, timesofisrael.com/jewish-iranian-mp-lauds-countrys-religious-freedom/

4 Thomas Erdbrink, "Jewish Hospital a Fixture in Tehran," *New York Times*, February 9, 2014, nytimes.com/2014/02/10/world/middleeast/jewish-hospital-at-home-in-iran.html?_r=0

5 Micah Goodman, "Making Jews out of Zionists," *Mosaic Magazine*, November 11, 2013, mosaicmagazine.com/supplemental/2013/11/making-jews-out-of-zionists/

6 Shlomo Shamir, "Aliyah? Fuggedaboudit," *Haaretz*, April 23, 2012, haaretz.com/opinion/aliyah-fuggedaboudit-1.425933

7 Caryn Aviv and David Shneer, *New Jews: The End of the Jewish Diaspora*, 2005, xv

8 "U.S. Jewish Population Substantially Larger Than Previously Estimated," *Jewish Philanathropy*, September 30, 2013, ejewishphilanthropy.com/u-s-jewish-population-substantially-larger-than-previously-estimated

9 Aviv and Shneer, *op. cit.*, 12

10 *Ibid.*, 12

11 Eric Hobsbawm, "Benefits of Diaspora," *London Review of Books*, October 20, 2005, lrb.co.uk/v27/n20/eric-hobsbawm/benefits-of-diaspora

12 Ella Shohat, "Sephardim in Israel: Zionism from the standpoint of its Jewish victims," *Social Text*, 1988, as reprinted in *Prophets Outcast: A Century of Dissident Jewish Writing about Zionism and Israel*, ed. Adam Shatz, 2004, 289

13 *Ibid.*, 316

14 David Shasha, *Sephardic Heritage Update*, November 14, 2013

A PALESTINIAN MUSLIM EXPERIENCE WITH ZIONISM
PAGES 49-54

1 Abu Sway, "A Palestinian Muslim Experience with Zionism," in Wagner and Davis, eds., *Zionism and the Quest for Justice in the Holy Land*, Wipf and Stock, forthcoming, 5

2 Neve Gordon, "Being honest about the dominant Zionist narrative," August 19, 2013, www.scoop.co.nz

3 This quotation and all subsequent quotations from the Holy *Qur'an* are from the Sahih International English version.

4 Barak Ahmad, *Muhammad and the Jews*, 1979, 46-47

5 *La Convivencia* ("the Coexistence") is a term used to describe the situation in Spanish history from about 711 to 1492 (roughly concurrent with the *Reconquista* ("Reconquest"), when Jews, Muslims, and Catholics in Spain lived in relative peace together within the different kingdoms. (During the same time, however, the Christian push to the south into Moorish land was ongoing.) The phrase often refers to the interplay of cultural ideas among the three groups and ideas of religious tolerance. www.websters-online-dictionary.org/definitions/Convivencia. [Editors' Note: In the field of Iberian studies there are other scholars who question the degree of "relative peace" during this period of history. www.google.com/#q=la+convivencia]

6 The Holy *Qur'an* 5:5

7 Abu Sway, *op. cit.*, 9

8 *Ibid.*, 4

9 Shimon Gapso, "If you think I'm a racist, then Israel is a racist state," *Haaretz*, August 7, 2013, haaretz.com/opinion/1.540278

10 adalah.org/eng/Israeli-Discriminatory-Law-Database. Many of these laws also affect Palestinians in the West Bank and Gaza, as well as Palestinian refugees outside Israel/Palestine.

11 Neve Gordon, *op.cit.*

12 Abu Sway, *op. cit.*, 17

13 Marc H. Ellis, *Judaism Does Not Equal Israel: The Rebirth of the Jewish Prophetic*, 2009

14 Abu Sway, *op. cit.*, 14

15 Ilan Pappe, *The Ethnic Cleansing of Palestine*, 2006, 90. Benny Morris, *Righteous Victims*, 2001, 204-209

16 Akiva Eldar, "Israel admits it revoked residency rights of a quarter million Palestinians," *Haaretz*, June 12, 2012, haaretz.com/news/diplomacy-defense/israel-admits-it-revoked-residency-rights-of-a-quarter-million-palestinians-1.435778

17 Pappe, *op. cit.*

18 *Ibid.* [Pappe footnotes this comment with "Walid Khalidi, 'Selected Documents on the 1948 War,' *Journal of Palestine Studies*, 107, Vol. 27/3 (Spring 1998), 60-105. Khalidi uses the British as well as the Arab Committee's correspondence."]

19 Akiva Eldar, *op. cit.*

20 btselem.org/jerusalem/revocation_statistics

21 Abu Sway, *op. cit.*, 25-26

22 A recent court ruling exposes the contradiction about what it means to be an Israeli citizen: Neve Gordon, "High court rules: It is impossible to be Israeli," *Al Jazeera*, October 21, 2013, aljazeera.com/indepth/opinion/2013/10/high-court-rules-it-impossible-be-israeli-201310201360824801.html

23 Abu Sway, *op. cit.*, 26

24 Meron Benvenisti, *Sacred Landscape*, 2002, 201

25 Theodor Herzl, *Complete Diaries*, entry of June 12, 1895

26 Randa Abdel-Fattah, "Illegal mourning: The Nakba Law and the erasure of Palestine," *ABC Religion and Ethics*, May 17, 2013, abc.net.au/religion/articles/2013/05/17/3761661.htm

27 haaretz.com/misc/writers/1.529297

28 haaretz.com/misc/writers/ali-ayyad-1.529297; www.haaretz.com/news/national/supreme-court-orders-israel-s-ag-to-explain-law-allowing-confiscation-of-palestinian-land-in-jerusalem.premium-1.525242

29 Josh Nathan-Kazis, "Jewish Agency Plans $300M-a-Year Push for Israel, *Forward*, August 15, 2013, forward.com/articles/182354/jewish-agency-plans-m-a-year-push-for-israel/?p=all

30 Barak Ravid, "Prime Minister's Office recruiting students to wage online hasbara battles," *Haaretz*, August 13, 2013, haaretz.com/news/national/.premium-1.541142

31 Akiva Eldar, "Frank Gehry steps down from Museum of Tolerance Project," *Haaretz*, January 15, 2010, haaretz.com/print-edition/news/frank-gehry-steps-down-from-museum-of-tolerance-project-1.261496

32 See mamillacampaign.org and ccrjustice.org/ourcases/current-cases/mamilla

MEMORICIDE
PAGE 55

1 Nur Masalha, *The Palestine Nakba: Decolonizing History*, 2012, 10

2 Jonathan Cook, "Canada Park and Israeli 'memoricide,'" *The Electronic Intifada*, March 10, 2009

3 Meron Benvenisti, *Sacred Landscape: The Buried History of the Holy Land since 1948*, 2002

A PALESTINIAN CHRISTIAN POSTSCRIPT
PAGES 56-58

1 Ben Ehrenreich, "Zionism is the Problem," *Los Angeles Times*, March 15, 2009

2 Or Kashi, "Israel's new Jewish identity initiative based on fascist values, consultant warns," *Haaretz*, July 10, 2013, haaretz.com/news/national/.premium-1.534791

3 kairospalestine.ps/sites/default/Documents/English.pdf

4 In 1982 the World Alliance of Reformed Churches (WARC) excluded the white Dutch Reformed Church of South Africa until it ended its support for apartheid. It was only readmitted to WARC in 1998 after it repudiated this racist doctrine. sahistory.org.za/dated-event/dutch-reformed-church-rejoins-world-alliance-reformed-churches

EMERGING FROM THE AMERICAN JEWISH "COCOON"
PAGE 59

1 Rachel Shabi, "Come, see Palestine!" Salon.com, June 5, 2006, salon.com/2006/06/05/birthright

2 Edward W. Said, *The End of the Peace Process: Oslo and After*, 2000, 267

3 Paul Krugman, "The Crisis of Zionism," *New York Times* (blogpost), "The Conscience of a Liberal," April 24, 2012

4 Peter Beinart, "The American Jewish cocoon," *New York Review of Books*, September 26, 2013, nybooks.com/articles/archives/2013/sep/26/american-jewish-cocoon/

5 *Ibid.*

"JUDAIZING" THE LAND
PAGES 60-61

1 "'Judaization' of the Galilee means racism," *Haaretz*, December 2, 2013, haaretz.com/opinion/.premium-1.561201

2 Eli Ashkenazi and Zafrir Rinat, "Arab council heads slam Israeli plan to build new Jewish towns in Galilee," *Haaretz*, December 2, 2013, haaretz.com/news/national/.premium-1.561257

3 "'Judaization' of the Galilee means racism," *Haaretz* December 2, 2013, *op. cit., haaretz.com/opinion/.premium-1.561201*

4 Dan Gazit, "The historical truth about Bedouin expulsion from the Negev," 972 blog, September 5, 2013, 972mag.com/the-historical-truth-about-bedouin-expulsion-from-the-negev/78404

5 "Settler Implantation and the Policy of 'Judaization,'" Badil Resource Center for Palestinian Residency and Refugee Rights, badil.org/en/component/k2/item/1370-judaization

6 "Israel approves plan to displace Negev Bedouins," Maan News Agency, May 6, 2013, occupiedpalestine.wordpress.com/2013/05/06/israel-approves-plan-to-displace-negev-bedouins

7 Neve Gordon, "Residents Only," *London Review of Books* (blogpost) October 22, 2013, lrb.co.uk/blog/2013/10/22/neve-gordon/residents-only

8 "Bedouins of Negev Desert Feel Betrayed by Israel Resettlement Plan" (Reuters), *Forward*, August 28, 2013, forward.com/articles/183073/bedouins-of-negev-desert-feel-betrayed-by-israel-r/?p=all#ixzz2nO3dzRTm

9 Dan Gazit, "The expulsion of the Bedouins from the Bsor Region after the War of Independence," *Kacha Ze*, August 2012, reprinted at 972mag.com/the-historical-truth-about-bedouin-expulsion-from-the-negev/78404

MAKING EXPLICIT THAT WHICH IS IMPLICIT
PAGE 74

1 *The Invention of History: A Century of Interplay Between Theology and Politics in Palestine*, Mitri Raheb, ed. 2011, 8-19

2 "A Cold Current," by Jesmyn Ward, Op-Ed, *New York Times*, August 7, 2013, opinionator.blogs.nytimes.com/2013/08/07/a-cold-current

40983

ABORTION

Roe v. Wade (1973)

By SUSAN DUDLEY GOLD

TWENTY-FIRST CENTURY
BOOKS
A Division of
Henry Holt and Company

New York

To my husband, John C. Gold, and my son, Samuel B. Morrison.

Twenty-First Century Books
A Division of Henry Holt and Company, Inc.
115 West 18th Street
New York, NY 10011

Henry Holt® and colophon are trademarks of
Henry Holt and Company, Inc.
Publishers since 1866

Published in Canada by Fitzhenry & Whiteside Ltd.,
195 Allstate Parkway, Markham, Ontario, L3R 4T8

Library of Congress Cataloging-in-Publication Data
Gold, Susan Dudley.
Roe v. Wade (1973) : abortion / Susan Dudley Gold. — 1st ed.
p. cm. — (Supreme Court decisions)
Includes bibliographical references and index.
1. Roe, Jane, 1947- —Trials, litigation, etc.—Juvenile literature. 2. Wade, Henry—Trials, litigation, etc.—
Juvenile literature. 3. Trials (Abortion)—Washington (D.C.)—Juvenile literature. 4. Abortion—Law and
legislation—United States—Juvenile literature. [1. Roe, Jane, 1947- —Trials, litigation, etc. 2. Wade, Henry—
Trials, litigation, etc. 3. Trials (Abortion) 4. Abortion—Law and legislation.]
I. Title. II.Title: Roe versus Wade. III. Series: Supreme Court decisions (New York, N.Y.)
KF228.R59G64 1994b   344.73'04192'0269— dc20   94-21860
[347.30441920269]   CIP AC

Photo Credits
Photos on pages 40 and 42 © *The Houston Post.*
Photo on page 56 courtesy of Sarah Weddington.
All other photos provided by AP / Wide World Photos.

Design
Tina Tarr-Emmons

Typesetting and Layout
Custom Communications

ISBN 0-8050-3659-8
First Edition 1994

Printed in Mexico
All first editions are printed on acid-free paper ∞.
10 9 8 7 6 5 4 3 2 1

Contents

A Constitutional Right

On January 23, 1973, the U.S. Supreme Court ruled that a woman has a constitutional right to abort a pregnancy. Only in the last three months of a pregnancy did the state have the right to ban abortion. Known as *Roe v. Wade*, the sweeping decision said the abortion right is as fundamental as the right to vote or the right to bear arms. It struck down the abortion laws in 31 states and required 18 more to rewrite theirs. New York state's abortion law, which was quite liberal, was unaffected by the decision.

Unlike most Supreme Court decisions in which the Court's ruling is accepted as the final word on a matter, the abortion decision marked the beginning of a bitter battle between those who opposed abortion and those who supported a woman's right to control her own body. That battle grows ever more violent today.

Sherri Finkbine, right, is interviewed by Swedish reporters in August 1962 about her decision to seek an abortion in Sweden. She had taken thalidomide, a drug blamed for severe deformities in fetuses. Her husband, Robert Finkbine, is next to her.

CHAPTER ONE

Sherri Finkbine's Ordeal

*One's philosophy, one's experiences, one's
exposure to the raw edges of human
existence, one's religious training . . . are
all likely to influence and to color one's
thinking and conclusions about abortion.*[1]

— **Justice Harry A. Blackmun**
in *Roe v. Wade*

The newspaper story sent chills down Sherri Finkbine's
spine. Several babies had been born in England with just heads and torsos—no
arms or legs. Apparently their mothers had taken sleeping pills during the early
part of their pregnancies.

Mrs. Finkbine loved children. Known as Sherri Chessen on TV, she
hosted the children's show "Romper Room," delighting her preschool audience. The Phoenix, Arizona, resident also was the mother of four children and
was pregnant with her fifth child.

Mrs. Finkbine read the story more carefully. The drug blamed for the
deformities was a sleeping pill called thalidomide. She thought back to the pills
she had taken during the first months of her pregnancy when morning sickness
had plagued her. Her husband, Robert Finkbine, had brought the pills home

7

from England. A history teacher, he had chaperoned his high-school students on a trip to Europe. While in England, he had had trouble sleeping and had obtained a prescription for the pills from an English doctor. Once home, he had stored the pills in the family medicine cabinet.

His wife had spied the pills on the shelf. Thinking they would calm her and help her nausea, she took about three dozen of the pills over the next two months. Now, reading the paper on this July morning in 1962, she thought apprehensively that the pills she had taken sounded suspiciously like the ones that had caused the deformities.

She ran to the bathroom and checked the bottle. Shaken by fear, she called her doctor and described the pills to him. They did indeed contain thalidomide, he told her. Even worse, the drug was most destructive to fetuses in the first three months of pregnancy.

She asked what she should do. The doctor recommended an abortion.

In Arizona in 1962, abortions were legal only if they were performed to save the life of the mother. In Phoenix, doctors performed between 18 and 25 abortions a year. Before an abortion was performed, a panel of doctors had to determine that the birth would endanger the mother's life.

During the first three months of pregnancy, doctors used a device to suck the fetus from the mother's womb. In later months, doctors had to operate to remove the fetus.

Finkbine, 30, was almost two and a half months pregnant when she learned she had taken thalidomide. An abortion performed at this stage would be a simple medical procedure. Beyond three months into her pregnancy, she would have to have surgery, a more complicated and more dangerous undertaking.

Reassured by her doctor, Finkbine sent a note to the three-doctor medical board at the hospital where she was seeking an abortion. She explained her situation and requested that she be given an abortion as soon as possible. The panel recommended to the hospital that the abortion be performed. Her doctor scheduled the procedure for the following Thursday.

Then, hoping to prevent other mothers from taking thalidomide, Finkbine called the editor of a Phoenix newspaper. By this time, 4,000 deformed babies whose mothers had taken thalidomide had been reported in Germany and another 1,000 in England, Canada, and Australia. The babies were born with flipperlike arms and legs. In some cases, their hands and feet were attached directly to their bodies. Though the drug had been banned in the United States in March 1962, it had been distributed since 1959 to more than 1,200 doctors throughout the country for tests on patients. Other U.S. residents had obtained the drug abroad, as Finkbine had.

Finkbine told her story to a medical reporter, asking that her name not be used. The next day, a front-page story blared out her tragedy: "Baby-deforming Drug May Cost Woman Her Child Here."[2] In the next few days, the story was carried by newspapers throughout the world.

Though the newspapers honored Finkbine's request not to publish her name, the media spotlight on Phoenix and its hospitals did not sit well with the medical community. Afraid they would be prosecuted for violating Arizona's abortion law, the hospital and doctors cancelled Finkbine's abortion.

Her doctor told her, "It is now a legal decision. It's no longer a medical or humanitarian one, I'm afraid."[3]

Finkbine and her husband decided to take their case to court. On July 25, 1962, they filed suit in superior court, asking the judge to declare the 1901 Arizona abortion law illegal. Joining in their suit was Steven Morris, administrator of the Good Samaritan Hospital, where the abortion had been scheduled. The hospital was willing to perform the abortion if the courts could reassure it that the action would be legal.

Once the court documents were filed, the Finkbines' names became public.

Every move they made was now recorded in newspapers nationwide. The *New York Times* reported that Finkbine had talked to two psychiatrists in an effort to show that the birth would endanger her life. "It would upset me terribly to have a deformed baby,"[4] she said, noting that her mental health would be affected.

While they waited for a court judgment, the Finkbines read about three babies born deformed in New York City. Their deformities were blamed on thalidomide.

On July 29, the Finkbines' attorney offered to drop the court suit if the state would guarantee it would not prosecute if the abortion were performed. The state would not give such an assurance.

The following day, Judge Yale McFate dismissed the case without a hearing. He said there was no legal controversy or dispute because all sides in the case agreed to the facts as presented by the Finkbines.

"As a human being I would like to hear the case," Judge McFate told the Finkbines. "As a judge, under existing Arizona law, I cannot."[5]

Time was running short. Mrs. Finkbine's pregnancy was progressing. The longer an abortion was delayed, the more dangerous it became.

Meanwhile, the *New York Times* reported that a New York woman who had taken thalidomide gave birth to a baby whose internal organs and all four limbs were deformed. The baby lived 41 minutes.[6]

The Finkbines desperately searched for a place where Mrs. Finkbine could obtain a legal abortion. In 1962, aborting a fetus was a felony in every state unless the life of the mother (or her health in some cases) was endangered. Alabama, the District of Columbia, and Oregon allowed abortions to preserve the mother's health. Maryland doctors had to prove an abortion was necessary for the mother's safety. In Colorado and New Mexico, an abortion was permitted to "prevent permanent bodily injury" to the mother. But there had

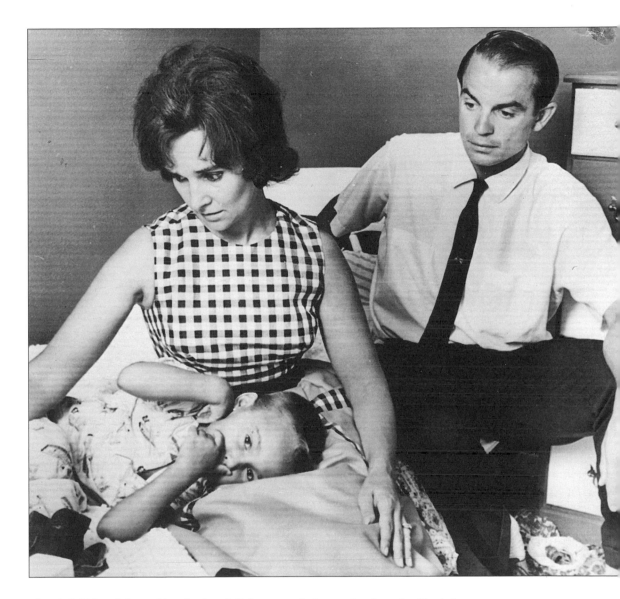

Sherri Finkbine, left, and her husband, Robert, put their son, Stevie, to bed in their home in Phoenix, Arizona, on July 25, 1962. The Finkbines had filed a suit earlier in the day to obtain court permission for an abortion for Mrs. Finkbine.

been few court rulings to define either "health," "safety," or "permanent bodily injury."[7]

No one seemed to be able to give the Finkbines a clear answer about the legality of the abortion they sought. On July 31, Robert Finkbine told the *New York Times* of the couple's decision to seek an abortion outside the country. They chose to go to a country where abortion was legal, because they did not want to break the law,[8] he told the news reporters.

At the time, seven countries permitted abortions: Japan, Finland, Norway, England, Sweden, Denmark, and the Soviet Union. The Finkbines' doctor recommended Japan, where those seeking abortions paid as little as $50 and encountered little red tape. Because of the publicity surrounding the Finkbines' case, however, the Japanese government was reluctant to allow Mrs. Finkbine to undergo an abortion there.[9]

Instead, the Finkbines decided to go to Sweden. A medical journalist from Sweden offered to arrange an appointment for Mrs. Finkbine with a Swedish doctor. They booked a flight to Sweden on August 3.

That same day, the Vatican broadcast a proclamation condemning those who seek abortions, even if the mother's life is in danger. "Every human being, from the first instant of conception, possesses all the rights that belong to any human person," the broadcast said. "Nothing justifies direct, voluntary suppression—not even the goal of saving the life of the mother."[10]

The radio broadcast did not mention the Finkbines by name, but Boston's auxiliary bishop, Thomas J. Riley, did. He likened Mrs. Finkbine's hoped-for abortion to "killing an innocent boy or girl."[11]

Other religious leaders, however, were not as harsh. Dr. Theodore R. Flaiz, world medical director of the Seventh Day Adventist Church, called the Finkbine abortion "therapeutic."[12] Protestant and Jewish religious leaders in the Finkbines' home state had not opposed the operation. The Finkbines' church, the Unitarian Universalist Association, had long been in the forefront of working for abortion reform.

Once in Sweden, Mrs. Finkbine had to undergo the same lengthy procedure Swedish women had to endure to obtain an abortion. She spent the next few days being examined and interviewed by social workers, psychiatrists, and an obstetrician. Once the examinations were complete, Finkbine submitted her application to the three-person Royal Medical Board of Sweden.

Composed of a gynecologist, a psychiatrist, and a woman specialist in social and political questions, the board made the final decision on whether to grant abortions. They were permitted if the mother's health or life were in danger, the mother's "physical or psychic health" would be affected by the birth of the child, if the mother was under 15 or had been raped, or if the mother would pass along genetic defects to the child.

On August 16—almost a month after learning that the fetus she was carrying might be deformed—Sherri Finkbine got a call from the Royal Medical Board. Her request for an abortion had been approved unanimously. She sobbed with relief, her husband told reporters. He added that they both thought it was "wonderful" that there was a country where abortions were "a medical decision, not obstructed by religious, legal, and social pressures."[13]

Doctors at the Royal Caroline Hospital in Stockholm, Sweden, performed an abortion on Mrs. Finkbine August 18, 1962. They estimated she was in her 13th week of pregnancy. The fetus was deformed.

Back in the United States, relieved to have the experience behind her, Finkbine told the press, "The Swedish people are the most intelligent, understanding in the world. Americans try to hide their heads in the sand like an ostrich and hope such problems will go away."[14]

She later wrote, "An abortion was to me a very sad, ugly experience, but [it was] definitely the lesser of two evils."[15]

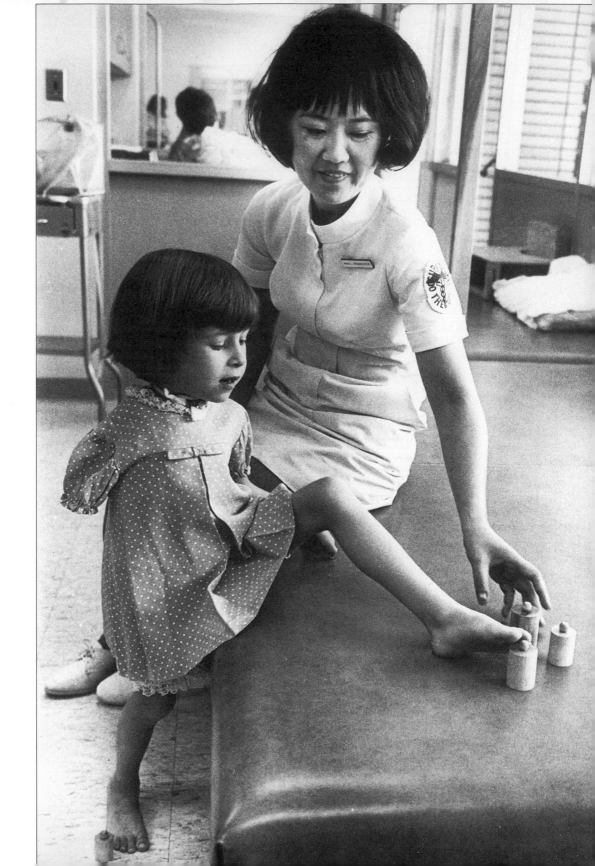

CHAPTER TWO

Efforts to Ease Abortion Laws

There is much dissatisfaction among physicians, lawyers, judges, legislators and the body politic in the United States with present archaic abortion laws.[1]

— Alan F. Guttmacher, M.D.
President, Planned Parenthood

The Finkbine tragedy highlighted for many people the need for more liberal abortion laws in the United States. The Finkbines had been able to go to Sweden for an abortion, but many others could not afford such a trip.

The birth of the "thalidomide babies" and a 1962-1965 epidemic of German measles in the United States that led to deformed fetuses upset people. Many in the health field and elsewhere began calling for legalized abortions when the baby might be born with physical or mental defects.

Though well-entrenched in 20th-century America, the ban on abortion had been only fairly recently established as law. The Greeks and Romans used

Occupational therapist Lynn Yasuda shows six-year-old Barbie Hanavan of Aurora, Colorado, how to use her feet to do various tasks. Barbie was born with only one arm, which is malformed. Her mother took thalidomide when she was pregnant with her.

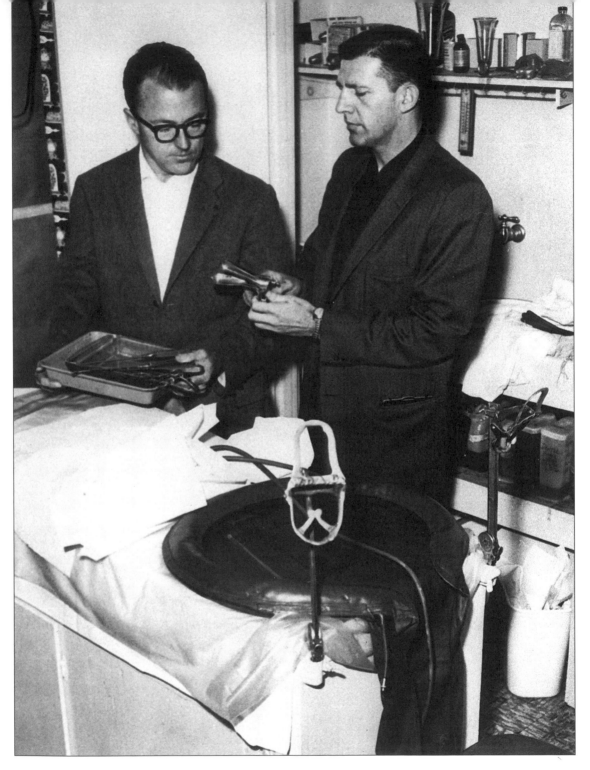

abortion as an accepted way to limit the size of their families. That attitude prevailed in much of England and other countries of Europe and their colonies through the 1700s. In the American colonies and later in the newly formed United States, abortion in the early months of pregnancy was left up to the discretion of the mother. Even in the later months of pregnancy, abortion was viewed as little more than a misdemeanor.[2]

It was not until the 19th century that states began to adopt laws regulating abortion, although they did so to protect the mother, not the fetus. During the early 1800s, 30 percent of the women undergoing abortions in New York died from the procedure.[3]

The first law, adopted by Connecticut in 1821, prohibited giving pregnant women poison to induce abortion. This was a common method at the time and one that was often fatal to both fetus and mother. The Connecticut law and others that followed applied only to mothers who had reached the "quickening" stage, the point when a woman can feel the fetus moving inside her.[4]

As the Industrial Revolution swept the country, the need for large families declined. People moved from farms and rural areas to the cities. Farmers began to use machines to do much of the work they had done by hand. By the late 1800s, women were entering the work force to supplement their families' incomes.

Between 1800 and 1900, the average number of children born to white women decreased from 7.04 to 3.56.[5] During this time, abortions became more common, and women turned to home remedies, such as plants and soap solutions. By the mid-1800s, one in five pregnancies ended in abortion, according to some estimates.[6]

The push to make abortion a crime came largely from medical doctors. The newly organized American Medical Association had several reasons for wanting to make abortions illegal. First, doctors feared for the safety of women who had abortions performed by unskilled practitioners or undertook to abort them-

Santa Clara County District Attorney Louis Bergna, left, and Detective Layton Gorham of the sheriff's office examine surgical tools and other equipment allegedly used in performing illegal abortions on women in the San Jose, California, area during the late 1950s.

selves. The medical profession also wanted to exert control over medical procedures. Licensed doctors believed they, not untrained practitioners, should be the ones to administer abortions. Many doctors, too, were morally opposed to performing abortions and believed they should be banned.[7]

The AMA lobbied legislatures and urged the public through newspaper articles to ban abortion. One physician, Horatio Storer, circulated flyers noting that more Protestant than Catholic women had abortions. These tracts fanned fears among the Protestant upper classes that Catholic immigrants would take over the population.[8]

The AMA campaign successfully turned society against abortion. During the last quarter of the 1800s, more than 40 states passed laws banning abortion.[9] Exceptions were made to save the mother's life, but most laws required at least one doctor to state that the abortion was necessary. The decision to have an abortion had effectively been removed from the woman's control and placed squarely under the doctor's authority.

Despite the widespread ban on abortion, women continued to have abortions. Estimates are that as many as one in three pregnancies ended in abortion during the early 20th century.[10] Rich, well-established women merely found a doctor willing to perform an abortion. Other women were forced to abort illegally through their own devices or at back-alley abortion mills. Often the illegal abortion clinics were no more than dirty rooms operated by untrained staff. Many women died at the hands of unskilled abortionists.

Ironically, it was doctors who, in the mid-1900s, once again worked to change attitudes about abortion—this time in favor of liberalizing the laws. Concerned over the numbers of women they saw injured and killed by illegal abortions, they sought to legalize abortions and thus move the procedure from the back alleys to sterile hospitals and clinics. Abortions done by skilled doctors under modern conditions had become as safe or safer than childbirth.

Doctors saw deformed babies born as the result of genetic defects, drugs such as thalidomide, and exposure to diseases such as German measles. Many doctors came to believe, as Sherri Finkbine did, that abortion was less repugnant than bringing a severely deformed baby into the world.

Doctors favoring the reform or repeal of abortion laws joined forces with women's groups and members of the clergy. Dr. Robert E. Hall, an assistant professor of obstetrics and gynecology at Columbia University's College of Physicians and Surgeons, noted that, because of advances in modern medicine, American women were rarely in physical danger from pregnancy. But, he said, damage to the mother's health and deformities to the fetus were much more common than death from childbirth. The New York abortion law, which permitted abortions only to save the life of the mother, was "inhumane and unrealistic,"[11] the doctor said.

As head of the Association for Humane Abortion, Dr. Hall sent questionnaires to New York obstetricians asking their views on abortion. Of the 1,372 who answered, 87 percent said they favored changes in the 83-year-old law.[12] They supported a model law proposed in 1959 by the American Law Institute. The proposed law would allow abortion in cases where the physical or mental health of the mother or the fetus was threatened or in cases of rape or incest.

Doctors were not alone in their efforts for abortion reform. By 1967, New York Governor Nelson Rockefeller was calling for revisions to the state's abortion law. The *New York Times* ran editorials that year urging the legislature to change the law. A National Opinion Research Center poll revealed that a majority of Americans, including Catholics, supported liberalized abortion laws.[13]

During the late 1960s, most of the opposition to abortion came from the Roman Catholic Church. In January 1967 a group with ties to the Catholic Church called the Right to Life Committee was formed to fight proposed

Demonstrators stand in front of the Allied Chemical Building in the Times Square area of New York City on March 12, 1967, to protest the defeat of a bill that would have made abortion legal. About 200 people attended the rally supporting legalized abortion.

changes in the New York State abortion law. The church said the procedure was "contrary to moral law" and forbade abortions even to save the life of the mother.[14] On Sunday, February 12, 1967, priests throughout New York State read a pastoral letter to their Catholic congregations urging them to fight the legislature's efforts to modify the law.[15]

Other religious groups, however, were taking opposite stands on abortion. In 1963, the General Assembly of the Unitarian Universalist Association passed a resolution calling the nation's abortion laws an "affront to human life and dignity."[16] Four years later, the Archbishop of Canterbury called for legalized abortion in Great Britain when the mental or physical health of the mother was in danger, there was a risk of a deformed child, or the pregnancy was the result of rape.[17]

The YWCA, the United Church of Christ, the United Methodist Church, the United Presbyterian Church, and the Episcopalian Church all lent support to the efforts to make abortion legal in New York.[18]

On May 22, 1967, New York City rabbis and Protestant ministers announced the formation of the Clergymen's Consultation Service on Abortion. Appearing on the front page of the *New York Times*, the story detailed the religious leaders' intention to help women obtain safe abortions.[19] The group's actions put the supporters of easing abortion laws firmly into the mainstream of American life.

The clergymen were joined in their stance the following month by the nation's most prestigious doctors association. On June 22, in another front-page *New York Times* story, the American Medical Association's House of Delegates declared its support of liberalized abortion laws.[20] It was the first time the doctors group had changed its position on abortion since 1871.

Slowly, a few states began to modify their abortion laws to include situations that endangered the health as well as the life of the mother and that might result in the birth of a deformed child. In 1967, Governor John Love of Colorado signed into law a bill that permitted abortions for those reasons and in the case of rape or incest. To obtain a legal abortion under Colorado law, however, a pregnant woman had to win the approval of a panel of three doctors.

California passed a similar bill in 1967 that permitted abortions when the mother's health was "gravely threatened." Governor Ronald Reagan "reluctantly" signed the bill, which had no residency requirement.[21]

By 1970, 12 states had passed liberalized abortion bills. Many more legislatures were considering bills that would make it easier to obtain abortions in their states. Even with the reforms, however, hundreds of thousands of American women continued to undergo illegal abortions. In California, an estimated 100,000 women had illegal abortions each year, while only 2,000 abortions were performed legally during the six months after the state's new law went into effect.[22]

Price, access to medical care, and abortion laws' restrictions all played a role in whether women resorted to illegal abortions. To obtain an abortion legally, women still had to fit certain guidelines set by the laws in their states. In most of the "reform" states, women had to convince a panel of doctors that childbirth would endanger their health or that they met the law's requirements in other ways.

Certification by psychiatrists or physicians was expensive, as was a hospital abortion. Charges could run as high as $700 (more than $2,600 in 1993 dollars), while an illegal abortion might cost only $200 (around $744 in 1993 dollars).[23] Women in search of abortions often had to travel long distances to states with more relaxed abortion laws. The trips added to the cost of the abortions and meant that poor and rural women seldom had access to legal abortions.

The reforms had done little to reduce the number of illegal abortions or to

California Governor Ronald Reagan talks to reporters during a news conference in March 1973. Reagan "reluctantly" signed a bill in 1967 that made abortions under certain conditions legal in California. In the 1980s, as president, Reagan opposed legalized abortion.

ease the terrible burdens placed on women seeking abortions. Led by women's groups, abortion rights activists began to lobby for the repeal of abortion laws. Mainstream organizations, such as Planned Parenthood Federation of America, the YWCA, and groups concerned with overpopulation, joined the battle to lift restrictions against abortion.

In 1970, the New York State Legislature voted to repeal its abortion law.

The bill passed by one vote after Assemblyman George Michaels changed his vote. Though it cost him reelection, Michaels said he voted for repeal because his son, a medical intern, had told him of the ghetto women who were suffering and dying because of illegal abortions.[24]

By the end of 1970, Alaska had joined New York and Hawaii in repealing laws that banned abortions during the first months of pregnancy. Washington State repealed its abortion law the following year, and 19 other states had liberalized their abortion laws by the end of 1973. Many others, however, continued to resist efforts to change the laws.

On another front, the push to legalize abortion began meeting with more success. In 1969, Federal District Judge Gerhard Gesell struck down a Washington, D.C., law that prohibited doctors from performing abortions except when the mother's health or life was in danger. Dr. Milan Vuitch, arrested by district police for performing illegal abortions, had appealed his conviction to the federal court. In his ruling, Judge Gesell said the district law was unconstitutionally vague and suggested Congress rewrite it to make it apply to specific circumstances. The Supreme Court later upheld the law.

Encouraged by the Gesell ruling, abortion rights activists decided they might have better luck in the courts than in individual state legislatures. In several states, the American Civil Liberties Union (ACLU)—an organization formed to protect people's constitutional rights—began filing cases seeking repeal of abortion laws. The ACLU and the James Madison Constitutional Law Institute filed suit in 1970 on behalf of the YWCA of Princeton, New Jersey, a group of doctors, and several other organizations against the state of New Jersey. The suit claimed the state's abortion law was unconstitutional because it violated the rights of women and hindered and threatened doctors. Many of these suits began making their way through the court system, as the losing side appealed the decision to the next higher court.

Women demonstrate against an abortion reform bill on the steps of the New York State Capitol in Albany on March 23, 1970. Others, at left, demonstrate in support of the reform bill, under consideration by the legislature.

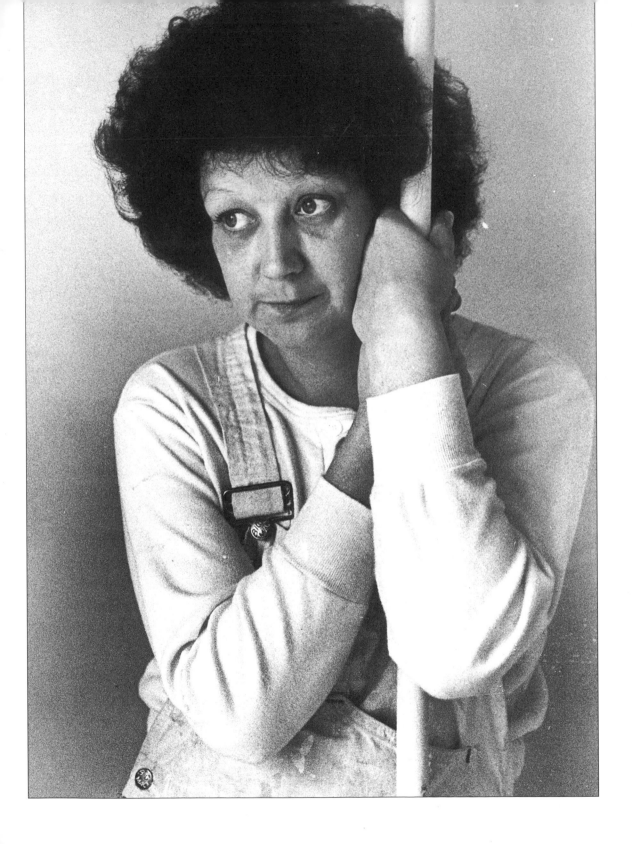

CHAPTER THREE

Search for Jane Roe

Rapid and simple abortion referral must be readily available through state and local public health departments, medical societies, or other nonprofit organizations.[1]

— Recommended standards for abortion services, adopted by the executive board of the American Public Health Association in 1970

In Texas, as elsewhere, abortion rights activists had been working to ease the state's laws on abortion. Under Texas law, abortion was permitted only to save the life of the mother.

By the 1960s, an extensive underground network had developed to advise women on abortions. There was even a package deal for women to get an abortion in Mexico. For $345, a woman could get a flight to El Paso from Dallas, a motel room, hospital care, counseling, and a carnation with breakfast.[2] Women would arrive in El Paso Friday night, cross the border, have an abortion Saturday morning, and be back in Dallas by Saturday night.

In October 1969, the Women's Liberation Birth Control Information

Norma McCorvey, 35, takes time from her job as a house painter to pose for a photograph in January 1983. McCorvey agreed to be the plaintiff in the *Roe v. Wade* abortion case in the 1970s. Her lawyers referred to her as Jane Roe to hide her identity.

Center in Austin, Texas—an abortion referral project—placed an ad in an alternative newspaper, the *Rag*, with a hotline number for women to call. With the publication of the ad and the growing number of people using their services, members of the referral project began to get nervous. They worried they would be arrested for helping Texas women get abortions. Members of the group asked a friend, Sarah Weddington, to research the law. A recent graduate of University of Texas School of Law, Weddington had been involved in a number of women's causes. Though not a volunteer at the referral service, she quickly volunteered to do the research.

At the time, Weddington was assisting one of her law professors in his work on the American Bar Association's Special Committee on the Reevaluation of Ethical Standards. The daughter of a Methodist minister, Sarah had married Ron Weddington in 1968. They lived in inexpensive student housing near the university, where Ron was attending law school. At 24, she was enthusiastic, energetic, and eager to put her law skills to good use.

Weddington's research soon led her to a number of cases that related to the abortion issue. In 1965, the U.S. Supreme Court had struck down a Connecticut law that banned the use of birth control devices. In *Griswold v. Connecticut*, the Court ruled that married couples were protected by the right of privacy to use contraceptives. In his majority opinion, Justice William O. Douglas said the right of privacy was protected by the First, Third, Fourth, Fifth, and Ninth amendments to the Constitution. Justice John Harlan, who voted with the majority, wrote that he believed marital privacy was protected by the Fourteenth Amendment, which states that no state can deprive "any person of life, liberty, or property, without due process of law" and that no person can be denied "the equal protection of the laws."

In a separate opinion, Justices Earl Warren, William Brennan, and Arthur Goldburg wrote that the privacy right was based in the Ninth Amend-

Associate Justice William O. Douglas, photographed in 1965

ment. That amendment says that certain rights exist even if they are not named specifically in the Constitution.

Weddington thought that abortion might well be considered a private matter and that the right to privacy might apply to women seeking abortions.

More recently, the California Supreme Court had voted 4 to 3 to overturn the conviction of a doctor convicted of helping a young woman obtain an abortion. The Court, in its 1969 ruling, said the California law in effect at the time was unconstitutionally vague. The law allowed abortion only "to preserve the life of the woman." But it did not define the meaning of the phrase. Did it apply to a woman's threatened suicide? What if the pregnancy damaged a woman's health or shortened her life?

The ruling in the case, *California v. Belous*, also described abortion as a "fundamental right." A fundamental right is one that is guaranteed to a person by the Constitution. To infringe on a fundamental right, a state must prove its interests in the case far outweigh the individual's right. The judges' opinion in the *Belous* case read:

> The fundamental right of the woman to choose
> whether to bear children follows from the Su-
> preme Court's and this Court's repeated acknowl-
> edgment of a "right of privacy" and of "liberty" in
> matters related to marriage, family, and sex.[3]

Weddington soon realized that the Texas efforts were part of a national move to change abortion laws. And the courts—at least some of the rulings—seemed to be favorable to the abortion activists' cause.

Excited by what she had learned, Weddington shared the results of her research with the referral project's volunteers. Judy Smith, one of the organizers of the project, suggested they go to court. She thought the group should challenge the constitutionality of the state's abortion law. Smith and the other group members agreed that Weddington should be the one to handle the case.

Weddington was overwhelmed by the idea. Young and inexperienced, she had never argued a contested case in court. A few divorce cases, wills, and an adoption amounted to the sum total of her court work. She urged Smith to find someone with more experience.

But the group members were insistent. They had been impressed with Weddington's research. Besides, she was willing to work for nothing, and the group had little money to spend on a lawsuit.

Weddington began to reconsider. She had never run from a challenge. As a law student, she had been one of five women out of a freshman class of 125. If she took on the case, it would give her experience in constitutional law. And with their few expenses, she and Ron could manage financially on savings, her work with the professor, and his part-time job.

Weddington had another reason for agreeing to take the case. In 1967, as an unmarried graduate student, she had become pregnant by Ron. The young couple, with little money and in the midst of school, decided not to have the child. They eventually found a doctor in Mexico, who performed an abortion on Sarah. Fortunately, the doctor was skilled, and Sarah had no ill effects from the procedure. But the fear and uncertainty she endured left their mark. She wanted to do what she could so that others wouldn't have to go through similar experiences.[4]

The pros outweighed the cons. Weddington agreed to take the case.

At the time she agreed to fight Texas's abortion law in court, Weddington had no idea it would one day take her to the Supreme Court. She did know, however, that she would need help. While a law student, Weddington had met Linda Coffee, a classmate with whom she often studied. Coffee worked for a small Dallas law firm that specialized in bankruptcy cases. Weddington called and asked if Coffee would be interested in helping with the abortion case. Coffee agreed.

The first order of business for the two lawyers was to find a plaintiff. A plaintiff is the person on whose behalf a lawsuit is filed. The court will not hear a case based solely on an abstract question. Weddington and Coffee could not simply ask the court to decide whether the Texas abortion law was constitutional. They had to find people who were directly affected by the law and who could prove to the court that the law unjustly harmed them. Plaintiffs in such a situation are said to have standing.

After researching the question, the two lawyers decided against using the referral project or its volunteers as plaintiffs. No one from the project had been arrested, and none of the volunteers suffered directly from the abortion law. Without the right plaintiff, Coffee and Weddington feared, the judge might throw the case out of court before it even had had a hearing.

Both Weddington and Coffee spread the word among friends and associates that they were looking for a plaintiff for their case. The Dallas Committee, a group of women involved in the effort to liberalize abortion, met frequently to discuss women's issues. At one of the meetings Linda Coffee spoke about the lawsuit she was working on with Weddington.

After her talk, a woman told Coffee she and her husband might be willing to be plaintiffs in the case. The woman, who was married, suffered from a condition that prevented her from taking birth control pills. Her doctor had told her a pregnancy might harm her health. She and her husband used another form of birth control, but it was less reliable than birth control pills. If she were to become pregnant, an abortion seemed the only way to ensure her health. But the Texas law allowed abortions only if pregnancy endangered the mother's life. Nothing was said about the mother's *health*. The woman and her husband believed that the state law put her health at risk and was therefore unconstitutional.

Coffee and Weddington decided to accept the woman's offer. They believed she and her husband could show that the law affected them directly. Because the couple did not want their names to be used in the case, Coffee and Weddington called them John and Mary Doe in the suit.

The two lawyers continued to look for another plaintiff. Lawyers often name more than one plaintiff to make sure their case is heard. That way, if one plaintiff lacks standing, the court may still hear the case of the second plaintiff. Their "ideal" plaintiff, Weddington and Coffee knew, would be a pregnant woman who wanted an abortion. Though the abortion referral project came in contact with many women who fit that description, involving them in the court case would have meant a long delay. That might have made an abortion risky or impossible. The women needed to undergo abortions while still in the early stages of their pregnancies.

A few weeks later, Coffee got a call from a young woman who had been referred by a lawyer she knew, Henry McCluskey. The woman was pregnant and wanted an abortion. Her name was Norma McCorvey.

Single and in her early 20s, McCorvey said she would lose her job as a waitress if she continued her pregnancy. She had little money and had already had one child, cared for by her mother. The young woman said she could not afford to pay for an out-of-state abortion. She also suggested that she had been raped. In response to the lawyers' questions, she acknowledged that she had never reported the rape, and she provided few details on how she became pregnant. The lawyers decided not to claim that McCorvey had been raped if she agreed to go to court. They believed all women should be able to choose whether to have an abortion, not just rape victims.[5] Years later, McCorvey changed her story and said she had not been raped.[6]

Weddington and Coffee explained the Texas law and why they wanted to challenge it in court. They told McCorvey what role she would play in the case if she agreed to be a plaintiff. McCorvey would have to sign an affidavit stating that she was pregnant and wanted an abortion. She would not have to appear in court or answer questions from other lawyers. The case would cost her nothing. The two lawyers worked free, and others paid court costs. And, Weddington and Coffee said, McCorvey wouldn't have to tell anyone she was the plaintiff in the case. They would use another name or pseudonym when they referred to her in court.

McCorvey agreed. She signed the affidavit. From then on, the lawyers would refer to her as Jane Roe. Under that name, she would become one of the most famous plaintiffs in U.S. history.

CHAPTER FOUR

A Case for Abortion Rights

[T]he state's position will be, and is, that the right of the child to life is superior to that of a woman's right to privacy.[1]

— John Tolle, Dallas DA's office
representing Texas in *Roe v. Wade*
in federal district court

Now that they had their plaintiffs, Weddington and Coffee had to decide where to file their suits. Most cases begin in state court. However, cases may be filed in federal court when a constitutional question, a federal law, or a treaty is at issue.

The lawyers decided to file their case in federal district court. They were challenging a state law on constitutional issues, so they believed the case qualified for federal review. Weddington and Coffee believed, too, that the federal courts were more liberal than the state courts. They hoped that a favorable verdict by a federal court would have impact on other abortion laws nationwide.

The cases would be filed against Henry Wade, district attorney of Dallas County. As DA, Wade was elected to enforce the laws of the state, including the abortion law. He had gained a measure of fame as the DA who won Jack Ruby's conviction for the murder of Lee Harvey Oswald, the accused assassin of President John F. Kennedy.

On March 3, 1970, Linda Coffee filed two cases in the federal courthouse in Dallas. Once docketed, the cases would become *Roe v. Wade* and *Doe v. Wade*.

The two lawyers worked hard to complete their briefs before the court deadline. Lawyers are required to state the arguments supporting their case in papers, or briefs, filed with the court. Weddington and Coffee also decided to file their cases as class action suits. That means that the plaintiff is joined in the suit by other people in similar circumstances. In the case of *Roe*, Weddington and Coffee would argue on behalf of all pregnant women in Texas who were seeking or would seek to have an abortion and whose lives were not endangered by their pregnancies.

As Coffee and Weddington had hoped, the two cases—because they were so similar—would be heard as one case. Three federal judges would hear the case: Federal District Judge William M. Taylor, Federal Circuit Judge Irving L. Goldberg, and Federal District Judge Sarah T. Hughes.

Weddington and Coffee were elated. After graduation, Coffee had been a clerk in Judge Hughes's office. The judge had made national news when she administered the oath of office to Lyndon B. Johnson aboard *Air Force One* after John F. Kennedy's assassination. Coffee viewed the judge as fair-minded and thought she might be more open than some other judges to the abortion case.

On May 22, 1970, Coffee and Weddington made their way to the Dallas Federal Courthouse for the hearing. Outside, demonstrators showed their support for the lawyers' case with signs that read: MY BODY, MY DECISION and

COMPULSORY PREGNANCY IS A CRUEL AND UNUSUAL PUNISHMENT.[2] Virginia Whitehill, a supporter of Zero Population Growth and an organizer of the Dallas Committee, had arranged the demonstration. She and other members of the committee sat in the courtroom waiting for the hearing to begin. Every seat was filled.

Before the hearing, Weddington and Coffee had agreed to join forces with two attorneys representing Dr. James H. Hallford. Dr. Hallford had been indicted and charged with performing illegal abortions. His attorneys, Fred Bruner and Roy L. Merrill, Jr., were challenging the legality of the Texas abortion law.

Standing before the three judges in the courtroom, Linda Coffee spoke first. She and Weddington would have 15 minutes to argue their case. Coffee had argued cases in court before, but most involved bankruptcy. This was the most important case the young lawyer had ever handled. Nevertheless, she set forth the technicalities of the case in her usual calm style.

First, she defended the plaintiffs' right to a hearing. They had standing and were entitled to sue in federal court, she argued, because the Texas law affected them directly and interfered with their constitutional rights. She contended that the law violated the First, Fourth, Fifth, Eighth, Ninth, and Fourteenth amendments. Coffee then discussed how the Texas law violated the First Amendment. She said the ban on abortions interfered with the right of doctors to talk to their clients about a medical procedure.

The judges didn't appear to be impressed by the argument. Judge Hughes asked her to comment on how the Ninth Amendment applied to the case. The Ninth Amendment says the people retain certain rights even though they are not specifically noted in the Constitution.

Coffee replied, "I don't think it makes any difference . . . whether you say that the rights involved are First Amendment rights or Ninth Amendment rights. I feel they are so important that they deserve the special protection that has been accorded to First Amendment rights."[3]

Coffee made a few other points, and then her time was up. Weddington took her place before the judges. She was 25 years old and had never before argued a contested case in court. Her voice shook as she began her statement, but she soon gained confidence. In a clear, strong voice, softened by her soft Texan drawl, Weddington began to state the facts of her case.

She noted that the state clung to the law to protect what it said were the rights of the fetus. But, she questioned, does the fetus have rights if it is not human? And how do we know when a fetus becomes human? "It is almost impossible to define a point at which life begins,"[4] Weddington told the court.

Goldberg asked her to talk about how the Texas law might violate the Ninth Amendment. Did the state have a "compelling reason," Goldberg asked, to override the "right" to an abortion?

The only compelling reason for the state to regulate abortion, Weddington replied, was to protect the woman. As long as abortions were performed by licensed doctors, she argued, the state had no good reason to ban the procedure. And, she noted, there was also no reason for the state to set up different standards for married and single women.

Once again, the court signalled that time was up.

During their allotted time, Bruner and Merrill, Dr. James H. Hallford's attorneys, argued that the Texas abortion law was unconstitutionally vague.

At the signal, they sat down. The hearing for the plaintiffs was over.

For the next 30 minutes, Jay Floyd and John Tolle argued the state's case. Neatly dressed and professional looking, Floyd worked as a lawyer in the enforcement division of the Texas attorney general's office. His specialty was liquor law.

Floyd argued that the plaintiffs had no right to sue in federal court. He noted that the state had never prosecuted a woman for undergoing an abortion. He said women could not say that the law hurt them. Therefore, he argued, Jane Roe and Mary Doe had no standing. Jane Roe, he noted, had probably already had her baby by now. Even if she were still pregnant, he noted, it was too late for her to undergo a safe abortion. Mary Doe, he continued, was not pregnant and never had been.

Judge Goldberg noted that some of the children involved in the school desegregation cases of the 1950s had long since graduated from high school by the time the court heard their cases.

"What would give them [Roe and Doe] standing in a case like this to test the constitutionality of this statute?" Judge Hughes asked Floyd. "Apparently you don't think that anybody has standing."[5]

Floyd went on to argue that the Constitution does not mention a "right" to abortion. He disputed Coffee's claim that the First Amendment protected abortion. Judge Hughes told him the court agreed with his view of the First Amendment in this case.

When questioned about the Ninth Amendment, Floyd went to the heart of the state's case. Texas, he asserted, had to protect the fetus. That was the state's "compelling interest" in limiting abortions. He argued further that the right to privacy cited in other cases means only the right to be left alone. It had nothing to do with abortion, Floyd contended.

John Tolle, a lawyer with the Dallas DA's office, took over for Floyd. Though he accepted the fact that no one knew when life began, he argued that the state still had "a right to protect life . . . in whatever stage it may be in."[6] He contended that it was up to the state legislature to decide when abortions should be allowed. Tolle ended by saying the state put the fetus's right to life ahead of the woman's right to privacy. The arguments were over. All either side could do now was wait for the judges to rule on the cases.

Linda Coffee in a 1970 photograph that ran in the *Houston Post* after she and Sarah Weddington won their abortion case in federal district court.

On June 17, 1970, the court handed down its 13-page decision. The Texas abortion law, all three judges said, was unconstitutional. They ruled that abortion was a fundamental right, and the law unconstitutionally interfered with that right. Women, the judges said, had a right to choose not to have children. That right, they said, was based on the Ninth Amendment.

The ruling supported Dr. Hallford's claim as well, that the law was too vague. According to the court, the Fourteenth Amendment protected Dr.

Hallford from being punished by the law. Under the Fourteenth Amendment, citizens can not be deprived "of life, liberty, or property, without due process of law." The judges also ruled that Jane Roe and Dr. Hallford had a right to sue. The Does, however, lacked standing.

Weddington and Coffee's victory celebration was short-lived. The court had ruled in their favor that the law was unconstitutional. But the judges had not ordered the state to stop enforcing the law. The court, it appeared, did not want to interfere further with state government.[7]

Henry Wade, the Dallas DA, announced publicly that he would continue to enforce the old law. "Apparently, we're still free to try them [doctors who perform abortions not allowed by the old law], so we'll do just that,"[8] he told the press shortly after the decision was announced. Despite the court decision, a woman still could not obtain a legal abortion in Texas unless her life was at risk.

For Norma McCorvey, the Jane Roe in the case, the decision came too late. Shortly after the court ruling, she had her baby and put her up for adoption.

Coffee and Weddington decided to appeal. Since the judges had not issued an order to enforce the law, the plaintiffs had a right to take the matter to a higher court. Usually, lawyers appealing cases will work their way through successively higher levels in the court system. Normally, a federal case would be appealed to the circuit court. Only then would it be appealed to the U.S. Supreme Court.

But the state had made it clear it would continue to enforce a law that had been ruled unconstitutional. Because of that, the law allowed Weddington and Coffee to skip a step. They appealed directly to the Supreme Court.

Each year the Supreme Court receives thousands of requests to hear cases. These requests are called petitions for certiorari. Most of the petitions are rejected outright. Some are ruled improper. Others don't qualify to be heard by the Supreme Court for other reasons. The other petitions are reviewed by

Sarah Weddington poses for the *Houston Post* in June 1970 after winning a victory in *Roe v. Wade* in federal district court in Dallas.

the Supreme Court justices. Four justices must vote for a case if the full Court is to consider it. Only about 150 cases are argued before the full Court each year.

Cases involving abortion were pending in 11 states in 1970. Three-judge federal courts were considering 20 cases. Lawyers in five cases, including *Roe*, had petitioned the Supreme Court for review.

On May 21, 1971, the Supreme Court published the list of cases it would hear during the coming October term. *Roe v. Wade*, number 808 on the Court docket, and *Doe v. Bolton*, a Georgia case, number 971 on the docket, were among those to be heard by the Court during its next session. The *Roe* brief, written arguments supporting the lawyers' case, would be due June 17. The state would have to submit its brief 30 days later. After the justices had reviewed the briefs, they would schedule oral arguments. At that time, lawyers for both sides would present their case in person before the Supreme Court.

Weddington and Coffee had a mountain of work to do before then.

CHAPTER FIVE

Work, Work, Work

*We deal with a right of privacy older
than the Bill of Rights—older than our
political parties, older than our school
system.[1]*

— Justice William O. Douglas
Griswold et al v. Connecticut

The Texas case had drawn the attention of abortion
rights activists nationwide. Harriet Pilpel, an attorney with Planned Parenthood Federation of America, phoned with advice. Pilpel had worked on the
Griswold case, winning a ruling from the Supreme Court that married couples
were protected by the right of privacy to use contraceptives.

Roy Lucas, who had worked on the *Vuitch* appeal to the Supreme Court,
offered his help. Milan Vuitch, the doctor arrested by District of Columbia
police for performing illegal abortions, had won a ruling in federal court that the
district's abortion law was unconstitutionally vague, but the Supreme Court
later upheld the law. As director and general counsel of the James Madison Law
Institute in New York, Lucas was deeply involved in the abortion issue. He told

The abortion issue began to draw large crowds of protesters on both sides in the
1960s and early 1970s. Here, demonstrators against abortions rally on the east steps
of the Capitol on November 20, 1971, in Washington, D.C. Those who favored making
abortion legal demonstrated on the west side of the Capitol.

Weddington the institute staff would help research the briefs for the Supreme Court. He also promised to help pay some of the costs.

The case would require a great deal of research, and both Coffee and Weddington had full-time jobs. Even though they were working free, they needed money to pay court fees and to print the thick stack of papers supporting their case. Hundreds of pages had to be printed for the Court and photocopied for the opposing lawyers. Coffee and Weddington accepted Lucas's offer of help.

Weddington had begun work as assistant city attorney in Fort Worth, Texas, in the fall of 1970. She was the first woman to hold the job. Once word got out that the *Roe* case was headed for the Supreme Court, Weddington's boss gave her a choice. She could continue to work for the city, or she could quit and work on the case. Weddington decided she couldn't pass up the chance to argue a case as important as *Roe* before the Supreme Court.

Lucas and the staff at the James Madison Institute had agreed to work on the briefs for the *Roe* case, but with the June 17 deadline looming, Weddington discovered little had been done. Lucas had asked the Court to postpone the deadline. The new deadline was August 1.

Weddington realized she had better get to New York and speed up the process. Lucas arranged for her to stay in a small room at the Women's Medical Center in Manhattan. Leaving Ron to run the couple's newly established law firm, she flew to New York in mid-June.

During the long, hot summer days, Weddington worked with the Institute staff researching and writing briefs for a stack of abortion cases. The cases were scheduled in Court that summer, and the overworked staff still had much work to do on them.

Work on the *Roe* case seemed always to be set aside. As the summer wore on, Weddington realized she would never be able to finish the *Roe* brief by

August 1. Again, the Supreme Court granted an extension—this time to August 17.

Weddington knew she needed help. Linda Coffee was working full-time with the bankruptcy firm in Dallas. The Institute staff was still swamped with work. Weddington called her husband, Ron. He was in the midst of remodeling their house. But the Supreme Court wouldn't wait much longer. Ron agreed to come to New York to help with the *Roe* brief.

For the next five weeks, the two young lawyers reviewed every abortion case and decision they could find. They studied other Supreme Court decisions that might relate to their case. These past decisions, called precedents, were used to bolster their arguments in the *Roe* brief.

Ron worked on the technical parts of the argument. Sarah focused on the merits of the case, the reasons why she believed the Court should decide in Roe's favor. Students at the institute pitched in. One helped with the research. Another proofread the brief.

The Supreme Court usually limits the length of briefs to 150 pages. Packed into those pages, the *Roe* lawyers had to list all their reasons for claiming that the Texas abortion law was unconstitutional. They argued that the abortion law violated their plaintiffs' rights guaranteed by the First, Fourth, Ninth, and Fourteenth amendments. Citing experts in several fields, the brief outlined the history of abortion law in the United States. It detailed the medical, legal, and religious aspects of abortion. The brief also described how pregnancy affected women's lives and mental health.

Abortion rights groups and others filed briefs that would also be submitted to the Supreme Court on behalf of the case. The amicus curiae ("friend of the court") briefs, as they are called, were filed by lawyers whose clients could be affected by the *Roe* decision. Each brief addressed one aspect of the *Roe* argument.

The U.S. Supreme Court in Washington, D.C. The slogan above proclaims "Equal Justice Under Law."

Jimmye Kimmey, executive director of the Association of the Study of Abortion, volunteered to organize the amicus briefs. Her association provided information on abortion to other organizations. Religious groups, Planned Parenthood Federation of America, the American Association of Planned Parenthood Physicians, Zero Population Growth, medical groups, law professors, and women's organizations all submitted briefs. In all, 42 amicus briefs were filed in support of *Roe*.

Among the few groups filing amicus briefs on the state's side were the National Right to Life Committee, the League for Infants, Fetuses and the Elderly, and the Association of Texas Diocesan Attorneys. The attorneys general in Arizona, Connecticut, Kentucky, Nebraska, and Utah also filed a brief supporting Texas. When they were finished, the briefs—along with the plaintiff's and the state's arguments in the case—stood a foot tall.[2]

The paper mound continued to grow. On Roy Lucas's advice, Weddington and the institute staff put together a 500-page appendix to the brief. The appendix included tables, graphs, statistics, articles, and other information related to abortion.

Ruth Bowers, a Texas philanthropist who donated generously to Planned Parenthood, footed much of the bill for printing and other expenses. The James Madison Law Institute picked up some of the Court filing costs and provided research assistance, as well as the free room, such as it was, for Ron and Sarah. Other funds came from supporters nationwide, who sent in donations. Among them was Thomas Cabot, a Boston businessman, who gave $15,000 to the cause.[3] A smaller gift came from a doctor in Harlem who wrote about the horror of seeing women suffer from illegal abortions.[4] Medical school professors, doctors, lawyers, law students, members of women's groups, and others volunteered to help get the brief done on time.

While Weddington and others were immersed in the paperwork involving the case, the plaintiff was far removed from the activity. Norma McCorvey, after giving birth, had disappeared from the scene. She had not attended the federal court hearing because of her pregnancy, and, later, she would not be at the Supreme Court hearings.

On August 17, the *Roe* lawyers delivered 40 copies of their brief to the U.S. Supreme Court. They had made the deadline. Now they had to prepare for oral arguments before the Court.

Lucas had listed himself as lead attorney when he filed the Court documents for *Roe*. Weddington and Coffee had been involved in the case from the start. Who would argue the case before the Supreme Court?

In July, Lucas had told the Court he would argue the case. Coffee and Weddington, who had not yet learned of Lucas's action, had agreed that Weddington would present the case before the Court. To compromise, Weddington asked the Court to allow each side one hour to argue its case. Usually, the Court limits arguments to one-half hour for each side. Weddington also asked that she and Lucas be allowed to take turns arguing the case. The Court denied both requests.

Lucas argued that he was more experienced than Weddington. But the plaintiffs in the case and many of those who had worked on it wanted a woman to argue before the Court. They urged Weddington to argue the case.

She accepted the challenge. On November 24, Linda Coffee sent a notice to the Supreme Court listing Weddington as the lawyer presenting oral arguments for *Roe*. She noted that both Jane Roe and Mary and John Doe, the plaintiffs, had requested Weddington. The court clerk recorded that Weddington would argue for *Roe*. Jay Floyd would argue the case for the state of Texas.

Few cases are won in oral arguments, according to court experts. But, the experts agree, some cases are lost because they were poorly argued in Court. Weddington wanted to make sure she was well-prepared.

The lawyers were to argue their cases in the Supreme Court on December 13, 1971. Weddington immersed herself in the case. She attended a Supreme Court hearing and watched the proceedings carefully. Preparing for her own appearance, she noted where each lawyer stood, what they wore, how the Court operated.

She rehearsed her performance in two moot courts. The moot, or pretend, courts were set up like the Supreme Court, with volunteers playing the roles of the justices. Weddington went through her arguments just as if the court were the real thing. The pretend justices interrupted her arguments with questions. In the real Supreme Court, justices often ask questions of the lawyers presenting their cases.

During their research for the brief, she and Ron had studied the decisions issued by each justice. They had read about the justices' politics, their interests, and their personal lives. Now Weddington reviewed that information, trying to tailor her arguments to each justice.

Warren E. Burger, chief justice of the Court, and Harry A. Blackmun had often been called the "Minnesota Twins." Both were from that state and had gone to Sunday school together as children.[5] Both had been appointed by President Richard Nixon, Burger in 1969 and Blackmun in 1970. Blackmun had voted with Burger on almost every case during his first term.[6] Burger was a social friend of Nixon, who opposed abortion. Court watchers put both justices in the conservative wing of the Court. They were likely to support strict abortion laws.

William O. Douglas had been appointed in 1939 by President Franklin D. Roosevelt. The oldest and most senior member, Douglas was considered the Court's most liberal justice. He most certainly would vote to strike down the abortion laws.

Joining Douglas in the liberal wing were William J. Brennan, Jr., and

President Richard Nixon, center, congratulates William H. Rehnquist, right, as Lewis F. Powell, Jr., left, looks on. Both men were commissioned as associate justices of the Supreme Court on December 22, 1971. They took their oath of office on January 7, 1972.

Thurgood Marshall. Brennan, appointed by President Dwight D. Eisenhower in 1956, had voted to strike down the law banning birth control devices in *Griswold v. Connecticut*. He would probably vote for *Roe*. Marshall, the first and only black member then on the Court, would also be likely to vote against abortion laws. Appointed by President Lyndon B. Johnson in 1967, Marshall was a strong supporter of civil and individual rights.

That left two remaining justices, Byron R. White and Potter Stewart. Stewart, appointed in 1958 by President Eisenhower, had voted against most of the liberal opinions of the Warren Court.[7] He had also voted against *Griswold*. But other votes had placed him in the middle of the Court. White, likewise, tended toward the middle with his votes. Appointed by President John F. Kennedy in 1962, White had cast his vote for the right of privacy in the *Griswold* case. But he was also "tough" on crime and voted with Burger on those issues.

Two other justices, John Marshall Harlan and Hugo Black, Jr., had resigned in September due to ill health. Nixon had appointed Lewis F. Powell, Jr., and William H. Rehnquist, to the Court. Because they had not yet been sworn in, they would not hear the case. The case would be heard by a seven-person Court.

Weddington would have 30 minutes to present her arguments. She would be followed by the state's attorney, who would argue his case for 30 minutes, also. During the same hearing, the Court would also hear arguments in the Georgia abortion case, *Doe v. Bolton*. The plaintiffs in that case claimed the more liberal Georgia abortion law was unconstitutional. Georgia allowed abortions but required the woman to get permission from a panel of doctors. The Court would review both types of laws: Texas's strict law and Georgia's liberal one. A decision in the cases would affect abortion laws throughout the nation.

CHAPTER SIX

To the Supreme Court

Because of the impact on the woman, this certainly . . . is a matter . . . of such fundamental and basic concern to the woman involved that she should be allowed to make the choice as to whether to continue or terminate her pregnancy.[1]

— Sarah Weddington
in her oral arguments in *Roe v. Wade*

The honorable, the chief justice, and the associate justices of the Supreme Court of the United States. Oyez, oyez, oyez. All persons having business before the honorable, the Supreme Court of the United States, are admonished to draw near and give their attention for the court is now sitting. God save the United States and this honorable court.[2]

This photograph shows the room where Supreme Court cases are argued. The justices enter through the velvet drapes and sit in the chairs before the wooden bench.

From left, Ron Weddington, Sarah Weddington, U.S. Representative George Mahon, and Sarah's mother, Lena Katherine Ragle, in Washington, D.C., on December 13, 1971, the day the Supreme Court heard the first arguments in *Roe v. Wade*

With those words the clerk announced the opening of the Supreme Court's session on December 13, 1971. Scheduled that morning were arguments on the two abortion cases. The seven justices stepped from behind velvet curtains and took their seats at the bench. Chief Justice Burger sat in the center, with Douglas on his right and Brennan on his left. The associate justices sat in order of how long they had served on the Court. Blackmun, the newest justice, sat on the far left. Next to him was White. To the far right sat Marshall, the second-newest associate justice. Next to Blackmun sat White. Stewart sat next to Marshall.

This was known as "ladies' day" among the court staff. Three women would be presenting cases. Weddington would argue for *Roe*, Margie Pitts Hames would argue for *Doe* in the Georgia case, and Dorothy Beasley would plead Georgia's case. Few women attended law school then, and even fewer appeared before the Supreme Court to argue cases. That fact was apparent to the women in the abortion cases when they discovered there was no women's restroom in the lawyers' lounge.[3]

Weddington would be the first to speak to the justices. She sat at the table on the left, directly in front of the bench. Sitting with her were Linda Coffee and Roy Lucas. Ron Weddington sat in the lawyers' section. Behind Weddington's table, Margie Pitts Hames and the other attorney for *Doe* in the Georgia case sat waiting for their turn to speak. At the front table to the right, Jay Floyd and Texas Attorney General Crawford Martin conferred with their team representing Texas in the *Roe* case. Behind them were Dorothy Beasley and the rest of the team for Georgia.

Among those in the audience were Weddington's mother and a crowd of supporters from Texas and elsewhere who had been active in the fight to legalize abortion. John and Mary Doe sat in seats reserved by Weddington for them. Norma McCorvey did not attend. About 350 people filled the small room. All 85 seats reserved for the press were filled.

Everyone rose as the justices walked in and took their seats. In hushed silence, the audience sat down. At 10:07 A.M., Chief Justice Burger addressed Weddington. "Mrs. Weddington, you may proceed whenever you are ready."[4]

The young lawyer rose and stepped to the lectern before the bench. It was only the second time she had appeared in court in a contested case.

Weddington spoke of the effect of pregnancy on a woman's life. She noted that the decision to have children is a fundamental right and should be made by the woman. "Because of the impact on the woman," Weddington told the Court, "this certainly . . . is a matter . . . of such fundamental and basic concern to the woman involved that she should be allowed to make the choice as to whether to continue or terminate her pregnancy."[5]

White asked her what part of the Constitution guaranteed a right to abortion. Weddington said the right could be based on both the Ninth and the Fourteenth amendments. In its majority opinion, the Court had already ruled in the *Griswold* case that the right to privacy is based on the Ninth Amendment.

The right to an abortion could also be found in the Fourteenth Amendment, Weddington said. The Fourteenth Amendment says the government cannot deprive anyone of "life, liberty, or property without due process of law." The due process clause of the Fourteenth Amendment had been used as a basis of Judge John Harlan's opinion in the *Griswold* case.

"I do feel that the Ninth Amendment is an appropriate place for the freedom to rest," Weddington told White. "I think the Fourteenth Amendment is an equally appropriate place, under the rights of persons to life [and] liberty. . . . In as far as liberty is meaningful, that liberty to these women would mean liberty from being forced to continue the unwanted pregnancy."[6]

In response to further questioning from White, Weddington said, "We originally brought the suit alleging . . . the due process clause, [the] equal protection clause, the Ninth Amendment, and a variety of others."[7]

"And anything else that might have been appropriate," added White.[8]

The audience, and Weddington, laughed. White made it sound like the plaintiffs were using everything—including the kitchen sink—to win their case.

After several other questions from the justices, Weddington noted that the state of Texas and the Constitution granted rights to people only after birth. The fetus had no rights in law. Asked if Texas law gave rights to unborn children regarding trusts and wills, she answered, "No, your honor, only if they are born alive."[9]

After a few more questions, the red light on the lectern lit up. That was the signal that Weddington's time was over. She had spoken for 25 minutes. Her final five minutes would be used later to argue points the state's attorney made. "Thank you, Mrs. Weddington," Burger said.[10] She sat down, and Jay Floyd stepped up to make his case.

"It's an old joke," Floyd began, "but when a man argues against two beautiful ladies like this, they're going to have the last word."[11] His attempt at humor failed. No one laughed.

Floyd continued by saying that Jane Roe had no right to plead her case in Court because she was no longer pregnant. A justice noted that the case was a class action, representing many women. Then Stewart remarked that "there are, at any given time, unmarried, pregnant females in the state of Texas."[12] That comment drew laughter from the audience.

Floyd persisted in saying that there was no way a pregnant woman could get a Supreme Court hearing because by the time a woman's case got to that Court, she would be no longer pregnant. "There are situations in which no remedy is provided," he noted. "I think [a woman] makes her choice prior to the time she becomes pregnant. That is the time of choice."[13]

"Maybe she makes her choice when she decides to live in Texas," came a justice's response.[14] Once again, the audience laughed.

A justice asked Floyd to explain what interest the state had in the abortion question. He replied that the state's primary interest was to protect the life of the fetus. "There is life from the moment of impregnation," he said.[15]

Marshall asked if he had scientific data to prove his statement. Floyd noted that he had outlined the development of the fetus "from about seven to nine days after conception."[16]

"Well, what about six days?" asked Marshall. "[T]his statute goes all the way back to one hour."[17]

Floyd stuttered out an answer. "I don't—Mr. Justice, it—there are

Chief Justice Warren E. Burger, photographed in 1970

unanswerable questions in this field, I—"[18] Laughter from the audience ended his comments, as Marshall said, "I appreciate it. I appreciate it."[19]

Weddington gave a short rebuttal, and the arguments in *Roe v. Wade* ended.

After a short break, the attorneys in the Georgia case presented their arguments. Hames argued that the state's abortion law, with all its requirements, was unconstitutional. The restrictions in the law made it too difficult for women to obtain abortions, she said. A woman seeking an abortion in Georgia had to get permission from two doctors and a hospital panel. The state's attorneys argued that it was up to the state to regulate abortion.

The red light on the lectern lit up for the fourth time that day. The abortion issue was now in the hands of the Supreme Court justices.

After oral arguments, the justices meet to discuss cases. They are the only ones allowed to attend the meeting. They review the points made in Court and in the briefs, and discuss precedents that relate to the case. The justices then vote on the case.

If the chief justice votes with the majority, he may assign one of the justices who also voted with the majority to write the opinion. Sometimes the chief justice writes the opinion himself. The opinion outlines the reasons behind the Court's decision in a case. If the chief justice votes with the minority, then the associate justice with the most seniority who is in the majority assigns the writing of the case.

A justice may spend several months researching and writing the opinion. During that time, other justices may be writing their own opinions. Those who go along with the majority but disagree with the reasons behind the vote may write concurring opinions. Those who oppose the majority vote may write dissents.

The final opinion may contain passages from a number of drafts written by several justices. To win support for the majority opinion, a justice may change the wording or include a section suggested by another justice.

Once the majority opinion has been written, the justices decide what their final positions will be on the case. Justices who agree with the opinion will join it—that is, agree to put their names on it. Others may choose to join a dissent or a separate, concurring opinion. Sometimes, the outcome of the case can change as justices who once supported the majority opinion decide, instead, to join a dissent. If a majority of the justices join the dissent, then it becomes the majority opinion.

After its final deliberations the Court then announces its decision, and the majority opinion is published. It is this document that becomes the basis of law. Attorneys will use it as a precedent when pleading cases.

Deciding the abortion case was particularly difficult for the justices. They knew what an emotional issue it was. White and Burger argued that the right to regulate abortions should remain with the states. White voted to uphold the law. Burger put off voting for the moment. The three liberals—Marshall, Douglas, and Brennan—voted as expected to strike down the laws as unconstitutional.

Blackmun had been an attorney for the Mayo Clinic for ten years. He saw the issue from the viewpoint of the doctor. Both he and Stewart favored lifting some restrictions against abortion because they hindered doctors from treating their patients. But they didn't vote to strike down the laws altogether.

Burger decided there weren't enough votes on either side to determine a majority. Instead, he asked Blackmun to write an opinion. The justices would vote on the case after the opinion was written.[20]

Blackmun devoted himself to the job. He spent hours at the Court's library, going over medical research and reviewing law texts. The term was to end by July 4. The justices would have to have a decision on the abortion cases by then.

Supreme Court Justice Harry A. Blackmun, author of the *Roe v. Wade* decision

Finally, in mid-May, Blackmun showed his draft to the other justices. Stewart, Douglas, Marshall, and Brennan agreed to join Blackmun's opinion. White disagreed with the opinion and issued a dissent. After reading White's opinion, Blackmun decided he needed to rewrite his own document. He withdrew this opinion and suggested that the case be argued again in the fall. He believed the case was an important one and should be decided by the full, nine-person Court.[21]

Douglas was angry over the delay. The two new justices, Rehnquist and Powell, were appointed by Nixon, a strong opponent of abortion. He believed Burger would try to pressure Blackmun into changing his vote, tipping the balance in favor of retaining the abortion laws. Douglas threatened to publish a memo severely criticizing Burger's handling of the case if the decision were delayed.[22]

The other justices urged Douglas not to publish the memo. It would weaken the Court, they argued. Blackmun told Douglas he would not change his vote. Finally, Douglas agreed not to publish the memo.[23] On the last day of the term, the Court announced its decision to ask for rearguments in the two abortion cases. Douglas dissented.

The Supreme Court's hearing of the abortion cases focused attention on the issue. It became one of the issues discussed during the 1972 presidential campaign. Both Nixon and Edmund S. Muskie, a Catholic who was running for the Democratic nomination, took stands against abortion. In February 1971 the American Bar Association had voted in favor of allowing abortion up to the 20th week of pregnancy. The following month, the Committee on Population Growth and the American Future issued a report calling for more liberal abortion laws. The report also recommended that the federal government finance abortion services and that birth control devices be made available to teens.

But opposition to abortion continued to grow. On April 16, 1972, a "Right

A protester in St. Louis, Missouri, carries a sign on March 8, 1972, favoring a woman's right to have an abortion. About 25 women marched in support of a campaign to repeal restrictive abortion laws in Missouri. The legislature was scheduled to hold a hearing on a bill to repeal the state law later in the day.

Governor Nelson Rockefeller delivers his fourth inaugural address as governor of New York in 1971. Rockefeller vetoed a bill in 1972 that would have reinstated limits on abortion in that state.

to Life Sunday" attracted 10,000 protesters in New York.[24] A smaller group of marchers, members of the Women's National Abortion Action Coalition, protested for a woman's right to choose an abortion.[25] A pro-choice rally on May 6, organized by abortion rights activists, drew the support of New York Mayor John Lindsay's wife, Mary Lindsay, and other prominent women.[26]

Lobbied by anti-abortionists, the New York State Legislature passed a bill that would have put limits on abortion in that state again. Governor Nelson Rockefeller vetoed the bill on May 13, 1972. He said, "I do not believe it is right for one group to impose its vision of morality on an entire society. . . . I can see no justification now for repealing this reform and thus condemning hundreds of thousands of women to the Dark Ages again."[27]

After arguing the *Roe* case before the Supreme Court, Sarah Weddington had returned to her Texas law firm. In late spring, she won a tough primary fight against three men as Democratic candidate for the Texas House of Representatives. That November, Weddington would win the general election for the House seat.

Meanwhile, the Court had announced the *Roe* and the Georgia cases would be heard on October 11. As the day approached, the lawyers once again headed for Washington, D.C. Ron Weddington joined Sarah and Linda Coffee at the table before the bench. Roy Lucas did not attend.

Weddington, standing this time before nine justices, was the first to speak. The arguments went much as before, though this time it seemed to observers that Weddington was better prepared.[28] Though the right to privacy was not spelled out in the Constitution, the Court had recognized the privacy right in a number of previous cases. The right of parents to send their children to private schools, the right to determine when to have offspring, the right to choose one's spouse, the right to use birth control devices—all had been granted by the Court. And all had been based on the right to privacy, Weddington noted. The abortion right, she argued, should fall into the same category.

White asked her if she would lose her case if the Court ruled that the fetus was a person.

Weddington answered that the Court would then have to balance the rights of the mother against the rights of the fetus. But, she noted, a fetus was not treated as a person under either the Constitution or its amendments.

Listening to the tapes of the oral arguments years later, researchers commented that the state's attorneys didn't seem prepared. Unlike Weddington, they didn't seem to have benefited from the chance to argue the case a second time.[29]

Robert Flowers, Texas assistant attorney general, argued the case this time for the state. He laid out his position: A fetus is a human being from conception and therefore has constitutional rights. Stewart asked if Flowers knew of any case where an unborn fetus was considered a person under the Fourteenth Amendment. Flowers had to admit he did not.

Later Blackmun asked if those in the medical profession disagreed over when life began. Flowers acknowledged that was so. He noted that the Texas law balanced the rights of the fetus and the mother. In cases where the mother's life was threatened, he said, the state chose to protect the mother. In all other cases, the state chose to protect the fetus. He also noted that the Court had protected the rights of the minority in the past.

"We say that this is a minority. . . ," he told the Court. "Who is speaking for these children? Where is the counsel for these unborn children, whose life is being taken?"[30]

Weddington used her final five minutes to rebut Flowers's statements.

"We are not here to advocate abortion . . ." she told the justices. "We are here to advocate that the decision as to whether or not a particular woman will continue to carry or will terminate a pregnancy is a decision that should be made by that individual, that in fact she has a constitutional right to make that decision for herself, and that the state has shown no interest in [or sufficient legal status to allow] interfering with that decision."[31]

Weddington sat down, and the lawyers in the Georgia case argued their case. The abortion issue was once again in the hands of the Court.

CHAPTER SEVEN

Decision and Aftermath

In a Constitution for a free people, there can be no doubt that the meaning of "liberty" must be broad indeed.[1]

— Justice Potter Stewart
quoting *Board of Regents v. Roth*
in *Roe v. Wade*

At 10:00 A.M. on January 22, 1973, the U.S. Supreme Court announced that the Texas abortion law was unconstitutional. The Georgia abortion law was also ruled unacceptable by the Court. The vote was 7 to 2, with Burger, Blackmun, Powell, Stewart, Brennan, Douglas, and Marshall in the majority. Rehnquist and White opposed the decision. Abortion throughout the nation had been declared legal.

Abortion laws in 31 states, including Texas, were overturned. Fifteen states, including Georgia, would have to rewrite their more liberal laws. Three other states, Hawaii, Washington, and Alaska—where rigid abortion laws had been repealed—had residency requirements or other limits that would have to be eliminated. Only the New York law, which allowed abortion without restrictions, was unaffected by the decision.

The opinion, written by Blackmun, was a compromise of sorts. It did not grant the woman the absolute right to decide when and whether to end her pregnancy, as the *Roe* attorneys had asked. Instead, it put certain limits on abortions performed after the first three months of pregnancy.

According to the opinion, during the first three months of her pregnancy, a woman and her doctor could decide to abort "without interference by the state." Beginning with the second three months, the state could pass laws that protected the health and welfare of the mother, but not prohibit an abortion. For example, the state might regulate the qualifications of the person performing the abortion or where the abortion was to be performed. In the third three months, the states, if they chose, could ban abortion except when the mother's life was at risk.

The decision noted that the Texas law violated the constitutional rights of pregnant women by violating their right to privacy. Blackmun's opinion acknowledged that the right to privacy is not explicitly mentioned in the Constitution. But, it noted, "the Court has recognized that a right of personal privacy, or a guarantee of certain areas or zones of privacy, does exist under the Constitution. . . ."[2] The "roots" of the privacy right, it read, are found in the First, Fourth, and Fifth amendments, in the "penumbras" (shades of meaning) of the Bill of Rights, and in the Ninth Amendment. The opinion noted that the privacy right is also found in the "concept of liberty guaranteed by the first section of the Fourteenth Amendment."[3]

"This right of privacy, whether it be founded in the Fourteenth Amendment's concept of personal liberty and restrictions upon state action, as we feel it is, or, as the District Court determined, in the Ninth Amendment's reservation of rights to the people, is broad enough to encompass a woman's decision whether or not to terminate her pregnancy."[4]

The state's interest in potential life becomes compelling enough to outweigh the right of privacy only when the fetus becomes viable, the opinion asserted. A fetus is viable when it can survive outside the mother's body. Doctors place viability at about six months, during the third term of pregnancy. With advances in medical science, however, some fetuses have been able to survive even earlier.

The opinion also agreed with Weddington's claim that Fourteenth Amendment rights apply only to persons already born, not to fetuses. The law has never recognized the unborn as persons. Since doctors, philosophers, and religious leaders cannot agree on when life begins, the opinion noted, the Court cannot be expected to have the answer.

As in the federal panel's decision, the opinion stated that John and Mary Doe had no standing to bring their case to Court. It also dismissed the claims of Dr. Hallford.

In a concurring opinion, Stewart based his reasoning on the first part of Section 1 of the Fourteenth Amendment. Abortion, he said, falls within the meaning of "liberty" as guaranteed by that clause, known as the "due process clause." Based on that clause, he noted, the Court had during the last term recognized the right of the individual to be free from "government intrusion into matters so fundamentally affecting a person as the decision whether to bear or beget a child."[5] That right, he concluded, also includes the right of a woman to choose whether or not to end her pregnancy.

Blackmun's revised opinion had won the support of the new justice, Lewis Powell, Jr. Powell had heard about the horrors of abortion from his father-in-law and his two brothers-in-law, all obstetricians.[6]

Burger finally agreed to go with the majority. Some believed Burger delayed his vote until after President Nixon's inauguration on January 20.[7] It would be an embarrassment to the president that the so-called Nixon Court had struck down the abortion laws that Nixon had so vehemently supported.

Members of the Supreme Court pose for photographers on April 20, 1972, in Washington, D.C. Front row, from left: Potter Stewart, William O. Douglas, Chief Justice Warren E. Burger, William J. Brennan, Jr., and Byron R. White. Back row, from left: Lewis F. Powell, Jr., Thurgood Marshall, Harry A. Blackmun, and William H. Rehnquist.

In his dissent, White said it was up to the states to regulate abortion. He called the Court decision "an exercise of raw judicial power."[8] Rehnquist, who also issued a dissent, questioned the right of Roe to bring the case to Court since she probably was not pregnant by then. He also argued, as White did, that the states, not the courts, should legislate abortion laws.

But Rehnquist's major difference with the decision revolved around the question of privacy. He contended that an abortion could not be considered a private act, because it required an operation (outside the home). Nor, he argued, were abortions protected by the right of people "to be secure . . . in their houses . . . against unreasonable searches and seizures" as guaranteed in the Fourth Amendment. Abortions occurred outside the home. The state did not "seize" a woman and invade her private property.

He also noted that the Fourteenth Amendment protected people from losing their liberty only when due process, or legal procedure, was not followed. A state, Rehnquist reasoned, could have a valid reason for limiting abortion. And, he said, it was up to Congress and the legislatures to weigh all the factors involved in the abortion question.

Rehnquist's dissent brought up many of the problems that would haunt the *Roe* decision. Constitutional scholars gave the opinion poor marks. They believed the Court never fully explained the concept of privacy and how it applied to abortion.[9] In past cases, privacy had referred to private property. Police couldn't enter someone's private property unless they had a legal reason to do so. They had to obtain a search warrant to invade the person's privacy.

In *Roe*, privacy referred not to a secure place but to a set of personal decisions.[10] According to *Roe*, the state could not interfere with a woman's private decision to have an abortion.

Some constitutional experts believed the decision would have been much stronger if it had been based on the *second* part of Section 1 of the Fourteenth Amendment:

> [States shall not] deny to any person within its
> jurisdiction the equal protection of the laws.

Their position was that women were not being treated equally under the law. Abortion laws, they contended, interfered with women's ability to control their reproductive process. No such laws existed for men.[11]

Blackmun's division of pregnancy into three terms raised other troubling questions. If the state had a compelling interest in preserving "potential life" in the third term, why not in the first term?[12]

Still others objected that the abortion question should have been resolved through the democratic process, by allowing the state legislators to decide the issue. The Court should not have overturned a law to enforce a right not mentioned in the Constitution, White and Rehnquist argued.[13] Once the Court issued the *Roe* decision, legislators could no longer ban abortion.

But defenders of *Roe* argued that the right to make one's own decisions in sexual matters was a fundamental right, basic to a person's liberty. They contended that state laws interfering with such a right had to be overturned.[14]

All of these questions—plus the fact that the right to an abortion was not spelled out in the Constitution—helped fan the controversy that would soon erupt over abortion. The *Roe* case played second fiddle to another news story that Monday. Former President Lyndon B. Johnson's death headlined the papers. But it quickly became clear that the decision would be at the heart of a raging battle.

John Cardinal Krol of Philadelphia, president of the National Conference of Catholic Bishops, issued a statement calling the abortion decision "an unspeakable tragedy for this nation."[15] Terence Cardinal Cooke of New York added that the decision was "shocking and horrifying" and called the opinion a "tragic judgment."[16]

From the Vatican came a pronouncement calling it "a decision of extreme gravity that deeply affects the concepts of human life—the dignity of the human person."[17]

On the other side, William Baird cheered the decision. Baird had won his own Supreme Court case during the previous term overturning his conviction for distributing birth control pills. "I'm delighted to see that our position—that women have the right to control their own bodies—has been vindicated,"[18] he told the *New York Times*.

Spokespeople for the Civil Liberties Union, Protestant and Jewish organizations, and others expressed similar views. A *New York Times* editorial said the Court had "made a major contribution to the preservation of individual liberties and of free decision-making." The ruling, the editorial continued, "could bring to an end the emotional and divisive public argument over what always should have been an intensely private and personal matter." It added that the *Roe* decision provided "a sound foundation for final and reasonable resolution of a debate that has divided America too long. . . . The country will be healthier with that division ended."[19]

The hope that the debate would end was soon dashed by Cardinal Cooke, who called on Americans to "reverse this injustice to the rights of the unborn child."[20] It was a call to action that many would heed.

Abortion rights activists assumed, like the *New York Times* editorial writer, that the *Roe* decision would be accepted as the law of the land. Many groups that had worked for liberalized abortion laws disbanded. Planned Parenthood and others shifted their focus to setting up abortion clinics. Now that abortion was legal, they wanted to provide low-cost, safe places where women could go for the procedure.

For those who opposed abortion, however, the fight was far from over. *Roe* became a rallying cry for them. They recruited members from the Catholic and Christian fundamentalist churches. The pro-lifers, as those against abortion call themselves, lobbied state legislatures to pass new limits on abortion. The Catholic Church played a major role in the lobbying effort. According to records filed with the government, the Catholic Church spent $4 million lobbying Congress on the issue in 1973.[21]

Pro-lifers voted only for those politicians who favored a ban on abortion.

Norma McCorvey, the plaintiff Jane Roe in the *Roe v. Wade* case, signs a petition in San Francisco, California, in July 1989 defending the right of women to have legal abortions.

As the abortion opponents targeted their votes against liberal candidates, the movement began to attract support from conservative Republicans. Their votes helped elect two antiabortion presidents, Ronald Reagan in 1980 and 1984 and George Bush in 1988. Reagan, despite his signing of California's liberalized abortion law in 1967, had won support from the pro-lifers during his 1976 presidential run. Bush had supported *Roe v. Wade* when the decision was first announced, but he changed his stand as Reagan's vice president in the early 1980s.[22]

With a pro-life president in place, the movement adopted several plans to ban abortion. In 1982 Senator Jesse Helms of North Carolina tried to pass the Human Life Statute. The bill defined a fetus as a human being. Helms hoped his bill would indirectly ban abortion. If the bill passed, fetuses would be entitled to the constitutional right to life. Senator Orrin Hatch of Utah tried a similar plan. The Hatch Amendment would give the states the right to decide whether to allow abortion. Neither bill passed the Senate.

But pro-life forces seemed to be making gains on another front. Pressed by pro-lifers, state legislatures in several states had passed limits on abortions. Those laws soon faced Court review. Between 1974 and 1993, the Supreme Court heard more than a dozen cases related to abortion.

The Court in 1973 had voted by a strong majority to support abortion rights. As time went on, several of the justices, faced with old age, retired. They were replaced by justices appointed by pro-life presidents, Reagan and Bush.

The Court's abortion decisions were a mixed bag. In the 1976 case of *Planned Parenthood v. Danforth*, the Court ruled that neither husbands nor parents can veto a woman's decision to have an abortion. But the next year, the Court ruled, in *Maher v. Roe*, that states don't have to pay for abortions for women on welfare. In 1980, in *Harris v. McRae*, the Supreme Court ruled that the Hyde Amendment was constitutional. The amendment, first passed by

Congress in 1976, prohibits the federal government from paying for abortions for poor women. In other decisions, the justices ruled that:

- Doctors, not the courts, have the power to decide when a fetus might be viable. The case, *Colautti v. Franklin*, was decided in January 1979.
- States may require women under 18 to get permission from their parents or from a judge for an abortion. The Court issued the decision in *Bellotti v. Baird* in July 1979.
- Abortions don't have to be performed in hospitals, according to a 1983 ruling in *Akron v. Akron Center for Reproductive Health*.
- Doctors don't have to tell women seeking abortions about programs to help with prenatal care and childbirth. The case, *Thornburgh v. American College of Obstetricians and Gynecologists*, was decided in June 1986.

In a split vote, the Court allowed states to place new limits on abortion in the 1989 case of *Webster v. Reproductive Health Services*. The ruling upheld a Missouri law that banned public money from being used for abortions. Public hospitals or staff paid by public funds could not perform abortions, according to the law. The ruling also allowed the state to require women who were at least 20 weeks pregnant to undergo tests to see if the fetus was viable. If it was, the law prohibited abortion. The Missouri law had also stated that life begins at conception. But the Court chose not to rule on that portion of the law. The justices issued five separate opinions in the case.

Although the ruling hadn't overturned *Roe*, it put serious roadblocks in the path of any woman seeking an abortion. Spurred by the ruling, pro-choice activists—as those who supported the right to an abortion called themselves—began their own campaign. They worked for pro-choice candidates, promoted their cause in newspaper ads, and held rallies. A pro-choice march on Washington in 1989 drew hundreds of thousands of people.

Stacey Bridges, left, a pro-choice advocate, argues her position with Ronald Ross, right, a pro-life supporter during a rally in Washington, D.C., on July 4, 1989.

Both sides closely watched a 1992 case, *Planned Parenthood v. Casey*. The Supreme Court, in a 5 to 4 vote, barred states from banning most abortions. But in a 7 to 2 vote, the Court granted states the right to impose more limits on abortion. The ruling also said that states, in adopting abortion regulations, must not place an "undue burden" on a woman's right to an abortion.

Pro-lifers were incensed that the so-called conservative Court continued to support abortion. Pro-choice advocates had mixed feelings about the decision. They objected that the ruling, by allowing more restrictions, prevented thousands of women from having access to abortion services. But the Court had upheld the basic right of a woman to have an abortion. In light of the *Casey* decision, it seemed unlikely that the Court would overturn *Roe* in the near future.

The pro-choice forces made further gains. In 1992, voters elected the pro-choice Bill Clinton as president. In one of his first acts as president, Clinton signed five decrees that eased restrictions on abortion imposed by Reagan and Bush.

Pro-choice supporters lobbied to keep abortion services in Clinton's health care reform package, still under consideration in Congress when this book was published.

They were also successful in winning passage of the Freedom of Access to Clinic Entrances Act. The bill, signed into law by President Clinton in May 1994, grants federal protection for women seeking abortions and clinic workers against acts of violence and terrorism.

Despite the pro-choice gains, however, women were finding it increasingly difficult to obtain abortions. Beginning in the 1980s, pro-life groups began to protest more aggressively. They picketed clinics, shouted at women seeking abortions, followed clinic staff members home. Their signs carried pictures of aborted fetuses.

Operation Rescue organizer and founder Randall Terry shows a crowd of antiabortion protesters a human fetus during a sit-in outside the Northeast Women's Center in Philadelphia, Pennsylvania, in July 1988. It was the second day of protests by the group at clinics that perform abortions in the Philadelphia area.

Some pro-life extremists resorted to violence. Between 1977 and 1990, more than 100 abortion clinics were bombed or set on fire. An additional 224 were vandalized.[23] One of the more aggressive pro-life groups, Operation Rescue, blocked clinics and prevented women from entering them. In their efforts to close clinics, more than 20,000 Operation Rescue members had been arrested by 1989.[24]

Because of the violence, fewer doctors and hospitals were willing to perform abortions. In 1973, Congress passed a bill that allowed doctors and hospitals to refuse to perform abortions if they opposed them. This permitted hospitals throughout the country to close their facilities to women seeking abortions. By 1988, 86 percent of the 1.6 million abortions performed in the United States were done in clinics. Only 40 percent of the nation's hospitals even allowed abortions to be performed.[25]

According to a 1988 survey, abortion services were provided in only 536 of 3,135 counties in the United States—17 percent. In Texas, where the *Roe* case began, only 22 of 254 counties provided abortion services. In South Dakota, abortions were available in only one county.[29]

In the 1990s the violence escalated. A man wearing a ski mask fired a sawed-off shotgun at staff members of a Springfield, Missouri, clinic. The office manager was paralyzed in the attack, and another staff member was injured.[26]

In March 1993, Dr. David Gunn, a 47-year-old doctor who performed abortions, was shot in the back three times outside his Florida clinic. He died two hours later. Michael Griffin, the 31-year-old man who admitted shooting the doctor, had done volunteer work for an antiabortion group called Rescue America. Before Gunn's death, pro-life supporters had distributed wanted posters with the doctor's name and photograph on them.[27]

The following August, Dr. George Tiller was shot in both arms outside a Wichita, Kansas, clinic. A pro-life demonstrator, Rachelle Renae Shannon, was charged in the shooting.[28]

While many pro-lifers denounced the violence, the shootings and burnings had an impact. Some clinics closed. Others hired armed guards or installed security systems.

In May 1994, a Texas jury awarded a clinic operated by Planned Parenthood of Southeast Texas $1.01 million in punitive damages from Opera-

An abortion rights advocate shouts at antiabortion demonstrators in front of Erie Medical Center in Buffalo, New York, in April 1992. The clinic was one of several targeted by Operation Rescue, an antiabortion group. The Supreme Court's decision in *Roe v. Wade* sparked a long and bitter fight between pro-choice and pro-life forces that continues today.

tion Rescue and another antiabortion group. Punitive damages are levied as punishment for actions done to deceive or cause injury. The money awarded for punitive damages is in addition to that given to cover an actual loss. Earlier in May, the jurors had awarded the clinic $204,585 for actual damages.

Planned Parenthood sued Operation Rescue, Rescue America, and the groups' two leaders after antiabortion protests during the Republican National Convention in 1992. According to Planned Parenthood, the clinic lost business and had to pay for fencing, extra security, and vandalism repairs because of the protests. It was the first time a jury had required protesters to pay for damages at a clinic. Abortion proponents and clinic operators are hopeful such suits will decrease violence at clinics.

Medical research may someday enable many women to have abortions peacefully and privately without having to go to clinics. In 1994 abortion rights activists were working to lift the U.S. ban on RU 486, the so-called abortion pill. A woman seeking an abortion early in her pregnancy could take RU 486 in a doctor's office. Later, she would take a follow-up pill at home, inducing an abortion. Having RU 486 available would make it easier for women to abort. It would also make it easier for doctors to avoid harassment from pro-life groups.

"I think a lot more private physicians would quietly give RU 486 in their practices," said Susan Hill, head of the National Women's Health Network, in an interview with *Time* magazine. "[I]f they felt it was safe and they weren't going to be protested every day, I think they would start offering it to their patients. . . . It's a lot easier to protest 400 clinics than 10,000 doctors."[30]

But pro-life supporters view the situation differently. In the same *Time* article, antiabortion author Joseph Scheidler said pro-lifers would ask doctors to supply them with RU 486, then picket the ones who granted their request.[31]

The two sides of the issue may never be able to find common ground. At one end of the scale are those who believe abortion is murder. At the other are those who believe the woman—and she alone—should have the right to decide whether to have an abortion.

Roe v. Wade brought the explosive issue of abortion to the forefront. After two decades of court fights, legislative battles, and fierce protests, the issue remains unresolved. But the major tenet of the *Roe* decision remains. A woman has a fundamental right, protected by the Constitution, to have an abortion if she chooses. The fact that the decision still stands is a testament to the strength of the Supreme Court and of the Constitution.

Source **N**otes

Chapter One

1. *Roe v. Wade*, 93 S. Ct. 705, p. 708.

2. Sherri Finkbine, "The Lesser of Two Evils," *The Case for Legalized Abortion*, ed. Alan F. Guttmacher, M.D. (Berkeley, Cal.: Diablo Press, 1967), pp. 15-26.

3. *New York Times* (July 25, 1962), p. 22.

4. *New York Times* (July 26, 1962), p. 22.

5. Finkbine, pp.15-26.

6. *New York Times* (July 31, 1962), p. 9.

7. *New York Times* (Aug. 1, 1962), p. 19.

8. Ibid.

9. Finkbine, pp. 15-26.

10. *New York Times* (Aug. 4, 1962), p. 20.

11. Ibid.

12. Ibid.

13. *New York Times* (Aug. 18, 1962), p. 43.

14. *New York Times* (Aug. 27, 1962), p. 20.

15. Finkbine, pp. 15-26.

Chapter Two

1. Guttmacher, p. 12.

2. Laurence H. Tribe, *Abortion: The Clash of Absolutes* (New York: W. W. Norton & Co., 1990), p. 28.

3. Ibid., p. 29.

4. Ibid.

5. Ibid.

6. Ibid.

7. Ibid., p. 30

8. Ibid.

9. Ibid., p. 34

10. Ibid.

11. *New York Times* (Jan. 31, 1965), p. 73.

12. Ibid.

13. *New York Times* (Jan. 26, 1967), p. 18.

14. Ibid.

15. *New York Times* (Feb. 13, 1967), p. 1.

16. Sarah Weddington, *A Question of Choice* (New York: G. P. Putnam's Sons, 1992), p. 63.

17. *New York Times* (Jan. 18, 1967), p. 14.

18. Tribe, p. 46

19. *New York Times* (May 22, 1967), p.1.

20. *New York Times* (June 22, 1967), p. 1.

21. *New York Times* (June 16, 1967), p. 24.

22. Tribe, p. 43.

23. Ibid.

24. Tribe, p. 48.

Chapter Three

1. Recommended Standards for Abortion Services, 61 Am. J. Pub. Health 396 (1971) as cited in *Roe v. Wade*.

2. Dana Rubin, "Roe Redux," *Texas Monthly*, vol. 21 (Feb. 1993), p. 185.

3. Weddington, p. 43.

4. Ibid., p. 46.

5. Ibid., p. 53.

6. *New York Times* (Sept. 9, 1987), p. 23.

Chapter Four

1. Weddington, p. 66.
2. Marian Faux, *Roe v. Wade: The Untold Story of the Landmark Supreme Court Decision That Made Abortion Legal* (New York: Penguin Books, 1993), p. 131.
3. Weddington, p. 63.
4. Ibid., p. 64.
5. Ibid., p. 66.
6. Ibid.
7. Faux, p. 168.
8. Ibid.

Chapter Five

1. *United States Reports*, vol. 381 (Washington, D. C.: U. S. Government Printing Office, 1965), p. 479.
2. Weddington, p. 99
3. Ibid., p. 93
4. Ibid.
5. Bob Woodward and Scott Armstrong, *The Brethren: Inside the Supreme Court* (New York: Simon and Schuster, 1979), p. 173.
6. Ibid., p. 171.
7. Ibid., p. 14.

Chapter Six

1. Weddington, p. 116
2. Transcript of oral arguments, *Roe v. Wade*, December 13, 1971.
3. Weddington, p. 111.
4. Transcript of oral arguments, *Roe v. Wade*, December 13, 1971.

5. Weddington, p. 116.

6. Ibid.

7. Ibid., pp. 116-117.

8. Ibid., p. 117.

9. Ibid., p. 118.

10. Ibid., p. 119.

11. Ibid.

12. Ibid.

13. Ibid.

14. Ibid., pp. 119-120.

15. Transcript of oral arguments, *Roe v. Wade*, December 13, 1971.

16. Ibid.

17. Ibid.

18. Ibid.

19. Ibid.

20. Woodward and Armstrong, p. 172.

21. Ibid., p. 186.

22. Ibid., p. 188.

23. Ibid.

24. *New York Times* (April 17, 1972), p. 27.

25. Ibid.

26. *New York Times* (May 7, 1972), p. 1.

27. *New York Times* (May 14, 1972), p. 1.

28. "Morning Edition," *National Public Radio*, Aug. 31, 1993.

29. Ibid.

30. Weddington, p. 141.

31. Ibid., p. 142.

Chapter Seven

1. *Roe v. Wade*, 93 S. Ct. 705, p. 734, quoting *Board of Regents v. Roth.*

2. Ibid., p. 726

3. Ibid.

4. Ibid., p. 727.

5. Ibid., p. 735.

6. Woodward and Armstrong, p. 230.

7. Ibid., p. 236.

8. *New York Times* (Jan. 23, 1973), p. 1.

9. Kermit L. Hall, ed., *The Oxford Companion to the Supreme Court of the United States* (New York: Oxford Univ. Press, 1992), p. 741.

10. Ibid., 672-675.

11. Ibid., p. 741.

12. Ibid.

13. Ibid.

14. Ibid.

15. *New York Times* (Jan. 23, 1973), p. 1.

16. Ibid.

17. Ibid.

18. Ibid.

19. Ibid., p. 20.

20. Ibid., p. 1

21. Tribe, p. 145.

22. Ibid., p. 164.

23. Ibid., p. 172.

24. Ibid.

25. *Glamour*, vol. 89 (Sept. 1991), pp. 280-283.

26. "Thou Shalt Not Kill," *Time*, vol. 141, No. 12 (March 22, 1993), p. 46.

27. Ibid., p. 45.

28. "Rising Tide of Zealotry/Abortion: Violence May Split the Pro-Life Forces," *Newsweek*, vol. CXXII, No. 9 (Aug. 30, 1993), p. 59.

29. *Glamour*, pp. 280-283.

30. Jill Smolowe, "New, Improved and Ready for Battle," *Time*, vol. 141, No. 24 (June 14, 1993), p. 54.

31. Ibid.

Further Reading

Beckman, Gunnel. *Mia Alone*. New York: Viking Press, 1975.

Bender, David L., and Bruno Leone. *Abortion: Opposing Viewpoints*. St. Paul, Minn.: Greenhaven Press, 1986.

The Bill of Rights and Beyond: 1791-1991. Washingon, D.C.: Commission on the Bicentennial of the United States Constitution, 1992.

Coy, Harold, (revised by Lorna Greenberg). *The Supreme Court*. New York: Franklin Watts, 1981.

Douglas, William O. *The Court Years, 1939-1975: The Autobiography of William O. Douglas*. New York: Random House, 1980.

Faber, Doris, and Harold Faber. *We the People: The Story of the U.S. Constitution since 1787*. New York: Charles Scribner's Sons, 1987.

Faux, Marian. *Crusaders: Voices from the Abortion Front*. New York: Carol Publishing Group, Birch Lane Press, 1990.

——. *Roe v. Wade: The Untold Story of the Landmark Supreme Court Decision That Made Abortion Legal*. New York: Penguin Books, 1993.

Forte, David F. *The Supreme Court*. New York: Franklin Watts, 1979.

Friedman, Leon. *Know Your Government: The Supreme Court*. New York: Chelsea House, 1987.

Goode, Stephen. *The Controversial Court: Supreme Court Influences on American Life*. New York: Messner, 1982.

Greene, Carol. *The Supreme Court*. Chicago: Childrens Press, 1985.

Katz, William Loren, and Bernard Gaughran. *The Constitutional Amendments*. New York: Franklin Watts, 1974.

Lader, Lawrence. *Abortion II: Making the Revolution*. Boston: Beacon Press, 1973.

Marquardt, Dorothy A. *A Guide to the Supreme Court*. Indianapolis: Bobbs-Merrill, 1977.

Meltzer, Milton. *The Bill of Rights: How We Got It and What It Means*. New York: Thomas Y. Crowell, 1990.

Morris, Richard Brandon. *The Constitution*. Minneapolis: Lerner, 1985.

Peterson, Helen Stone. *The Supreme Court in America's Story*. Scarsdale, New York: Garrard, 1976.

Pierson, Anne, and Carol Risser. *52 Simple Things You Can Do to Be Pro-Life*. Minneapolis, Bethany House, 1990.

Stein, R. Conrad. *The Story of the Powers of the Supreme Court*. Chicago: Childrens Press, 1989.

The Supreme Court of the United States: Its Beginnings and Its Justices, 1790-1991. Washingon, D.C.: Commission on the Bicentennial of the United States Constitution, 1992.

Terkel, Susan Neiburg. *Abortion: Facing the Issues*. New York: Franklin Watts, 1988.

Tribe, Laurence H. *Abortion: The Clash of Absolutes*. New York: W. W. Norton, 1990.

Weiss, Ann E. *God and Government: The Separation of Church and State*. Boston: Houghton Mifflin, 1982.

Woodward, Bob, and Scott Armstrong. *The Brethren: Inside the Supreme Court*. New York: Simon and Schuster, 1979.

Index